WIDENING HORIZONS

The story of INTERSERVE

Katharine Makower

Illustrated by Timothy Makower

Sequel to *Shadows Fall Apart*
by John Pollock

HODDER AND STOUGHTON
LONDON SYDNEY AUCKLAND

By the same author

Follow my Leader
Don't Cry for Me

All maps provided by Interserve.

British Library Cataloguing in Publication Data

A catalogue record for this title is
available from the British Library.

ISBN 0-340-58045-3

Published by Hodder and Stoughton,
a division of Hodder and Stoughton Ltd,
Mill Road, Dunton Green, Sevenoaks, Kent TN13 2YA
Editorial Office: 47 Bedford Square, London WC1B 3DP

Typeset by Hewer Text Composition Services, Edinburgh
Printed in Great Britain by Cox & Wyman Ltd, Reading.

Contents

Foreword

It is a privilege and honour for me to write the Foreword to this history of Interserve. My acquaintance with BMMF, as it was then known, goes back to 1966. I attended the United Conference of BMMF at Edgehill, Landour in 1966 at the invitation of Mr Alan Norrish. After that he invited me to attend the formation meeting of the International Afghan (later Assistance) Mission, representing the Indian Evangelical Mission. It was through his effort that the IEM-BMMF partnership began to blossom with the sending of our first missionary, Mr T. M. John to Afghanistan under the BMMF.

I have always looked upon BMMF as a selfless missionary organisation which existed to serve other indigenous agencies in India, such as the Indian Evangelical Mission, the Evangelical Fellowship of India, Union Biblical Seminary and the Union of Evangelical Students of India. In this role BMMF may not have a very high profile or a visible identity. But it has certainly served the Church in India. I trust and hope that Interserve will continue to have this servant role in India and in other countries.

I also have great admiration for the flexibility and freedom found in its approach to world missions. By emphasising the role of tentmakers to reach the restricted access countries, Interserve plays a vital role in world missions today. I pray that the Lord will guide the mission in its future endeavours in partnership and servanthood.

I have great joy in commending this history to the world Church.

The Rev Dr Theodore Williams
President, Indian Evangelical Mission

Author's note

It has been a privilege to meet and to write about the enter-prising and godly band of people who make up Interserve. This book is about them, and is a sequel to John Pollock's *Shadows Fall Apart*, a history of the Zenana Bible and Medical Mission which was published in 1958. This account starts in 1952, ZBMM's centenary year, so there is some overlap.

It has not been possible to mention everyone. Had I done so the book would have been an unreadable catalogue of names, but I have tried to present a balanced picture of a complex and widespread network of effort, and to give some idea of the sweep and progress of events. I am very conscious too of the adverse effect exposure by the media can have. Some vital work of Interserve is going on quietly and effectively and is best not publicised. Because it is not mentioned here, it does not mean it is not happening. And don't be surprised, Interserve Partners, if you find the work you are currently engaged in – and even yourselves – described in the past tense. Interservers move so fast that the book would soon have become hopelessly dated had it been written in the present tense!

So many people have helped me in my research: those in the Cyprus and London offices who have responded gra-ciously and helpfully to requests for information, National Directors who have done the same; those who have patiently read and corrected drafts; Regional Representatives in vari-ous countries who have arranged programmes of visits and all those who have given hospitality, time and information as I have visited and interviewed them. This is their story, and I thank them all.

KM

Note on names

Interserve has had various names over the years. The dates of the introduction of each new name are as follows:

1852 Calcutta Normal School
1864 Indian Female Normal School and Instruction Society
1880 Zenana Bible and Medical Mission (ZBMM)
1957 Bible and Medical Missionary Fellowship (BMMF)
1978 BMMF International (although it actually became international in 1966)
1987 International Service Fellowship, or Interserve (new name phased in at different speeds by different national Councils)

As a rough guide, I have tried in the text to use which ever name was current at the time about which I am writing.

Other terms used in the book:

Field Partners: Former name for members of Interserve who were employed by other groups and not by Interserve itself.
Partners: In 1987 this became the name used for all full members of Interserve.
Tentmakers: Partners of Interserve who are employed primarily in secular jobs (see Paul in Acts 18.3).

Initials and their meanings

ACTS	Association for Community Training Services, Pakistan
ARC	Assist Refugee Co-ordination
BMMF	Bible and Medical Missionary Fellowship
BPC	Butwal Power Company, Nepal
BSFB	Bible Students' Fellowship of Bangladesh
BTI	Butwal Technical Institute, Nepal
CEZMS	Church of England Zenana Missionary Society
CHAP	Christian Hospital Association of Pakistan
CMEF	Christian Medical and Educational Fellowship
CMS	Church Missionary Society
CTTC	Christian Technical Training Centre
DCS	Development and Consulting Services, Butwal, Nepal
EFI	Evangelical Fellowship of India
EFICOR	Evangelical Fellowship of India Commission On Relief
EHA	Emmanuel Hospital Association
EMFI	Evangelical Missionary Fellowship of India
ENFI	Evangelical Nurses' Fellowship of India
HASP	Horticulture and Agronomy Support Project, Nepal
HBI	Hindustan Bible Institute

HEED	Health, Education and Economic Development, Bangladesh
IAM	International Assistance Mission, Afghanistan
IEM	Indian Evangelical Mission
IFES	International Fellowship of Evangelical Students
IMTI	Indian Missionary Training Institute
INF	International Nepal Fellowship
ISA	International Service Associates
KLS	Khristiya Lekhan Sanstha – the School for Indian Christian Writing
MAB	Ministry among Asians in Britain
MAP	Medical Assistance Programme, Afghanistan
MEM	Middle East Media
MIK	Masihi Isha' at Khana – Christian Publishing House, Lahore
NOOR	National Organisation for Ophthalmic Rehabilitation
OMF	Overseas Missionary Fellowship
OTI	Outreach Training Institute (formerly IMTI)
PBCS	Pakistan Bible Correspondence School
PFES	Pakistan Fellowship of Evangelical Students
RBMU	Regions Beyond Missionary Union
SCD	Society for Community Development
SEAN	Study by Extension for All Nations
TAFTEE	The Association for Theological Education by Extension
TEAR Fund	The Evangelical Alliance Relief Fund
TEE	Theological Education by Extension
TESL	Teaching English as a Second Language
TRACI	Theological Research and Communication Institute, India
UBS	Union Biblical Seminary, Yavatmal, India

UBTC	United Bible Training Centre, Gujranwala, Pakistan
UESI	Union of Evangelical Students of India
UFCS	United Fellowship for Christian Service
UMN	United Mission to Nepal
USAID	United States Agency for International Development
WUMS	Women's Union Missionary Society
YCLT	Yavatmal College for Leadership Training
ZBMM	Zenana Bible and Medical Mission

THE WORLD OF
INTERSERVE

Introduction

The courteous Indian neurophysiologist in a white coat ushered me into his consulting room at one of London's big teaching hospitals. Actually I hadn't come to consult Dr Raju Abraham on a medical matter, but to hear a little, over lunch, of his life story, his ideas on Christian mission, and in particular his connections with Interserve.

'I was a late entrant into Interserve,' he said. 'Initially I was quite suspicious of it as coming from the West. But my ideas changed to such an extent that I not only became involved myself, but persuaded my brother Viju, who is a pastor in the slums of Bombay, to do the same. He is now the Chairman of Interserve India. It was another Indian Christian, Dr M. C. Mathew of Madras, who encouraged me to look more deeply into the work of Interserve. He said, "If you want to understand Interserve, you must read its early history – a book called *Shadows Fall Apart*."'

Shadows Fall Apart, written by John Pollock and published in 1958, was the story of a remarkable organisation known formerly as the Zenana Bible and Medical Mission (ZBMM), later as the Bible and Medical Missionary Fellowship (BMMF), and now as Interserve. It described how in 1852 a group of visionary and courageous ladies met at 1, Pall Mall, London, to consider how best to help the women of India. At that time there were no women doctors in India and many women and girls died needlessly and in pain. Male doctors did not see female patients. Only a few hundred women in India could read and there were no colleges training women teachers.

Worse still to these ladies was the spiritual darkness in which most Indian women lived, shut away in the zenanas (female quarters), deprived of freedom, oppressed by fear of the unknown and with the expectation of the agony of sati (widow-burning). Bound by their religion and superstition, they were totally ignorant of the love of a forgiving God and unaware that Christ offered them hope and salvation. As Mary Kinnaird wrote then, 'If we can give the women of India the power to read, and the Book to read, God will bless his word.'

To meet the need for women teachers, these Victorian ladies founded a society in 1852, seventy years before they themselves were given the vote. 'Normal Schools' was the name given to teacher training schools, so they called the society the Indian Female Normal School and Instruction Society. In 1871, when the establishment of 'female medical missions' was first proposed, medicine as a career for women was considered indecent. Only two English women, Elizabeth Blackwell and Elizabeth Garrett Anderson, had qualified as doctors. The latter founded her hospital in 1873, and this opened the way for women to engage in medical as well as educational work. As the trickle of volunteers increased and the zenanas opened to them, the women changed the name to the Zenana Bible and Medical Mission. For a hundred years they worked tirelessly to bring the knowledge of God, medical help and Christian education to thousands of Indian women. Clinics were formed, hospitals started, orphanages established, schools and colleges founded. The great work of caring and sharing gathered momentum and the Gospel of reconciliation transformed the lives of thousands. The cost to missionaries was high, and many laid down their lives for Christ. But the cost to converts was equally high. Prayer cells sprang up all over Britain, public meetings attracted large audiences, the great and the godly were enrolled for their support – including the Duchess of

Teck, mother of Queen Mary, who became President of the society.

Intrepid personalities stride through the pages of the book: Mrs Mackenzie from Inverness who first had the vision of training women teachers in Calcutta; Lady Kinnaird, wife of the banker, MP and Scottish laird the 10th Lord Kinnaird; Dr Elizabeth Bielby who brought a message in a locket from the Maharani of Pune to Queen Victoria asking for more help for the women of India; Miss Rosalie Harvey who set up not only a Babies' Home and a Leper Asylum, but also a Veterinary Hospital; 'Granny' Pollen who with her great friend Qulsam Begum engaged in village evangelism based at Khurja and Bulandshahr; Dr Ethel Douglas who was in charge of the Kinnaird Hospital, Lucknow for thirty-six years, establishing its fine reputation; and many more.

The book was out of print by the time Raju Abraham heard about it, but he eventually tracked down a copy and read it carefully, making notes. He was fascinated by what he read. As he told me: 'I was deeply impressed by the sheer energy released by these women. As I observed in my own mother in this century, who rose from a poor Christian family in Kerala to become a doctor and a magistrate, so in the previous century where you had an ostensibly repressed section of society, this apparent repression released a lot of creative activity. Instead of moaning or campaigning, they got on and did something. Society may have appeared less progressive than it is now, but they had more audacity, creativity and tenacity than many women of today. I was amazed by their boldness in penetrating the zenanas: they saw a need, heard God's call and went ahead and got on with it. Rosalie Harvey, founding the first veterinary hospital in Nasik – wonderful! And the relationships they formed: Granny Pollen and the Begum working together as friends and equals. I saw what M. C. Mathew meant – "If you want to understand Interserve, look at what those women did!" He was right.

'I also met leaders of BMMF at that time, who impressed

me: Jack Dain and Alan Norrish – people with gifts of leadership and servant-hearts. They were highly professional in the way they worked, humble, tenacious, consistent in their devotion to Christ. There were women too who seemed to be models of Christian leadership and servanthood: Vivienne Stacey with her burden for the women of Islam, and Margaret Parkinson. This lady from Australia had no desire for leadership – she simply wanted to get on quietly with her work of training Indian Christians in Maharashtra. But as things turned out, most of the leadership left, and for four years she was holding Interserve together in India. I admired this, and recognised the spirit of the early ZBMM women. It seemed to me a model for Christian leadership. I longed to see Indians, and particularly Indian women, developing the same blend of leadership and servanthood, the same determination to go for what was important in God's plan – not necessarily for what was easy.'

Raju Abraham linked up with Interserve, and has been on its UK Council for some years. Now Dr Abraham, inspired by the dedication of those women who long ago were called by God to reach out to women less privileged than themselves, seeks to build on that foundation and to continue God's work of seeking the lost and needy for Christ. My hope is that this sequel to *Shadows Fall Apart*, an account of the last forty years of the work of BMMF/Interserve, will similarly inspire others to push the boundaries forward and to attempt the important things, no matter how difficult they are, as God leads.

1

Independence, centenary, change

When India became independent in 1947, the fruit of
ZBMM's labours could be seen in physical form in an
array of institutions, all run by women and all serving the
girls and women of India. Among them were the Kinnaird
Memorial Hospital at Lucknow, the Duchess of Teck Hospital at Patna, the Canada Hospital at Nasik, Queen Mary
High School, Bombay, Kimmins High School, Panchgani,
Kinnaird High School for Girls, Kinnaird College and
Kinnaird Training Centre at Lahore, orphanages at Nasik,
Manmad and Sholapur and the Sharp Memorial School for
the Blind at Rajpur, as well as several evangelistic missions
among tribal peoples. Over the years thousands of girls
had received a good education and thousands of women
had received medical help. The reputation of these schools
and hospitals was high.

During the war years things had not been easy. Travel was
difficult, if not impossible. New staff could not be recruited
from abroad, and those already there could not get away
for leave. The institutions kept going, but there was no
real advance. By 1947 the war was over, swaraj – Indian
Independence – was declared, and India was no longer one
country but two. ZBMM hospitals had worked hard to help
mop up the carnage following partition between India and
Pakistan, but what would its role in these independent
countries be now?

At this crucial moment Jack Dain, with experience both
as a missionary and in the forces in India, was appointed

as the General Secretary of ZBMM. Traditionally this was
the one post in ZBMM which was held by a man. Jack's
qualities of leadership had developed during his time as an
officer in the Gurkhas and then as a lieutenant commander
in the Navy. He saw at once that with staffing and income
static and the very real possibility of ZBMM only having
a few years' welcome left in India, this could be either
a moment of retreat or of opportunity and advance. For
Jack there was only one answer, but the financial situation
must be sorted out first. The Committee had just passed
a budget for £25,000 for the coming year, while their
income was only £20,000; so Jack promptly telephoned
Paul Broomhall, a chartered surveyor, whose wife Rosalind
was on the Committee.

Both Paul and Rosalind came from impressive families:
Paul's grandmother was Amelia Hudson Taylor, the sister
of the founder of the China Inland Mission; his father had
worked for thirty years in China, and his brother Jim was
deeply involved in Chinese and Far Eastern missionary
work as well. Rosalind's family had been in India for
five generations: one of her grandfathers, Colonel Jacob,
was the Chief Engineer in the Punjab, and the other,
George Allen, established the famous Indian newspaper
the *Pioneer*, on which Kipling worked. Rosalind herself had
worked in a children's home at Gorakhpur until coming
back to England on their marriage, and was now serving
energetically on the Committee.

For thirty-five years Paul and Rosalind Broomhall were
to be key members of ZBMM, taking over the leading role
of Major and Mrs Mainwaring-Burton who preceded them.
Paul became involved on the financial side; Rosalind, a great
judge of character, was on the Personnel Committee and
made an invaluable contribution in the selection of candidates. Over many years, all potential ZBMM candidates
were invited to their home at Addington near Croydon, and
later to their beautiful seventeenth-century manor house at
Penhurst, East Sussex, where not only were their strengths
and weaknesses assessed, but they absorbed something of

the sense of 'family' which was characteristic of the mission. When eventually Paul and Rosalind retired in 1982, a tribute in the Mission's magazine announced that they had given over one hundred years' service to ZBMM. 'What?' said Paul. 'We're not that old!' But adding up Paul's time on the Finance Committee, his time as Chairman of the Council and Rosalind's years on the Committee, the total was correct.

'Paul,' said Jack over the telephone, 'these dear ladies have just passed a budget for £25,000 and their income is only £20,000. Something must be done. We need your help!' If male chauvinism can be detected as invading ZBMM's portals from this moment, the ladies seem graciously to have ignored it over the years. Soon Paul's inimitable voice was ringing round the Surrey Street office: 'Well, Jack, I know nothing about missionary accounts, but if this were a business we'd look first at our assets.'

The main asset of ZBMM was its lovely Georgian house in Surrey Street, London, built over a Roman bath; and over the next few decades, judicious selling of relatively valuable properties and moving to cheaper areas – from Surrey Street to Ladbroke Grove, from Ladbroke Grove to Kennington – contributed to the sound financial basis of the Mission. Other factors contributed too. As a result of earnest prayer and without appeals, giving increased. Also, in 1950 Jack, his wife Edith, Paul and Rosalind took a trip to India, visiting all the hospitals and schools. They were impressed by what they saw, but as Paul Broomhall observed:

The Duchess of Teck Hospital at Patna was running at a loss. Poor people were treated free – that was good. But in a private ward I saw a Maharani with three servants at the door. When I heard what they charged her, I said that a wealthy woman like that should be paying ten times as much. The missionaries were shocked at such a commercial view, but I pointed out that we were spending more than we were getting, and this could not go on. Similarly at Queen Mary High School in Bombay, there were a thousand girls or more from the wealthiest families in West India, arriving with chauffeurs and with servants who set out their lunches in the grandest style. These families would have to pay more. And they did.

But an organisation based in India can't run successfully with people from London calling the tune, and soon an important development took place. The Council decided that a 'Field Secretary' was needed, based in India – somebody who knew the country well. The person they appointed was Alan Norrish, who proved to be God's man for the job. When his father lost everything in the Depression, Alan had gone to India and found work in the mail-order department of a big store. In the process he got to know India well, and made a point of getting to know the missionaries wherever he went. Rising to lieutenant colonel in the 9th Gurkhas during the war and then serving in Colonial Administration, he was well equipped, together with his wife Sylvia who had nursed at a missionary hospital on the border with Nepal, to accept the invitation to become ZBMM's first Field Secretary in 1952, its centenary year.

When he and Sylvia married, he had promised God that their union would make two missionaries in the place of one (Sylvia), and this proved to be the case. They were making ZBMM history in that Alan was the first man on the field, although in an administrative rather than a missionary capacity.

This marked another big change which took place in the centenary year: a shift from the 'women only' policy of the first one hundred years. For many more years the work of ZBMM was to continue mainly among women, but with women gradually gaining more recognition and opportunities in the subcontinent, it seemed appropriate to widen the scope of the work and of the candidates to include both sexes. The mission had been founded under God by women who felt called to minister to the special needs of their own sex, but times and needs were changing. Although it caused some heart-searching, especially among the older members, and anxiety about the extra financial support necessary for families with children, ZBMM showed the flexibility which has always been one of its main characteristics, and was able to respond to a changing situation and move forward. Alan and Sylvia Norrish were followed soon afterwards by BMMF's first missionary couple, Peter and Alison Bagnall, who did village evangelism based at Bulandshahr and then moved to Pakistan where they worked among students and nurses in Karachi. Ken and Barbara Jolley and Jock and Gwendy Anderson were the other two couples to join ZBMM at about the same time. Good on team work and yet allowing for individuality, the Mission was attractive to people with drive and initiative, and became more so now that married couples could serve in it together.

Alan and Sylvia began work straight away. Alan had flair and vision for policy, Sylvia for personnel. Both brought a breath of fresh air and new ideas. They were based at Landour, a beautiful place in the Himalayan foothills of North India, where Sylvia soon found herself running Edgehill, the guest house which provided a refuge for ZBMM missionaries in the hot season. It really was on the edge of a hill, and sometimes appeared in danger of falling off. The rambling old bungalow with its various satellite buildings housed not only visiting missionaries but also the Norrish family and the office and staff. Alan's office consisted of a small wooden lean-to, something like an army bivouac, with one army-issue tin box as filing cabinet with all the BMMF files neatly suspended inside. The two secretaries, Moonyeen Littleton and Sheila McColl, typed indomitably from Alan's audio-cassettes in the corners of their bedrooms which doubled as offices. Alan began administering the various large properties owned by ZBMM – seeing that the schools and hospital buildings were kept in good repair and well managed. As he travelled from one institution to another he grew to know the missionaries, as Sylvia was doing at Edgehill, and also gained valuable insight into the work of the various institutions.

At the Duchess of Teck Hospital in Patna, for example,

Lodi tombs, Delhi

founded almost sixty years before, he met three very
different people, who seemed to him to reflect the old
regime and the new. Miss Win Emery was there, a gracious
and humble evangelist; there was Dr Winifred 'Sandy'
Anderson, a gynaecologist and doctor in charge: decisive,
professionally competent, well trained in pre-war days. And
there was Dr Marjory Foyle – small, slight, a junior doctor
just arrived. She made a point of speaking to Alan about
the changes which would have to be made. This was a
pre-war hospital and she was post-war trained. Marjory had
worked at both the Kinnaird Hospital, Lucknow and at the
Duchess of Teck, Patna, since coming out to India in 1949.
Impressed as she was by the work being done by doctors
who had been virtually cut off by the war and unable to
keep up with medical progress, and by the respect in which
the hospitals were held in the community, she nevertheless
became frustrated by the old-fashioned approach and the
rigid hierarchy – an approach she felt was unsuited to
her generation which had coped with the bombing of the
Blitz. She was aware that change must come, including the
advent of men onto the hospital staffs; and with Jack and
Alan quick to sense what she describes as the 'screaming
frustration' of her generation, change – too slow for some,
too fast for others – was soon on its way.

1952. Once again a woman was on the British throne.
A hundred years of sterling work by dedicated women
for women, in medicine, education and evangelism had
established ZBMM as an interdenominational organisation
which had the confidence of church leaders throughout India and Pakistan. Now men were beginning to
be involved. The challenge of Indian independence had
been faced, and the determination reached to use every
moment of time still available in the subcontinent. The
financial side of the work was on a firmer footing and a
Field Secretary who knew India well had been appointed.
Here indeed was a time of opportunity. The year before,
the Skylon, an elegant and futuristic metal structure, had
soared up by the Thames as a symbol of man's aspirations

for the future. It was part of the Festival of Britain, which looked back one hundred years to the Great Exhibition of 1851 when Britain was the heart of a huge empire. It also looked forward, after the destruction and stagnation of the war years, to a brave new world. But how was God, the Lord of creation and of history, planning to lead his people in ZBMM now?

2

Training and co-operative work

One thing was clear. If, as seemed all too possible, ZBMM had only a few years left in India and Pakistan, and with the two countries now eager to manage their own affairs, it was vital to train nationals in medicine, theology and in general education, and to hand more and more of the leadership over to them. Both Indians and Anglo-Indians had long been working in the various ZBMM institutions, but not in positions of leadership. Far-sighted members of ZBMM had wished for this long before. For example, in 1922 the Hon Gertrude Kinnaird had commented in a report:

> After seventy years of work it seemed sad that we met in conference in the Punjab without a single Indian or Anglo-Indian as a member. One felt that somehow or other our work had not developed as it should and that something must be done to change this ... I have met women trained in our schools who did offer themselves to our society years ago and were told the only opening was to become a Biblewoman. These women should have been invited to join us as full missionaries.

Commenting in the same report on ZBMM's work in Lahore she made a similar point: 'There are Indians on the staff of school and college. They should also be on the committee. The more we can take the Indians into our confidence and not appear to be a foreign group trying to manage the work without consulting them, the better it will be.'

Now the time was ripe to act on that vision. The key lay in training, and this was steadily achieved as ZBMM missionaries took posts in Christian higher educational establishments and hospitals and helped to train Indian and Pakistani teachers, pastors, nurses, and doctors to take increasing responsibility. For example an Indian lady, Dr Shanti Lal, took over the medical leadership of the Duchess of Teck Hospital in 1954. Her father had been the cook at Edgehill, and she had been educated through ZBMM and then trained at the Christian hospital at Vellore. She was one of the first Indians to have full missionary status with ZBMM.

Requests kept coming in from various churches and institutions – particularly those involved in the training of nationals – for well-qualified ZBMM workers to join their staffs. ZBMM – interdenominational and eager to serve God as a 'hand-maid of all the churches' – was able to provide these, and as it did so, the realisation came that the name of the society must change. The idea of a mission, with its connotation of Western superiority, was becoming an anachronism: '"Mission" speaks of control and must go. We envisage a Fellowship serving with and under Asian leadership.' For this reason, and with its work no longer limited to the women in the zenanas, the name was changed in 1957 to the Bible and Medical Missionary Fellowship. Less and less were workers attached to specifically BMMF institutions – more and more they were attached to and served in a variety of co-operative Christian ventures. As Jack Dain has pointed out, when he arrived in the ZBMM office in 1947, only one ZBMM worker was working outside a ZBMM institution; when he ceased to be General Secretary in 1959, almost half the total number of workers were involved in co-operative work.

Indeed, due largely to its interdenominational constitution which went back to Lady Kinnaird's original vision, ZBMM had been involved in co-operative work for some time. The Kinnaird College for Women in Lahore, founded in 1913 to provide higher education for girls, in a Christian environment, became co-operative in 1920 and was run jointly by ZBMM, the Church Missionary Society, the United Presbyterians and the Punjab Indian Christian Conference. The Kinnaird Training Centre – a Christian teacher-training college – developed in much the same way. In 1947 a women's Bible school which had been set up some years before by the United Presbyterians for training evangelists at Gujranwala in West Pakistan opened its doors to other denominations and became known as the United Bible Training Centre. For eight years ZBMM's support was limited to a grant and to representation on the governing body. Then in 1954, as part of the new wave of enthusiastic and well-qualified young Christians offering to serve God with ZBMM, a member of staff arrived who was to play a major part in training Pakistani Christians for many years to come.

Vivienne Stacey, a small determined lady with a cherubic round face and short curly hair, and with degrees in English and theology, was well qualified for Bible college work, and felt called to the training of women. She sailed for Karachi and eventually reached Gujranwala, some fifty miles north of Lahore in Pakistan. Here was a large American mission centre with a United Theological Seminary for men, a girls' school and an industrial school as well as the Bible Training Centre which was run by Miss Marian Peterson of the United Presbyterian Mission. Although now a Muslim country, there had been a sizeable Christian community in this part of what had been India going back to mass movements among the poorer people in the nineteenth century. The first five students of the college had named themselves after the five rivers of the Punjab, praying that God would use them to bring the water of life to a thirsty land. Much of the Christianity, though, was nominal. Vivienne found herself teaching not only two-year courses for girls committed to serving God as Bible teachers in hospitals or villages, but also a three-year part-time course for the wives of men studying in the Theological Seminary – women who as she tactfully put it, 'are not all as consecrated

Kinnaird College, Lahore

as they might be'. Short courses were also held for hospital nurses, school-teachers and Sunday school-teachers, mostly in Urdu, which Vivienne worked hard to learn.

She found one truly dedicated Pakistani Christian in her colleague Annie Budh Singh, who had joined the staff in 1951. The daughter of a converted Sikh, Annie had studied at Kinnaird College in Lahore. Brought up as a Christian, it was the catastrophic experiences of Partition which caused her to seek the reality of Christ for herself. Her father's home and farm were near the new border and during the weeks of violence she and her parents hid many Sikhs in their home and helped them to escape massacre. At night Annie dreamed her guidance for the next day. When things settled down she went back to teaching, and in 1951 God called her to the staff of UBTC, as a lecturer and matron. Also on the staff was Jean Mullinger, who like Vivienne had studied at the London Bible College. She had come out to Pakistan in 1957, and after a spell of teaching at Kinnaird High School, came to UBTC where she worked for twenty-seven years, taking over as Principal in 1975.

The constitution of the new country of Pakistan provided for toleration of all beliefs, but it did not exclude the persecution of converts by their own families. So people born into Christian families could continue to live and worship as Christians, but converts might even be threatened with death. Indeed in 1960 an outstanding Pakistani Christian who had trained as an evangelist at Gujranwala was murdered for her faith. She had been converted through the witness of a teacher at the Christian school she attended and through reading Isaiah chapter 53. Her real name was Qamar and for six years she continued to live out her Christian faith quietly in her Muslim home, reading her New Testament secretly. When a marriage with a Muslim was arranged for her, the almost inevitable fate of Christian girls, she left home and was baptised, taking the name of Esther John, partly to conceal her identity, and went to Gujranwala. Her studies finished, she left and joined an American couple in village evangelism, cycling

round with them on a bicycle – most unusual for a Pakistani
woman. A few years later she was murdered one night in
her room at the American Reformed Presbyterian Mission
in the little town of Chichawatni, her skull smashed in as
she slept. Police, seeking a clue, perhaps a note from a
disappointed lover, went through her papers and reported
to the missionary, 'Sir, we have found no clue. This girl
was in love only with your Christ.' As Vivienne, who had
taught her, commented, 'She was the real teacher, for she
showed me much about living the Christian life and how
to share Christ with Muslims.' A chapel was built in her
memory at Sahiwal Christian Hospital.

However, this was an exceptional event, and although
things were not always easy, and Christians were accused
from time to time of being political agents who were using
religion and philanthropy as a cloak for their real intentions,
the work of the college continued. One valuable development was the setting up of short courses for leadership
training in other parts of the country. In 1967 Vivienne
took over from Miss Peterson as Principal. The two-year
course of studies was closed and more stress was put on
short courses, extension work, and on a new Christian
Education course – a vital step in preparing qualified
teachers to specialise in Christian Education.

The aim was to help women of varying backgrounds
to learn, to think, in some cases to reach positions of
leadership, in others simply to struggle slowly from darkness to light. Like Rakhia, a young girl from a nominal
Christian background who had only recently learnt to read
through an adult literacy programme in her home village
and who found Christ for herself while on a course at
Gujranwala. She returned to her village transformed, full
of joy and enthusiasm, and started a prayer meeting for the
few Christian families in the village. More than that, she
sent eight more girls from her village to the next available
courses at UBTC, and was fortunate (and unusual) enough
to find a committed Christian man to marry – an electrician
who had been badly burnt in an electrical accident, but was

healed by God and decided to become a pastor. One of the eight girls who followed Rakhia to the Bible Centre was her sister, who was also converted and as a tribute to God's goodness to her family gave her baby boy the unusual name of UBTC . . .

Visiting Gujranwala in February 1992, travelling by bus the flat canal-irrigated fifty miles from Lahore, I found a varied and flourishing work, founded by the United Presbyterian Church but now interdenominational and with considerable input by Interserve. Christine Sorensen, an Interserver from New Zealand, had taken over recently from Jean Mullinger as Principal of UBTC, which continues to offer Bible training through short courses, retreats and extension work for women and girls. There are refresher retreats for Bible teachers and pastors' wives; short residential courses for college students or for girls who have just completed a phase of their schooling; and courses for nurses, usually from mission hospitals, teaching them how to share their faith. Often, with the help of the three Pakistani women on the staff and others, the girls come into a living relationship with Jesus Christ for the first time during their stay here, as many of them are only nominally Christian. There are also courses for primary school-teachers, Sunday school-teachers and newly-literate women, as well as a three-year part-time course covering Bible subjects, health education, budgeting etc for the wives of students training to be pastors at the Theological Seminary over the road. One-day retreats for local women had been particularly encouraging recently, with about seventy women coming each time and enjoying Christian teaching, fellowship and a good meal.

The Theological Seminary, having been through a troubled time, was moving forward under the new (Pakistani) Principal, the Rev Arthur James, with Interserve Partners seconded to the staff. Also in Gujranwala are Christian primary and secondary schools, some of whose teachers benefit from courses at UBTC, a Christian Technical Training Centre and an English Language Institute. These

three all come under the interchurch 'umbrella' organisation
SCD – the Society for Community Development – which
aims to provide the opportunity for literacy and training for
disadvantaged Christian children living within the Muslim
culture of the Punjab as well as to local Muslim young
people.

The Christian Technical Training Centre (CTTC), has a
long history. It was established by the Presbyterians in 1900
after a severe famine in the area, as the Industrial Home
for Orphaned Boys, with the aim of providing not only
a home but also Christian teaching and training in various
trades. Over the years, and particularly under the inspired
and energetic leadership of Ken Old, a civil engineer, it had
expanded and developed and now had a metalwork-shop, a
draughtsmens' room, and courses in electrical engineering,
electronics, and the maintenance of hospital equipment. The
Barr Institute, a separate project under SCD, was providing
computer training. Boys trained here have some hope of
finding work, and as the Pakistani Principal, Nathaniel
Nawab, put it simply, 'We are most of all eager to help
the poor.'

The SCD, whose Secretary was Wing Commander
Evert Lal and whose accountant was Interserver Sally
Davies, also includes the English Language Institute, which
offers English conversation courses at various levels. Mike
Thomas, an Interserve Partner from the UK, was Principal.
The students are mostly Muslims, and although their
favourite topics of conversation are politics and religion,
Mike was careful to bear in mind that in the classroom
he is primarily a teacher of English, and not an evangelist.
He was always available after class if a student wished
to pursue a topic with him, but would never push this.
Getting involved with individuals takes time, and this is
an area where the short-term service of young people can
be particularly useful, as the students enjoy talking to them
and having them as friends.

As well as UBTC at Gujranwala, another key venture in
co-operative theological education was the Union Biblical

Seminary at Yeotmal (now Yavatmal), near Nagpur in Central India. It began as a Free Methodist theological seminary, but in 1951 the Principal, Frank Kline, had the vision of making it an interdenominational college under the auspices of the newly formed Evangelical Fellowship of India. Here, as at Gujranwala and at other united colleges – the Hindustan Bible Institute of Madras, Kalvari Bible School for women, Allahabad, and the Allahabad Bible Seminary – BMMF was able to contribute senior members of staff. As Jack Dain noted, it was remarkable how just as requests were reaching him for well-qualified staff to teach in these colleges at a time when training national Christian leaders was of crucial importance, so at the same time God was leading young people with excellent teaching qualifications to offer their services to BMMF.

Two of these were Bruce and Kathleen Nicholls, a dedicated couple from New Zealand whose work in India over nearly forty years has been important for the growth of the Church in India. It is illuminating to see the way in which God has used their complementary gifts and led them from one area of work to another. They actually joined ZBMM in England, having heard Jack Dain lecture at the London Bible College where both were students. Arriving back in New Zealand by ship, they were given a tumultuous welcome by ZBMM supporters, who unknown to them had been praying for years for two new missionaries.

For nearly twenty years they worked at the Union Biblical Seminary, Yavatmal, helping to train pastors and Christian leaders, and now wherever they travel in India, they find their students in positions of leadership. As Bruce told me when I met them in their spacious flat in Greater Kailash-II in New Delhi, 'In our time we've trained five bishops, principals of various theological colleges, pastors of big city churches and small rural ones, and people heading key Christian organisations.' Bruce specialised in theology, while Kathleen was put in charge of English and drama, speech and communication, an unexpected assignment which was to lead to exciting developments.

BMMF's contribution to UBS was further strengthened over the next few years with the arrival of Ian and Elizabeth Kemp, also from New Zealand, and Dr Alexa ('Lexy') Cameron from Canada who was Head of the Christian Education Department and Warden of Women at the time of her premature death in 1974. She died of hepatitis while on holiday on a houseboat in Kashmir.

In 1974, too, Bruce and Kathleen moved to Delhi, from which base Bruce worked as Theological Secretary for the World Evangelical Fellowship, setting up a Theological Commission in 1975 and co-ordinating a world conference on the mission of the church. Working with him was Lionel Holmes, later Publications Secretary of Interserve (UK). At the same time Bruce and Kathleen set up an important new study community: the Theological Research and Communication Institute, or TRACI, in a large house which they were able to buy near their home in Delhi in 1976. They had already become aware while at UBS of the need of a centre where people could spend time grappling with the issues of the Christian faith, and had started there under the name Evangelical Research Centre in 1972. Now in Delhi they changed the name to TRACI, conscious that theologians and philosophers need to learn to communicate and that artists and communicators too often have little of true value to say. As in all their ventures, their concern was to strengthen the Indian Church. BMMF encouraged and seconded them to this work, with funding coming from various agencies, including BMMF.

The idea was to live and work as a community of about fifteen to twenty people who shared a common commitment to Christ, to each other and to the communication of Christian truth. A researcher would stay for two to six months, with the help of a scholarship where needed and the use of a good library which gradually built up at the Institute. The members would then read the resulting paper and discuss it together – sometimes a painful process for the author, but worth it as the work was honed to excellence. For various reasons,

TRACI did not develop fully as conceived. However, seminars were also held, lasting perhaps a week, on a wide range of subjects: evangelism, pastoral care, counselling, social justice, family matters, medical ethics. Articles and a journal were produced. A publishing firm was founded, Select Books, with the aim of getting the writings out of the Christian ghetto and to the attention of secular readers.

One book which resulted was Anthony Stone's work on astrology. He first came to India to teach mathematics at Alwaye Christian College, Kerala. He then moved to Delhi and taught maths at St Stephen's College. He and his wife Bertha met on board ship: she was a nurse working in Ethiopia with another mission. After a time in England they came back to India with BMMF and Tony researched and wrote his book, having learnt Sanskrit by way of preparation. Although the last chapter questions the scientific basis of astrology, the book was so scholarly and well researched that it was well received by the Hindu readership for whom it was intended.

A book which received attention at the World Book Fair in Delhi was Kathleen Nicholls' *Asian Arts and Christian Hope*, first published in 1983, which gives a fascinating overview of traditional Indian art, craft, drama, mime, dance and puppetry. In it she discusses the way in which these art forms have spread to other countries in Asia, and in particular ways in which Christians can use them, learning to discern what must be rejected, what can be transformed or accepted and where new dimensions can be added. While at UBS, Kathleen realised that the use of drama is a very Indian way of teaching, and her work in drama and communication developed into an effective form of evangelism. She became an authority on the diverse arts of India, but refused to remain academic, preferring to put her expertise to practical use wherever she could – travelling and speaking, arranging Christian arts festivals, making videos and films, encouraging young artists and using her gifts in the church where Bruce ministers.

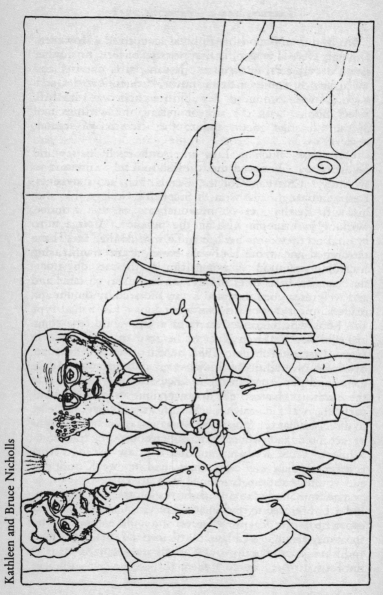

Kathleen and Bruce Nicholls

In 1986 the Nicholls' lives once again took a new turn. Leaving TRACI under the Directorship of Dr Christopher Raj, Associate Professor at the Jawaharlal University and with Alex Joseph as Administrator, they followed God's lead again to something new. Still seconded by BMMF, Bruce was ordained into the ministry of the Church of North India, and became pastor of the church of Gurgaon, a town of 300,000 people in the state of Haryana and the Diocese of Delhi. Like Interserve itself, Bruce and Kathleen are convinced that they should be committed to working through and for the local church, as its servants, strengthening it in its witness and work.

As Bruce put it, 'A missionary is on the frontier. We see our role as helping the people at Gurgaon to reach out to their neighbours.' For example, they have developed an annual four-day event in the town, using indigenous methods of evangelism. In the satsung, a dais is set up in the market place, with colourful curtains and good lighting. Accompanied by an Indian harmonium and drums, an Indian Christian poet sings his ballad-type Bible-based songs and then talks a little about the song. In this way he can speak to the soul of the people in their traditional idiom. Then another Indian Christian, dressed in the white dhoti, will sit cross-legged on the dais, guru-style, and speak, expounding Scripture, relating it to the Hindu scriptures, not down-grading them, but taking them further. Similarly in a Muslim community in Delhi, TRACI arranged a Christian musa'ira, or poetry reading of poems written by Christians. This being a traditional Muslim mode of communication, it was received with respect and appreciation. Drama, shadow-drama, puppetry or any other appropriate medium is used.

Although in the Indian culture response takes time, some are drawn to Christ by what they see and hear. This can cause problems regarding means of livelihood, and has led Bruce and Kathleen to help set up a project called FARMS India which aims to provide small interest-free loans to poor Christians, enabling them to become self-sufficient, on the basis that 'little is much when God is in it'. For example one man was struggling to carry a fruit basket on his head, selling from door to door; FARMS helped him to buy a tricycle which lightened his burden and increased his income.

Bruce has seen his role in India as a catalyst in the Church: helping to get things started and then handing them over. This was true of TRACI and of an offshoot of it: Sahara House (known previously as Ashiana). The word 'sahara' means 'refuge', and this is an Indian community for drug rehabilitation, first set up by David Andrews of BMMF Australia in the 1970s. The leadership has always had close links with TRACI, and the two houses are just across the road from one another. Neville Selhore, the young Indian in charge, showed us round and described the daily programme for the thirty-two residents, who come voluntarily and stay for six months to a year: sport and exercise, prayer, singing and Bible study, discussion, mastering practical skills and sessions of group dynamics. In addition, anyone who is actually in the process of withdrawing from drugs will be given round-the-clock attention, support and prayer, and counselling is available to those who need it. The success rate is high, with people being helped not only to come off drugs but also to rebuild their lives. The aim is to give people the love and care of an extended family which some of them have never known, and the knowledge, as they find themselves helping each other at Sahara, that they too can be useful in the world. Or as they put it themselves, 'to give people adrift in the hurly burly of modern life an anchor, some roots, a feeling of centredness and groundedness; so that they can spread their wings, and fly.'

As Bruce and Kathleen saw it, they may have been among the last of the classical missionaries in India. But they were also part of the new missionary era, where missionaries are integrated into national structures, serving with them and bringing to the church their experience to enrich it and widen its vision. And right up to their last moment in India before retirement they were hard at it, helping to make a film about the 'father of modern missions', William Carey of Serampore, for his bicentenary, and also arranging the first missionary conference in the state of Haryana. As Bruce summed up, 'Although I'm a regular pastor, I'm helping the church to get a missionary vision and to develop structures appropriate to the task. I work through the church, and help to raise its vision.'

In the field of medicine, BMMF's work in India followed a similar trend as in education: withdrawal from specifically BMMF institutions and involvement in co-operative work, notably in the two great Indian Christian hospitals and medical schools of Ludhiana in the north and Vellore in the south. The work at Ludhiana sprang from a small beginning in 1881 when Miss Greenfield, a qualified teacher with the American Presbyterians, became aware of immense medical needs in the area, and opened a small dispensary. She wrote for her sister, a nursing sister at the Great Ormond Street Hospital for Children in London, and together they obtained the use of a small unused church building and put in a few beds. With financial backing from their brother, an Edinburgh businessman, they opened a hospital, and here in 1894 Dame Edith Brown founded a college for training women doctors. At the time of partition between India and Pakistan in 1947 the hospital made a notable contribution in caring for the wounded of all communities, and true to its original purpose, it still trains doctors to help women and their families living in the villages of India. The college has pioneered community healthcare, mobile eye hospitals, and the care of women being delivered in their homes. Many of Ludhiana's graduates, instead of choosing the more prestigious and remunerative posts in the cities, are serving the less privileged rural communities in mission hospitals.

Here, to Ludhiana, from the early 1950s, BMMF workers were seconded in various capacities. Eileen Platts, for example, served there as a nurse for thirty-five years from 1953, happiest spending time with patients on the wards, or else visiting from house to house on her bicycle nicknamed

'My Maruti' after one of India's popular makes of car. Also in 1963 Alan Norrish, BMMF's Field Secretary, who had served on the Board for several years, was appointed as Chairman of the Governing Body. He had earlier protested that he knew nothing about medicine. They responded that he did know about administration, and that was what they needed. In the 1960s, '70s and '80s a steady stream of BMMF personnel was seconded to CMC Ludhiana, a significant proportion from North America.

The story of Vellore is well known: how in 1884 Ida Scudder, a carefree young American woman with no thought of becoming a missionary or a doctor, came to visit her missionary parents in south India. While she was there, a man came to the mission bungalow desperate for help for his fourteen-year-old child bride who was dying in child-birth. Could Ida help? She told him that it was her father who was medically qualified and she was not, but as the rules of purdah meant that the girl could only be seen by a woman, there was nothing to be done and the girl died. The event spurred Ida Scudder to go back to the States for medical training, and six years later in 1900 she founded her first hospital with only one ward – the spare bedroom in her father's bungalow. Later, in 1918, she opened a medical college for women, which eventually opened its doors to men in 1947.

The hospital, now employing 4,000 staff and training 600 doctors and 800 nurses, has had marked successes – among them Dr Paul Brand's development of reconstructive surgery for leprosy of the hand; also, as at Ludhiana, it led the way in community health care. In 1969 the first BMMF workers, Ben and Peggy Walkey, came to Vellore. They already had experience of southern India, having worked at Dohnavur, and now Ben joined the staff of Vellore Medical College and Hospital, practising and teaching surgery, particularly hand-repair for leprosy patients. From then onwards, over the years, there were usually BMMF members on the staff of Vellore. As F. T. Davey comments, 'The great centre at Vellore became what it is because during the years of development the hospital and medical school were supported by forty-two missionary societies from several countries.'* BMMF was one of them, ready as always to contribute professionalism and expertise to Christian ventures and to co-operate with other Christians in serving the needy in the name of Jesus Christ.

And what of the three hospitals for women set up in India by the ZBMM pioneers themselves – the Kinnaird Memorial Hospital, Lucknow, started in a rickety house by Miss Bielby in 1878, the Duchess of Teck Hospital, Patna, opened in 1895, and the Canada Hospital, Nasik, opened in 1914? They all reached and maintained high standards in the provision of medical care for women. Dr Ethel Douglas of ZBMM, who ran the Kinnaird Hospital for thirty-six years until 1946 was so respected that the hospital was known locally as the Douglas Hospital. She was awarded the Kaiser-i-Hind Gold Medal and the OBE for her work. However, the role even of this excellent hospital was altered by the weakening of purdah, especially among Hindus, in the 1940s and the establishment, just opposite the front gate, of the King George V Medical College (government) hospital. By 1960 all three BMMF hospitals were struggling with shortages of funds and of staff. Curiously, at this time it became impossible to recruit women doctors for these hospitals. The single lady doctors who were offering to BMMF at that time all seemed to be called to Nepal. As Alan Norrish has commented, this was puzzling and frustrating at the time, but looking back it could be seen as part of the pattern of God's will moving on. The era of the large women's hospitals was past, and the Indian Government was making adequate provision. The call now was for BMMF to move on, out into the community into new areas of need.

One after another the hospitals closed. First to go, in 1961, was the Duchess of Teck Hospital, Patna, and several

* Stanley G. Browne, ed., *Heralds of Faith* (CMF, London, 1985).

of its staff members, both expatriate and Indian, transferred to the newly developing work in Nepal. The property was sold to a Roman Catholic order who continued to run it as a women's hospital. Next, in 1962, the Canada Hospital at Nasik closed down and was sold in two parts, one of which is now part of the telephone network of India. The other part was retained by BMMF, and allocated to an exciting new venture – a writing institute called Khristiya Lekhan Sanstha – with the aim of continuing the writers' workshops recently started by BMMF member Maureen Clarke.

Finally in 1965 the Kinnaird Hospital was closed after almost seventy-five years of service. Rising costs had placed the running of a city hospital beyond the resources of BMMF. Such was the prestige of the hospital that BMMF was reluctant to close it. Indeed Marjory Foyle was called back – equally reluctantly – from Tansen, Nepal, where she had begun work, to see if it could be modernised and kept going in some way. The stress she was under was too much, especially as she did not really believe in the proposed course of action. Her health broke down ('possibly in retrospect the best thing which ever happened to me'). Requests to the Government for permission to convert to a general rather than a purdah hospital were unsuccessful, as the original lease stipulated that the land be used solely for a hospital for women and children. With Marjory unable to work, Dr Shanti Lal struggled to keep the hospital going. It was impossible, and eventually the property reverted to the Government and was re-opened in 1971 as a psychiatric unit attached to the King George V Medical College over the road.

It was sad, and the end of an era. The hospital had won wide respect in the community over the years. Nonetheless such had been the progress of modern India that the Government was now well able to provide necessary health services in the cities. As Ray Windsor (later General Director of BMMF) commented, 'The place where medical missions should make their contribution in developing countries is in the rural areas.' Indeed, an unusual example of this sort of rural community health care work had been started some years before in Pakistan.

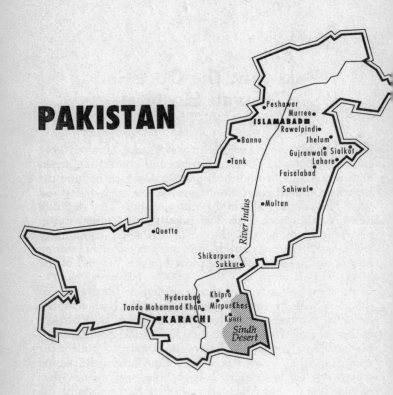

3

Pakistan: the Christian Caravan Hospital

Pakistan, or West Pakistan as it was known between 1947 and 1971, consists of three distinct and contrasting areas: high mountains to the north and west, which include the world's second highest mountain, K2; the great valley and flood plain of the Indus in the centre, and the Thar or Sindh desert in the south east. The population is ninety-seven per cent Muslim, and the small Christian community are mostly descendants of the mass movement among Hindu outcastes which took place towards the end of the nineteenth century.

The beautiful city of Lahore, capital of the Punjab to the east, with its fort, Mogul mosque and Sikh temples, home of Kipling's *Kim*, had been a centre of ZBMM's work since the 1860s. There they had established Kinnaird High School, Kinnaird College – the first degree college for women in what is now Pakistan, and the Kinnaird Training Centre – a teacher-training college, also for women. Other missionary societies had also worked here, notably the Presbyterians and the Church Missionary Society, whose Thomas Valpy French became the first Anglican Bishop of Lahore. Another CMS missionary, Henry Holland, a pioneer opthalmologist and general surgeon working on the North West Frontier, came to work at the hospital at Quetta, in Baluchistan, not far from the Afghanistan border. Here he built up a great reputation as an eye specialist, and also started the famous eye clinic at Shikarpur, a Hindu city in the north of Sindh province, travelling between the two places according to the season. In addition, he was the innovator of 'eye camps' where small teams took their ophthalmic skills out into rural communities. His two sons, Harry and Ronnie, both qualified in medicine and eye surgery, Ronnie becoming even more skilled than his father. It was Ronnie who asked Jack Dain, visiting the hospital in the early 1950s, whether ZBMM might be able to lend a doctor to Quetta. Jack, who always seemed to know the right person to fit into any slot, thought at once of Dr Jock Anderson, newly qualified, who with his wife Gwendy was eager to serve the Lord in that part of the world. So Jock and Gwendy went to Quetta in 1955, and Jock was soon learning all he could about eyes. There was a high incidence of cataract in Pakistan, even among relatively young people, and already in March 1955 Jock found himself doing nineteen cataract operations on one of Ronnie Holland's eye camps. His time at Quetta was immensely valuable. The hospital had a high reputation, and medically it was demanding and excellent experience, as he was called on to do things that a junior doctor would never have a chance to tackle at home.

Already too he was becoming concerned about the right way to share the Gospel. There was preaching on the wards and among the outpatients at Quetta, but Jock had mixed feelings about preaching to a captive audience. Loyally he took his turn, but felt that the way he treated his patients would speak most for Christ. Certainly it was important that the hospital be known as a Christian one, and that careful loving treatment should be given. He and Gwendy did all they could to encourage the Pakistani members of the hospital staff, some of whom were only nominal Christians in much need of teaching, and they regularly invited them to their home. The hospital was sometimes accused in the press of pressurising people to become Christians, and here at Quetta Jock began to ponder the difference between proselytism (trying to make you change from your group to mine) and introducing people to a Saviour – preaching

Empress Market, Karachi

the Kingdom of God and sharing his love, 'against which
there is no law'. This distinction, he came more and more
to feel, was crucial in Pakistan and in other countries where
proselytism was not allowed.

Often the eye team would leave the cool heights of Quetta
and set up eye camps in the grounds of a wealthy landlord
in the sweltering Sindh desert, performing hundreds of
cataract operations in a short space of time. Driving back
from an eye camp one day, Jock reflected on the possibility
of doing more for the people in these country areas. Many
travelled for days to reach Quetta and arrived exhausted.
Others could not attempt the journey at all and so received
no treatment. The work of the eye camps was limited.
Wasn't there some way of taking modern medicine to these
villages . . . the hospital to the people . . . something clean,
dust-proof, fly-proof for surgery. What about a series of
caravans?

So the idea of the Christian Caravan Hospital was born.
But it wasn't born in a vacuum. As so often happens, God
had been preparing the way through a remarkable movement of his Spirit among the Kohli tribe in Sindh. Some
years before, Chandu Ray, a Sindhi pastor and convert from
Hinduism, led an evangelistic campaign among the Kohlis.
These were a Hindu tribe living not far from the Indian
border, an insecure minority since partition, in a Muslim
state. Many whole villages turned to Christ and asked for
Christian teaching – a call to which BMMF responded,
especially through some of its Australian members. Chandu
Ray, who subsequently became Assistant Bishop of the
Anglican Diocese of Lahore and then Bishop of Karachi,
was a man of prodigious energy, purpose and vision.
In 1958 he invited a number of Sindhi church leaders
and missionaries to his home in Karachi, including Jack
Dain. The need for medical work in Sindh was discussed
and Jack, to whom Jock had put his idea of a caravan
hospital, suggested that BMMF might be able to help.
In response to Chandu Ray's appeal for help, the West
Pakistan Conference of BMMF held in Lahore a week

later recommended that Jock undertake a six months pilot scheme among the Kohli, working in close co-operation with the local church.

The result was that in October 1958 the Anderson family arrived at Hyderabad, the ancient capital city of Sindh with its old fortress on the hill, its miles of narrow bazaar streets and its famous university. Forty miles on, near the village of Mirpur Khas, they set up the Christian Rural Eye Clinic with the help of a Pakistani Christian couple, Samuel and Maryam Gill. One room in a tiny bungalow became the operating room, the adjoining passage became the consulting room, two car batteries provided power for the operating lamp, and the operating table consisted of two halves of a chest of drawers placed end to end. Three eye camps were held at different places; all were eagerly welcomed and successful, and as Dr Anderson recorded, 'In every place we visited, healing and preaching went hand in hand. On the second eye camp, at Mirpur Khas, for example, Samuel's faithful witness and selfless nursing opened a number of hearts to the Gospel, particularly three Hindu men who turned to Christ on Christmas Day.'

'What has the pilot scheme shown us?' Dr Anderson asked. He continued:

Essentially three things: inaccessibility, need and responsiveness. The need has to be seen to be believed – TB and malaria sapping vitality and taking their toll of lives; trachoma evident everywhere; vitamin deficiency and malnutrition ... and dozens of eyes blinded through the ravages of smallpox, where a timely vaccination would have kept it away. And the responsiveness just makes us cry to God to show us his plan – to send us the means so that we can fulfil Christ's commission to preach the gospel to every creature.

Already the door was opening. As well as the initial appeal for help from Chandu Ray, the land-owner on whose land the last eye camp was held asked eagerly that if the dream of the caravan hospital did indeed materialise, they would promise to come back to his premises first. But could it happen, or was it only a dream?

Back in Britain, Christians were asked to give financial support, but only if it did not come at the expense of other work. As a result of enterprising and sacrificial giving, the money was soon coming in, and there was further encouragement in the form of an unexpected God-send: George Dolby, an agriculturalist, practical and experienced with vehicles and machines, offered his services free to help with fitting up the caravans. Eventually two land-rovers and the six gleaming caravans were ready and formed an integrated but small-scale hospital. An Open Day was held in September 1960 in the grounds of Bedford General Hospital, England, and in the presence of Colonel Sahim Khan, medical adviser to the Pakistani High Commission in London, it was given as a gift from the Christians of Britain to the Pakistani Government and people, and dedicated to God for the service of the people of Sindh. A promise was received in return that on arrival at Karachi the caravan hospital would be swept through Customs. It was, and the caravans were then transported one at a time on trailers through the narrow bazaar streets of Hyderabad where they caused a considerable stir, and on along the 164 rough slow miles to Mirpur Khas.

Soon the hospital was set up, its own generators providing air conditioning for the operating theatre and a bamboo frame covered in reed matting providing extra shelter from the sun. The patients came pouring in, including one lady who had been so grateful for the frequent visits of Nurse Pat Davis during the pilot scheme of 1958 that she said simply, 'I have seen Christ', and turning to him in faith was baptised: a seal on the work of the caravan hospital at its start. As well as Jock and Gwendy Anderson, the staff included Valerie Baker, an evangelist, Betty Cox and Pat Davis, both nurses, Samuel Gill as Registrar and Drs Peter and Carol Hover. These two young doctors had married in 1957 and when they heard about the plans for the Christian

Caravan Hospital, felt sure that this was where God wanted them to be. Jock taught Peter eye surgery and reckoned that his pupil soon overtook him in skill.

Life on the site was demanding. The hospital staff lived in simple mud houses much like those of the local people. The Hover family lived for some time in a tent, and then in a small 10'×6' caravan. Maintenance work on the generators, medical equipment and vehicles had often to be done by the doctors when there was no engineer. Mercifully much of the general nursing and feeding of the patients was seen to by their relatives. In spite of this, the pressure of work was enormous, and sometimes overwork exacerbated problems in personal relationships. Peter and Jock, for example, had serious differences – Peter tending to come to rapid conclusions, quick to act, Jock with a more contemplative approach. On other occasions Pakistani staff felt left out when discussion took place in English, or Samuel felt that his authority as Registrar was being undermined. But with humility and prayer these problems were resolved.

So the Christian Caravan Hospital continued its work, inundated with eager and appreciative patients. Every year or two it moved on – a process involving enormous labour each time in packing up and re-assembling the hospital. In 1965 Jock Anderson handed over the leadership of the hospital team to Peter Hover and moved on into a new area of service with BMMF. The caravan hospital went then to Umerkot on the edge of the desert, a place with no Christian community and no hospital. Peter and Carol were in their element here, pioneering in both medicine and evangelism, but tragically in 1969, with the hospital all packed up in Hyderabad ready for the monsoons and the Hovers about to set off for leave in England, Peter's car collided with a bus on the rough dusty road. He was killed, aged only thirty-seven. In less than ten years with the caravan hospital, his achievement had been immense.

Dr Ralph Heaton continued the medical work, helped, among others, by Norman and Jean Norris; Jean a nurse, and Norman maintaining and moving the caravans and the equipment. After two to three years at Umerkot and another spell at Mirpur Khas, the hospital ceased to be mobile, and a settled hospital using some of the caravans was set up in a disused Roman Catholic hospital at Kunri, as a rural health care and TB hospital reaching out into the desert. Its other specialities were obstetrics and gynaecology and ophthalmology. The thinking had come almost full circle, from the idea of a stationary hospital with its emphasis on treatment, through the imaginative innovation of the caravan hospital, to the outreach hospital with a fixed base again but with its emphasis on preventative medicine.

The work at Kunri was not easy. Indeed perhaps because of the special movement of God which was seen in Sindh, workers there have seemed specially under attack. As Ian Lacy reflected in 1988, having worked there for seven years:

> Over the years, far more than the average number of people working there have become ill or been hurt. Two have died, and no-one working there has not experienced pressure and pain of some sort. There is darkness round Kunri – the darkness of those without hope and without God in the world. Someone wants to keep it that way, so he uses the power at his disposal to assault all those, expatriate and Pakistani, who are sent to keep the light burning.

Ian and his wife Gerry experienced this attack, as their daughter Emma was diagnosed as having leukaemia at the same time as Ian's father died of an infection he had picked up while working in the operating theatre at Kunri. And Juliet Smith, who at the beginning of 1986 came to Kunri as part of the School Leavers Overseas Training Programme (SLOT) – now 'On Track' – became ill and died aged eighteen after being there only three months. On top of all this, in 1988 two Pakistani staff members of the hospital were killed in a road accident. One of these was Mukhtar, the head eye-assistant, a keen Christian and key worker in the hospital; the other was a Hindu sweeper. They had been on their way to set up an eye camp in the desert. But as Dr Maureen Yates, another person who came through 'the Kunri experience', was shown in a vision – yes, there is darkness, but there is also a shining light which the darkness cannot put out.

I visited Kunri, and saw for myself something of the hard work that goes into keeping the light shining in this remote place on the edge of the desert. Starting from Karachi, a train took us through flat, irrigated, fertile countryside to Mirpur Khas. A prosperous-looking land-owner, hearing that we were going to Kunri, spoke appreciatively of the hospital. From Mirpur Khas we needed a police escort, as there had been kidnappings recently in the area, and it would reflect badly on the government should foreigners be kidnapped. In Mirpur Khas events took over, and we just let them happen: a young man came and took us in a horse-drawn cart or tonga to a Church of Pakistan boys' hostel where we were to wait for the escort. Here we met an American Interserver, Pat Stock, whose husband Paul was the Administrator of the hostel. Paul's parents were veteran workers with the American Presbyterian Church – we were soon to meet them at Kunri – and Pat had first come to Pakistan with YWAM (Youth with a Mission). As Pat told me, when she and Paul married, they were uncertain what to do, as both the American Presbyterian Church and YWAM had special strengths – the former its structure and long history, the latter its creativity and freedom in the Spirit. In the end they opted for Interserve, as suiting them both and having all these qualities; and also for its good support structure for its partners, something well demonstrated on our visit, for we were travelling with Denis Roche, Interserve's Medical Adviser, who was visiting Partners from his base at Interserve's International Office in Cyprus.

The boys' hostel seemed a happy place, with space

for football and cricket, and a menagerie of rabbits and budgerigars. The boys, who come from Christian families from the small desert communities, go to local government schools. We saw their dormitories, tight-packed with beds covered with the boys' own brightly coloured quilts, well worn and not over clean. Paul did many creative things with them. Very musical, and fluent in several languages having been brought up in Pakistan, he composed himself, and also picked up songs composed by local Christians in Sindhi, Punjabi, Gujerati and Urdu. He played the tablas (drums) and harmonium and with infectious enthusiasm taught the boys to play instruments too. Every Christmas he wrote a play and the boys performed it and took it to nearby villages. This taught them a lot about working together and discipline, as well as getting them involved in outreach among their own people.

Eventually our escort – two young policemen – arrived, and we set off in a land-rover along the endless straight road to Kunri, sometimes through desert, sometimes through mango orchards and other crops where irrigation made this possible. Intricately decorated buses hurtled along the narrow dusty road, small donkeys gamely and daintily pulled loaded carts, lordly camels and flocks of goats ambled by, and sometimes we passed small groups of round thatched huts where the tribespeople lived. At last, on the edge of the hot and dusty town of Kunri we arrived at the peaceful oasis which is the hospital: surrounded by fields of wheat and mango trees, with flowers everywhere, and people in twos and threes working quietly in the fields. The Roman Catholics had built the hospital here years earlier. They still have an active church and schools, and provide pastoral care for Roman Catholic patients. Here in 1975 BMMF's caravan hospital had come to rest. Indeed we saw one of the caravans, a real piece of mission history, now the watchman's hut. Another of the caravans – the erstwhile operating theatre – is still in use at Rattanabad, as the base of a maternity and TB clinic run by the Church of Pakistan.

Both Kunri hospital and the outreach among the neighbouring tribes come under the auspices of the Church of Pakistan, and the Bishop of Hyderabad, Bashir Jiwan, is closely involved in the work of the hospital, helping, among other things, with finding staff from local Christian families. Expatriate staff, from United Presbyterians, Interserve, CMS and Wycliffe Bible Translators, are all seconded to the Diocese of Hyderabad. People we met included Dr Don Curry from Canada, and his wife Nancy. Nancy was deeply interested in Pakistani handicrafts and in her contacts with the local tribal women, hoping to get cottage industries going among them. Don was training TB workers and supervising local TB clinics; he had recently been ordained into the Church of Pakistan and was now giving more time to pastoral and evangelistic than to medical work. The village outreach was encouraging, with four villages with groups of Christians, several of them ex-TB patients. Through contact with the hospital over several years they had gradually come to faith.

The Currys are a remarkable family. Don came to Pakistan in the late 1970s and adopted a radically simple lifestyle, becoming notably fluent in Sindhi and later Dhatki. He and Nancy established a bridgehead for the Gospel in a small village called Gordi, where Nancy, dark and attractive with fine-boned features, dressed like the tribal women, complete with arm bangles, colourful sarees and bare feet, walking five kilometres to get water for cooking. They had many adventures in Gordi before coming to Kunri. Don's brother Doug and his sister Joanne both worked with UMN in Nepal.

Sara Smith, an Interserve Partner from England, the hospital evangelist, had also moved from medical to pastoral work. Coming first to Kunri as a nurse, she helped with Yvonne Dorey and Jean and Norman Norris to get the hospital ready for re-opening after the Roman Catholics had left. Norman, who was officially in charge of maintenance, supervised the building, liaising with ZOR engineers, the joint venture of his brother Dennis and another engineer

from England. Initially the hospital was planned as a base
for a community health programme, but gradually the work
became more curative and hospital-based, apart from the TB
clinics and a World Health Organisation programme called
EPI (Expanded Programme of Immunisation), which was
run by another Interserve Partner from Scotland, Dr Derek
McHardy. In 1983 Sara sensed that the Lord was leading
her away from nursing and into evangelism and pastoral
work within the hospital, and this is what she was now
doing: sharing the love of Christ, particularly among
women patients, helping those who were frightened or
didn't understand the system, praying with them. As she
put it, 'It's all right to talk about God in Pakistan' – often
the patients welcome and expect it.

I was shown round the hospital, with its cool concrete
buildings and shady, well-irrigated compound, its two big
eye wards and the operating theatre. Three ophthalmic
patients are wheeled up to three entrances to the theatre
so that their heads protrude simultaneously into the sterile
area. One is prepared for surgery, another is operated on
and the third is given dressings, as the quickest and most
efficient way of getting them done. Regular eye camps,
with even faster 'conveyor-belt' methods, treat patients in
a marquee in the hospital courtyard. The eye work was
directed by a Pakistani doctor, Dr Jacob – there were no
expatriates on the eye team.

Beyond the hospital, past the old caravan and the watch-
men, a peaceful walk leads to the Kunri Ashram or Christian
community, where some of the hospital workers live near
to the round thatched church. Here I met the pastor, Fred
Stock and his wife Margie. They were fraternal workers of
the American Presbyterian Church, whose two sons Paul
and Dale both worked with Interserve in Pakistan: Dale
as Maintenance Manager here at Kunri and Paul at Mirpur
Khas. Fred and Margie had worked for thirty-five years in
Pakistan: in the Punjab, then at the Pakistan Bible Training
Institute, Hyderabad, and for the last five years at Kunri,
where at the Bishop's request Fred came to be pastor of

Outpatients waiting, Kunri

the Ashram church. Fred and Margie are the authors of an important book, *People Movements in the Punjab*.* They told me about their methods of teaching Christian truth to the largely illiterate tribal people using pictures; and they introduced me to a tall tribesman, emaciated by TB, who, deciding to be baptised after contacts with the hospital over many years because of his illness, brought twenty-three others with him for baptism.

I went to morning prayers in the round Ashram church: shoes off, women with heads covered, we sat cross-legged on mats on the floor. Songs were sung, accompanied by local instruments, Margie told a Bible story using a picture-Bible, and men and women gathered separately in small groups for extempore prayer. The church was built by Jim Hunter of Interserve, who after a time as engineer on the caravan hospital worked here on hospital maintenance but moved on to become Project Director and was then ordained. Many other Interserve Partners have been involved with Kunri, among them Dr Malcolm Dunjey from Australia who served as Director for the rural health project for a time, based in Karachi, and Dr John Parsons who led the community health team and pastored the church.

Two other Interserve Partners whom I met in Karachi also had Kunri links: Philip and Florence James first came to Pakistan from the UK and Australia respectively to work as nurses in the days of the caravan hospital: Florence (as Florence Hastings) first at Umerkot and then at Rattanabad where she and Philip both helped Dr Ralph Heaton and other medical personnel on his eye team. When BMMF transferred its medical work from the caravan hospital to Kunri, both Flo and Philip were transferred. They were married in 1979. Gradually Philip became more involved in evangelism and village work, and in 1981 the Bishop invited them to move to Rattanabad where they ran a TB clinic and a Christian conference centre. Four years later they moved again – this time to Khipro, north-east

* Published by William Carey Library, 1975.

of Mirpur Khas, where John Self of CMS had started a small Christian community centre. Here they did TB clinic work, linked with Kunri hospital, and helped the pastor, the Rev Qaiser Lal, the evangelist, Mr Emmanuel, and other local church leaders in their work. When they arrived only about a dozen Christians met to worship; by 1992 there were about sixty to seventy. A round church has been built there, slowly over many years as gifts came in. It was finally consecrated by the Bishop as the 'Church of Reconciliation' in 1989, the name expressing the hope that here in this agricultural community people from all backgrounds would be reconciled in Christ.

Looking back on the effectiveness of the Christian Caravan Hospital, Jock Anderson observed that in a sense it fell between two stools, being neither a proper base hospital nor fully mobile, since setting up on a new site took weeks or even months. But the main failure, he felt, lay in not allowing local people more share in the planning, the decision-making and the work. Somehow they had never been able to stop working for long enough to arrange this. Yet if it had been done, it would have made an indelible mark on the Sindh community as local people were involved in serving their own community. At all events it was a remarkable venture, visionary and innovative. To a considerable extent Jock Anderson anticipated the general move towards community and preventative medicine in poor rural parts of the world, responding to a clear need in the name of Christ. But the caravan hospital was the last major purely BMMF venture of its kind to be launched. From now onwards, the way forward lay in co-operative work.

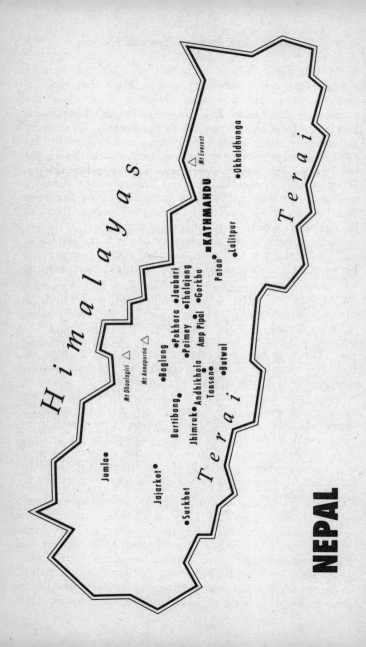

4

Into Nepal, under an umbrella

Nepal! The very name breathes beauty and mystery. Beauty because of the towering Himalayas on its northern borders, mystery because for so many centuries it was a closed land, to all intents and purposes cut off from the rest of the world. Eighty to ninety per cent of the population in this poor and undeveloped country follow a folk version of Hinduism involving idol-worship, blood-sacrifice, ancestor-worship and spirit-appeasement. Others are Buddhists, and here in Nepal Hinduism and Buddhism are closely intertwined. The ruler of this unique Hindu kingdom is traditionally regarded as the incarnation of the Hindu god Vishnu. What room then in Nepal, if any, for the Christian faith?

For many years the country was ruled not by the king but by the repressive regime of the hereditary prime ministers of the Rana family. Under them the country remained closed, isolated, locked in the inflexible, medieval structure of a rigidly Hindu society, shut off from influences from outside. Yet even during those years the influence of the Gospel was known in Nepal: in 1704 Capuchin Fathers had established missions in Bhatgaon and Kathmandu, only to be expelled when the King of Gorkha conquered the small kingdoms of the Kathmandu valley in 1769. From then onwards the policy of excluding all foreigners and Christians was maintained, but in the nineteenth and early twentieth centuries the Bible was translated into Nepali by missionaries in India, and portions were widely distributed among Nepalis living in India and on the borders. Over the years Scriptures were distributed too among Gurkha soldiers in the regiments, from Burma to the Punjab and later in Hong Kong and England.

In the nineteenth century many Nepalis went to India looking for work. They mostly entered the Darjeeling district and became the dominant people there. Some became Christians, composing this prayer for their homeland:

> O Lord, hear our petition, open the door of salvation
>   For the Gorkhalis.
> Father, Son, Holy Spirit, hear our petition,
>   Show us the way by a cloudy fiery pillar.
> Peoples of different religions are to east, west and south;
>   Tibet is north, and Nepal our home is in the middle.
> There are cities: Thapathali, Bhatgaon, Patan, Kathmandu:
>   Our desire is to make them your devotees.
> Up, brothers: we must go, ignoring hate and shame,
>   Leaving wealth, people, comfort, to do the holy task.

To one group of about forty people, God gave a vision to go back to live and work and witness as Christians in Nepal. So in 1913 they packed up everything and undertook the arduous journey to Kathmandu, only to be expelled once they were discovered to be Christians. But this prayer and concern led to the founding by Nepali Christians of the Gorkha Mission which placed evangelists along the Nepal border to preach and give Scriptures to people travelling in and out; they also did some school-teaching and simple medical work. ZBMM did similar border work, notably through Kitty Harbord, a much loved and respected doctor who after working in the ZBMM hospitals felt God calling her to move on to Nautanwa on the border and even once spent six weeks in Nepal attending the daughter of the Governor of West Nepal for her confinement. In Nautanwa she printed her own Gospel tracts, which she distributed each day in the bazaar after her morning dispensary. Jonathan Lindell remembers her in later life like this:

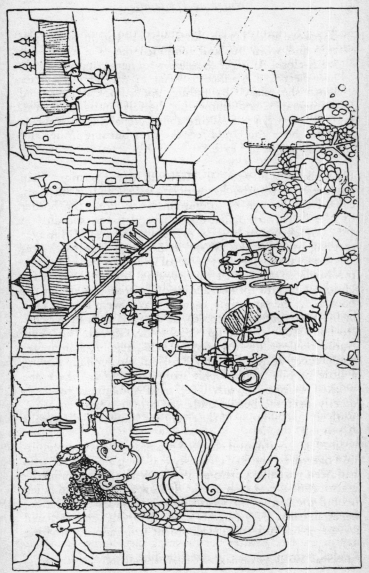

Durbar Square, Kathmandu

She wore ankle length skirts, had her hair in a bun, was thin and worn out and reminded me of a wrung-out wash-cloth. At night she slept with newspapers between her sheet and blanket to keep in the warmth. After lunch she relaxed by pulling out a book of advanced mathematics and immersing herself in its problems. When you got her talking about Nepal and missionary work there you could feel the fires burning in her and see flashes in her eyes.*

He reckoned it was Dr Harbord, perhaps more than anyone else, who by her articles, letters and enthusiasm, caused the growth of interest in work along the border of Nepal. Having defied death several times, she died in 1952, knocked over by a car on her way to a ZBMM prayer meeting at Ladbroke Grove in London. Her work was eventually taken over by the Nepal Evangelistic Band, while the Medical Mission of the Regions Beyond Missionary Union at Raxaul formed another Christian beacon on the border. At the same time, earnest prayer went up that God in his own time would break down the 'walls of Jericho' (Joshua 6:20) and open up Nepal to the Gospel. The Nepal Border Fellowship, founded in 1935, held regular prayer conferences at Raxaul, and Rosalind Broomhall, driving a little mobile medical unit from Gorakhpur where she worked before her marriage, used sometimes to cross quietly over the border and hold a little prayer meeting. With all this 'blowing of the trumpets', how could the walls fail to fall?

In 1950 the situation changed dramatically, when revolution overthrew the Rana dynasty and King Tribhuvan, who had been virtually a prisoner in his own palace, became the constitutional monarch. Realising how far Nepal had fallen behind the rest of the world during its years of isolation, he established 'His Majesty's Government' and initiated sweeping reforms and development programmes, inviting

* Jonathan Lindell, *Nepal and the Gospel of God* (UMN 1979), p 97.

people from other countries to help. When he died in 1954 his initiatives were continued by his successor, King Mahendra, who soon reversed the democratic changes and clamped down on new freedoms so that Nepal continued as a one-party Hindu state. Amidst all the new government-sponsored activity – building roads and bridges, educational and medical work – there was need and room enough for Christian workers, but the law of the land still insisted that 'No person shall propagate Christianity, Islam, or any other faith so as to disrupt the traditional religion of the Hindu community within Nepal, or convert any adherent of the Hindu religion into these faiths.' The penalty for baptising converts was six years' imprisonment, while the convert could be jailed for one year. When, in 1952, Christian missions were permitted to enter the country, it was made clear that they were given visas in order to serve the people in areas of medicine, education and development and not to propagate their religion or convert the people. But these agreements applied only to foreign mission organisations; Indian and Nepali Christians could now freely enter and live in Nepal, although for them too there were severe penalties if their activities led to conversions.

As far as medical aid was concerned, the Government already had contact with people who might help. One link had been created gradually over the years as one faithful person after another followed God's leading towards Nepal. Kitty Harbord's work at Nautanwa was continued by Dr Lily O'Hanlon and Miss Hilda Steele, who had worked with ZBMM. Dr O'Hanlon had started at the Duchess of Teck Hospital at Patna, not far across the border in India, but then felt called to Nepal, as did Hilda Steele. They were released with good will and prayer by ZBMM and continued Kitty Harbord's work by forming the Nepal Evangelistic Band in 1940 – a band of foreign and Nepali Christians working together in the dispensary and distributing Christian literature at the railway station and the bazaar at Nautanwa. When eventually the new Nepali Government began asking for medical help, the

British Ambassador suggested Dr O'Hanlon, who had been a neighbour of his in England. As a result, she and Miss Steele moved from the border to Pokhara and established the 'Shining Hospital' – so called because of the way its metal roofing shone in the sun. Christian work in Pokhara still continues under the auspices of what is now the International Nepal Fellowship, to which Interserve people are seconded.

The other link came about remarkably. In the neighbouring Himalayan mountains of India, to the west of Nepal, was the well-known Woodstock School sponsored by a group of missions, including ZBMM. In the 1940s an American, Dr Bob Fleming, taught science there and his wife Bethel was the school doctor. An enthusiastic student of the bird life of the Indian Himalyas, Bob was surprised and delighted when his request to the Nepali Government to extend his studies eastwards into the mountains of Nepal was granted, and for several years running he and Bethel spent their winter holidays bird-watching in Nepal. Latterly they were accompanied by doctors Carl Taylor and Carl Friedericks, and in 1952 while Bob Fleming joyfully studied the bird life, the three doctors organised a simple medical dispensary in Tansen for the local people. So much was this appreciated, that when Nepal began seeking aid, it was the Flemings and Friederickses who were asked to start medical work in Kathmandu and Tansen respectively.

When the doctors, who came from Presbyterian and Methodist churches in the United States, received this invitation, in May 1953, it was felt that it would be unwise and unwieldy for too many different missionary groups to obtain special agreements with the government to set up medical work. So apart from the International Nepal Fellowship who already had permission, it was decided that all further work would be done unitedly by any other interested missions. As Jonathan Lindell commented:

These two missions, full of the belief that this was the way God wanted his people to live and work on the earth, 'died' to their personal possessiveness of this permission and gave it up to the world church for the widest possible co-operative basis of work . . . so that out of the womb of church and mission in India, by the work of God's Spirit, there was born a new kind of united mission.*

Among the thirty-nine different missions from various countries which eventually joined what has become known as the United Mission to Nepal, ZBMM was prominent from the start. Indeed, this united venture suited ZBMM perfectly – interdenominational, eager to be involved in united efforts, ready to respond to needs as they arose.

The United Mission to Nepal, originally called the United Christian Mission to Nepal and born out of two important meetings in India in 1954, was an early example of an important development in missionary work: the 'umbrella' organisation working under protocol or by agreement with government. UMN's authorisation to work in Nepal was set out in an Agreement which stated: 'I have the honour to inform you that His Majesty's Government of Nepal do permit the United Mission to Nepal to undertake work in this country . . . ' What an answer to much faithful prayer! And although evangelistic work as such was prohibited, individuals, both expatriate and national Christians, were free to share their faith, vision and expertise, and in the words of the constitution of UMN, 'to minister to the needs of the people of Nepal in the name and spirit of Jesus Christ, and to make Christ known by word and life'.

The invitation received and the organisation set up (not an easy matter, as the theological stances of the contributing groups did not always agree), work began at once. For ZBMM God's timing, as usual, was perfect in that the opening of Nepal coincided with a rethinking of ZBMM's medical policy in India. As it gradually became clear that Indian personnel could and should take responsibility for

* Jonathan Lindell, *Nepal and the Gospel of God*, pp 143, 149.

India's medical work, ZBMM staff – particularly those at
Patna – responded to the need and challenge of work in
Nepal. The first of these was Dr Marjory Foyle from
England, who in March 1956 went as the much-needed
woman doctor to work with Carl Friedericks and a small
international team in Tansen, the hill-top town where Kitty
Harbord had attended the Governor's daughter almost
thirty years before and where Bethel Fleming and the
other doctors had set up their clinic. They started work in
a converted private house, where conditions were primitive,
but were eventually given land on the hill outside the town,
'the hill of ghosts and jackals' unwanted by anyone else.
There a new hospital was built.

Here too in 1957 came Mary Cundy, also from England.
Trained as a medical social worker, she was called by
a remarkable series of circumstances to serve God in
the then little-known country of Nepal. From language
school in India a bus brought her across the border
as far as Butwal. From there onwards there were no
roads. Eventually, together with fellow missionaries from
America and their small children, the Nepali carriers and
one horse, she reached Tansen on foot, 4,500 feet up in
the terraced middle hills of Nepal. Despite her training,
she was asked to be Business Manager at the hospital, a
job she tackled with her usual humour and determination.
After ten years at Tansen she ran dispensaries in two villages
for a further twenty. First, in 1968, she moved to Pyersingh,
a mountain village some forty miles south of Pokhara,
where Hilda Steele had set up, with the co-operation of
the local panchayat (village council) a dispensary and small
demonstration farm, helped by two local girls who became
Christians. Later Mary was forced to leave after vandalism
of the building at Pyersingh, and continued the dispensary
work at nearby Paimey: like Pyersingh, within view of the
magnificent snow-capped Annapurna mountain range and
about five hours walk uphill from the nearest road. The
village people lived in stone and mud thatched houses with
cooking fires on the floors of smoke-filled rooms. They

would own maybe one worn change of clothes; lice and bed-bugs abounded, and most had no access to medical help or education. Triumphs and tragedies filled her days as she continued to serve the community and little church, helped when Hilda Steele retired by Valerie Collett of Interserve. When Mary herself retired in 1989 the group of believers numbered nearly a hundred, including children. The work was taken over by Nepali Christians Prabhu Dan and Jyoti who had come to Christ through her friendship and witness, which had been like a beacon of light for miles around.

Kathmandu, the capital of Nepal, lies in the centre of the great clay bowl of the Kathmandu valley. The old part of the city is a maze of narrow streets and close-packed three and four storey brick buildings with balconies and wide roof eaves reaching out. Through intricately carved and decorated doorways one enters courtyards of palaces and temples where both the richness of the wood-carving and the primitive nature of some of the shrines take one by surprise, bringing home the difference and the darkness of the culture. Everywhere in streets and squares are tiny shops and stalls selling a rich variety of wares: fruit and vegetables piled high, bales of cloth, brass, pottery, the goods weighed out on archaic metal scales. It feels like part of the mediaeval world. Beyond the old city, though, Kathmandu is growing, with high-rise buildings spreading outwards into the valley.

Here, what was first planned to be a group of women's and children's clinics soon developed into a general hospital, based first in a government-loaned cholera hospital and then in a former Rana palace just across the river in Patan – Shanta Bhawan Hospital. When the mission first moved in, there were still large chandeliers, grand furniture from Europe and huge oil-paintings on the walls. Here, to work with the Flemings, came Dr 'Sandy' (Winifred) Anderson from Patna – at first just visiting and helping out, but soon to work full time – and Sister Margaret Fleming; also Brian Richards as pharmacist with his wife Pat. With considerable resources from abroad and a rapidly growing international

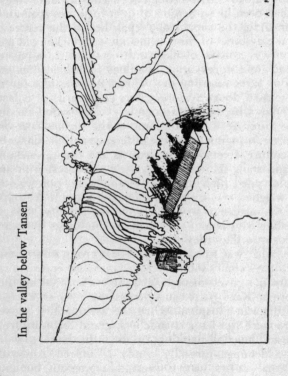

In the valley below Tansen

staff, the hospital provided high-quality medical care at a crucial time in Nepal's development. Its name and fine reputation became known throughout the land.

In 1958 yet another hospital opened, nine miles east of Kathmandu in the ancient city of Bhatgaon (now Bhaktapur) with its narrow streets and hundreds of Hindu shrines and temples. Here came Dr Pamela Dodson, who had worked at the Canada Hospital in Nasik, hoping one day to transfer to Nepal. Wiry and energetic, she was always game for adventure, as when she and Val Collett, a nurse then newly recruited for Nepal by BMMF, managed to buy a jeep for UMN in Delhi against all the odds at a time of acute postwar scarcity and then drove it up to Kathmandu along a road that was only then being built, surmounting obstacles, getting coated in dust and sleeping in a railway station on the way.

In 1961 Pam became ill and Dr Denis Roche, then working at Shanta Bhawan, was asked to take her place as Medical Superintendent for a few weeks. In fact Pam was then posted to Tansen, and thirteen years later Denis was still at Bhaktapur. There were encouragements, especially in the area of TB prevention and cure, but in 1974 the Government built its own hospital, and the UMN hospital, which in its final year had treated 22,150 outpatients and 1,063 inpatients, had to close. It was hard for those who had put so much into the work there to pull out, but they did it with grace and faith, transferring where possible to other projects within Nepal.

Of his time at Bhaktapur, Denis remembers the complete absence of electricity when they first arrived; a tense three months when a man-eating leopard hunted and killed in the area; Cliff Richard visiting in 1974 in connection with a TEAR Fund road-building project, to be entertained by the Roche's young daughter Patsy, in bed with hepatitis; and his wife Ann's many roles, especially in entertaining. A jeep on the road below meant she had ten minutes to prepare for visitors – without a phone, there was no other warning. In the church in Bhaktapur they saw slow, steady growth

under the Nepali pastor Tir Bahadur who, imprisoned and
beaten only a few years ago at the age of seventy-five, still
continues his work and is now seeing a number of people
turning to Christ, many from seeds sown twenty to thirty
years ago. Denis and Ann were also founders, with support
and encouragement from the British Council and Embassy,
of the British Primary School in Kathmandu, which arose
out of the educational needs of their own and a few other
children. Returning from their first home leave in 1966 they
brought back with them Margaret Thoday of BMMF to be
the first Headmistress of the tiny school which started in
rented property with eight pupils. Since then it has grown
and flourished, with BMMF well represented on the staff,
and continues to be a lifeline to many UMN and other
expatriate families.

In all these places, the medical work was not done in
a spiritual vacuum. As John Pollock wrote, 'No public
preaching is permitted in Nepal, but in the hospitals and
in their homes the Nepali and Indian Christians and the
Westerners are seeing the growth of a Church on simple
apostolic lines.' In Kathmandu there was already one
Christian man before the country opened up in 1951.
An aristocratic Hindu of the ruling Rana family, Colonel
Nararaj Shamshere had met Christ when accompanying a
sick grandson to the hospital at Raxaul. Back in Nepal,
he continued to read the Bible he had been given, 'in a
shut door room'. He made a second journey to India in
order to be baptised, and as soon as Christians began to
enter the city in 1951 he opened his home to them and
others for Bible study and for Sunday worship. Among
the first Christians meeting there were three Mar Thoma
Christians from South India who had studied at the Union
Biblical Seminary at Yeotmal and responded to God's call
to Nepal. There was someone too whose mother, then a
child of nine, had been part of the group of believers who
travelled from India and were expelled in 1913. Jack Dain
remembers going there with his wife Edith in 1956: 'It was
in an upper room on the main street of Kathmandu. We

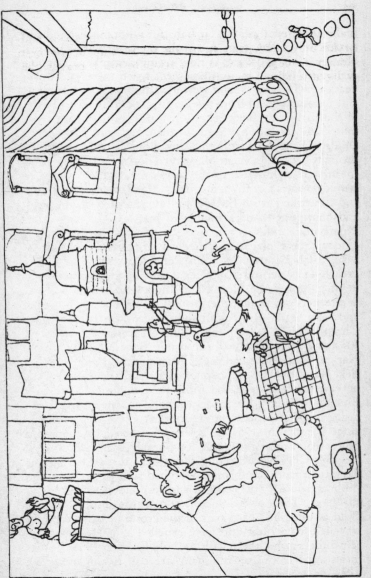

Sweta Machhendranath Temple, Kathmandu

went upstairs, took off our shoes, sat on the floor and broke bread. What a joy it was to worship in the first church in Nepal!' Indeed, in answer to much prayer, the walls of Jericho were tumbling down.

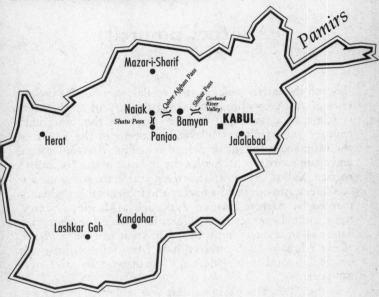

5

Another umbrella

Beyond the north-west frontier of Pakistan lies the mountainous and gloweringly beautiful country of Afghanistan – scene of devastating frontier wars in the nineteenth century and rarely off television screens in the 1980s, as the Mujahedin fought to defend it against Russian troops, and again more recently, with the collapse of the Najibullah regime. Kabul, the capital, lies deep within the mountains at 6,000 feet, surrounded by barren and inhospitable highlands pierced by narrow ravines. Although a Muslim country, there have been scattered Christians here for centuries. There is an ancient tomb of a Christian martyr at Herat. Many Afghans have received help from mission hospitals on India's and now Pakistan's north-west frontier over the years.

In the 1950s, when Afghanistan was still ruled by its king, the country began to open its doors to help from the West. Teachers in particular were invited, and among those to respond, convinced that this was where God wanted him to go, was an American Presbyterian minister, Christy Wilson, whose parents had been missionaries in Iran. He went out with his wife in 1951 to teach English at Habibia Secondary School, but as the international community grew and he was the only ordained Protestant minister in the country, he was often asked to take weddings and funerals. In 1952 he was asked to pastor the new Community Christian Church which met in a rented house, its members being foreign diplomats and other professionals – teachers, doctors, engineers – and eventually he became the full-time pastor. A specially built church building was dedicated on May 17th 1970.

In the 1950s, too, USAID (the United States Agency for International Development) had built a hospital in the new desert town of Lashkar Gah. A fine building and adequately staffed by Peace Corps nurses and CARE-MEDICO doctors, it attracted few patients because it had no surgeon. The situation soon changed dramatically with the arrival of Dr Howard Harper, a New Zealand doctor who had worked with the Brethren in Pakistan. He started operating, and at once the hospital filled up to such an extent that not only the wards but also the corridors were overflowing with patients. He also ran successful eye camps. Waiting one day in 1966 at Kabul airport for a consignment of human corneas for grafting, Dr Harper was hailed by someone he knew from Lashkar Gah:

'Nice to see you, Dr Harper. What are you doing here?'

'Waiting for corneas. And you?'

'I'm waiting for His Excellency the Minister of Health – I'll introduce you.' So His Excellency got off the plane, Howard got his eyes and was introduced to the Minister of Health: 'This is Dr Harper, who has done so much for our people . . .' As they chatted, the Minister asked Howard what he thought were the priority medical needs for the country, to which he replied – praying, no doubt, as Nehemiah did when asked a similar question by a king – 'An eye hospital, a blind school and a corneal bank.'

'Come and see me tomorrow, and we'll talk about this.' And so, in God's providence, an open door.

Here as in Nepal, God had already been at work. Shortly before, in April 1966, a group including Alan Norrish of BMMF had met in Peshawar, over the border in North Pakistan, and had formed the International Afghan Mission – I AM. Like the UMN, it was to be an 'umbrella organisation' involving CMS, BMMF, the Presbyterians and others. The hope was to work, like UMN, under protocol to the

Government, but as yet it had no projects and no openings. So when Howard Harper met the Minister of Health, and he was asked how he thought the ophthalmic needs he had mentioned might be met, Howard was able to say that he knew people who might be able to help.

With IAM already set up, and an open door before them, the first thought was to initiate an eye project as a way of introducing IAM to the country. And as the first British participants in this exciting new project, the Anderson family – Jock, Gwendy and their three children, flew out to Kabul in 1966, ready to tackle the new challenge in the same spirit as they had set up the Christian Caravan Hospital some ten years before. The inspired name for the new project was NOOR. This stood, apparently prosaically, for National Organisation for Ophthalmic Rehabilitation. But the word 'noor' also means 'light', and so in this choice of name Jesus took his rightful place: 'I AM NOOR – I am the Light of the world.

After lengthy negotiations, a signature of agreement between NOOR and the Afghan government was eventually obtained from the new Minister of Health, Miss Kobra Nurzayi, and NOOR's work began. It was a frustrating time. NOOR had no building as yet, so eye wards were set up in two existing government hospitals – one Russian and one American-built. Fastest progress was made in the rehabilitation of the blind, a field in which Christy Wilson and his wife Betty had already made a start, teaching braille reading, knitting and other skills. Developing this work, IAM set up a Blind School in a rented building next to the church in Kabul. Soon it was thriving, and there were notable conversions: so much so that the Government began to clamp down and forbid proseletysing. But quality of life and service could still proclaim Christ as King, and in this spirit IAM continued its work. Visiting Kabul in 1968, Arthur Pont of BMMF found

teeming, swarthy faces all around. Bourka-covered women with no flesh to be seen anywhere – not even the eyes. Meat hanging in the doorways, strong Pathan faces with flowing robes, marked poverty alongside marble embassies and lovely houses; the whole contrasting impact can be almost overwhelming. I was so conscious that I was in a land that had been closed to the outside world up till only ten years ago.

Later, walking round the bazaars and the old city with BMMF workers there, he absorbed more impressions of

a city alive with people, ragged clothes, piles of dirt, millions of flies, narrow alley-ways and darkened shops too gloomy to see inside. Yet elsewhere wealth and plenty. I was told of an Afghan boy who had been thrown out of his home that afternoon for being a Christian. He could be punished by death. A sense of the old formerly closed country came sweeping over me. The people are bound by the people.

He visited the Community Christian Church: 'a little Christian oasis in a desert of harsh prejudice on a plateau of 6,000 feet surrounded by mountains on all sides, landlocked, remote, previously inaccessible. Here we raised our voices in praise of the King of Kings.'

Various things besides the rehabilitation of the blind were planned under the NOOR project: an eye hospital, the training of Afghan doctors and opticians and the holding of eye camps round the country. An eye camp held in 1968 was described in BMMF's *Go* magazine:

'Come over and help us,' came the call. In response came a small medical team and by land-rover from Britain a party of nine lively young people (including a Scot and a South African) – two medical students, two nursing sisters, a mental health social worker, ophthalmologist, pharmacist, solicitor and orthoptist – to give a helping hand. Tents, matting, rope, operating table and other equipment were transported by lorry, and on arrival they all worked flat out to pitch a canvas eye hospital. The following day the clinical work began. In three weeks 800 outpatients were seen, suffering from trachoma and other eye conditions. Inpatients were housed in tents and under canvas awnings, and about 130 operations were performed.

Progress on the other proposals was slow, and the Health Minister began asking, 'Where is this hospital you have promised us?' She was getting worried, as she had promised it to the people and it reflected badly on her if what was promised failed to be delivered. The main reason for the delay was funding. Donor agencies were not keen on building a large Western-style hospital in Afghanistan. They thought that the real need was for preventative eye work. This may well have been correct, but in a country like Afghanistan, only recently accepting help from the West, the Government first wanted a show-piece – something for the people to see, and a place for training doctors – before it would give serious consideration to preventative measures.

So how to get the funding and build the hospital? Oxfam had given generously to IAM for the building of an Eye Institute, but the Minister of Health insisted that the hospital must be built first. Soon IAM was under pressure not only from the Government as to why the hospital was not being built, but from Oxfam as to why the Blind Institute was not going up either. Eventually a solution was reached: the Blind Institute was built but used as a temporary eye hospital. Honour was satisfied all round. Miss Nurzayi laid the foundation stone and soon the NOOR team were performing about 1,500 eye operations a year, with a special consignment of human eyes flown courtesy of Royal Afghan Airlines from London to Kabul each month. Not long afterwards the money for the hospital came through as well. This gift was announced in BMMF's *Go* magazine of April 1971 as follows:

Christian Aid has given one of their largest and most generous gifts to the International Afghan Mission via the BMMF in London. For this kindness we thank God and the Council of Christian Aid. The gift is for the erection of a 60-bed eye hospital in Kabul for the NOOR team of doctors and nurses ... But even in Afghanistan £50,000 will not build an adequate modern eye hospital. The promise followed by the first instalment of the gift primed the pump which encouraged other donor agencies to share in the project. The German Christian agency Zentralstelle has promised 2½ million Deutsche Marks. The capital costs of building a new hospital today are far beyond the resources of a single society. The creation of the major donor agencies and their willingness to assist missions in their capital needs for buildings and equipment are part of God's sovereign timing in history.

There were setbacks. In May 1972 a mobile eye clinic, known as 'the Box' and destined for NOOR, was involved in a crash on its way out through Yugoslavia, and badly damaged. 'Why did God allow this?' Jock Anderson wrote. 'The Box is broken. Two thousand years ago another box was broken – it was made of alabaster ... The disciples asked why this waste; but the Lord knew it was a love-gift to himself. I believe the Mobile Clinic was primarily a love-gift to Christ. I believe he has accepted it as such.' The hospital – known as the NOOR Eye Institute – was built on the outskirts of Kabul and opened in 1973. In the entrance hall was a striking wall-carving of Jesus touching the blind beggar's eyes. A training scheme in ophthalmology was negotiated with the University, and the expatriate doctors' main task was to develop this course, and to teach.

As well as NOOR, IAM had another programme – MAP (Medical Assistance Programme). Unlike NOOR, which specialised in ophthalmic work and was based in Kabul, MAP staff ran a twenty-bedded hospital in the Yakaolang valley 8,000 feet up in the mountains of the Hazarajat, and satellite stations and clinics in other distant places. They were assisted by the Missionary Aviation Fellowship, as without the use of their small aeroplane it would be impossible to reach such inaccessible sites. The MAP project was led by Drs Rex and Jeanne Blumhagen from America, with a team drawn from many different countries – Finland, Sweden, USA, Canada, India, Australia, New Zealand and the UK. Among them, Marcia Sayre came from the USA with BMMF, having previously been in Afghanistan as a secretary with USAID, the American Development agency. Rex had been medical attaché to the US Embassy in Kabul. They conducted a medical survey for MAP, and began taking a mobile medical unit into the central highlands of Afghanistan. In the winter when the mountains were wrapped in a thick blanket of snow and all roads closed, a small fleet of 'skidoos' (motorised sledges) served otherwise inaccessible people and places.

One of their 'camp clinics' was described by Dan Condit, a retired chemist and Trustee of the USA Council of BMMF. He and his wife went out in 1973 to help as volunteers. As he wrote, organising a completely self-contained medical clinic for twenty to thirty people – doctors, nurses, ophthalmologist, dentist, nutritionist, lab. technician, pharmacist and supporting personnel – in the remote mountains of Afghanistan was not easy. After a long drive from Kabul up the Gorband river valley, they made the sharp ascent to the Shibar Pass, over 11,000 feet up. Then came the Qabre Afghan Pass, even higher at 12,000 feet. Near midnight they reached the MAP hospital at Naiak and eventually next day after crossing the spectacular Shatu Pass they reached the planned clinic site at Panjao. There for the whole summer a camp-based clinic was held; patients assembling in their hundreds by 7 a.m., the camp humming with activity, Doctors Rex and Jeanne seeing men and women respectively while an Afghan doctor, Raffin Miazed, worked with them and liaised with everyone in Farsi. All too soon the summer was over and the clinic dispersed, but the work of MAP, based in the government-built hospital at Naiak, continued until political events made it impossible. The community health-workers developed good rapport with the village women who would ask, 'Who sent you here?'

'We've been sent by the Government in Kabul.'

'We don't believe that – they've never done anything for us.'

'God sent us. He's a sending sort of God. Long ago his Son Jesus told us to come and show his love.'

In 1970, the work of IAM was greatly strengthened by the appointment of Alan Norrish as its Executive Secretary. From his initial post as BMMF Field Secretary, he had become International Secretary in 1966. In 1968 his wife Sylvia had died suddenly, aged only fifty-five. As Superintendent of Edgehill, the BMMF guest house at Landour, she had been a help and confidante to hundreds of people of many nationalities. Alan had already warned the BMMF Council that he intended to resign as International Secretary, feeling that a younger person who could carry the growing organisation forward should take over by 1970 at the latest. Having been involved in the setting up of IAM, he was now invited to become its full-time Executive Secretary. In November 1969 he married Noel Matheson, a good friend of Sylvia's who had been seconded from BMMF to Ludhiana Medical College and worked there for many years. As Warden to the medical students' hostel she had looked after Indian women students at the time when the college became co-educational, a major change. She had then done various administrative jobs. Alan and Noel were married in Afghanistan and started their new work based in Kabul. IAM initially had only a few workers, but with foreign aid pouring in it expanded rapidly. By 1973 there were eighty IAM workers in Afghanistan and more due to come, when in a revolution King Zahir Shah was ousted and first a socialist government and then in 1978 the Communists took power.

For some years the work of IAM (re-registered as the International Assistance Mission in 1978) was not too badly affected by the change. Some IAM members were told to leave, but although for a time the team grew very small the medical work was welcomed by the new Government, and in 1978 Dr Murray McGavin, the Scottish Project Director, reported that the Afghan Minister of Health had encouraged expansion of the work of NOOR and that a forty-bed satellite hospital was under construction 600 miles from Kabul. Eye camps continued to be held in increasing number, and a vitamin A project to give protection against blindness in children was being integrated into the country's immunisation programme. MAP, however, was not able to continue. The programme reached its peak between 1971–73, establishing three health clinics and a small hospital with supporting airstrips. And as the Director of the programme wrote,

> For those brief years there moved up and down the valleys of that remote mountain fastness a quality of human compassion expressed through medical care and concern which the people of the area had not known from the beginning of time. In the 'sarais' of the khan, in the mud-walled homes of the villagers and farmers, and around the smouldering 'boota' fires the word got around, 'A new thing is happening'.

Then in 1973 and, after a brief reprieve finally in 1974, the protocol between MAP and the Ministry of Health was terminated. By June 20th all MAP personnel had left.

Spiritually, too, things were not easy. A church for foreign workers was acceptable to the Government, but Christians were forbidden to preach the faith with a view to converting Muslims. Afghans who became Christians were persecuted, and this made it difficult for Christian workers from abroad even to attempt to have fellowship with them for fear of getting them into trouble with the authorities. In 1973 the Kabul Community Christian Church, dedicated as a 'place of prayer for all nations' was destroyed by agents of the Government. The timing of this destruction was significant. Hearing that Christians had an 'underground church', the bulldozers flattened the building and proceeded to dig up the foundations. Within an hour of the bulldozer finishing the work and leaving, the Government was toppled in a coup and the King overthrown, never, to date, to return. Some Muslims said this was God's retribution for destroying a holy place of worship.

In 1979 things became much worse when the Russians entered Afghanistan. All IAM work in the provinces was stopped, the work in Kabul being all that continued. Work at the hospital became almost impossible. Being a government hospital although most of the workers were Christians, political meetings would be held on the premises with no prior consultation. All the staff would have suddenly to drop tools and go and listen to a visiting politician. It was no way to run an efficient hospital. Then at Christmas 1980 two members of the hospital staff were brutally murdered – the Dutch pharmacist Erik Barendsen and his Finnish wife had their throats cut in front of their two small children. No one knew why this happened, or who the attackers were. To make matters worse, a blind Christian leader was arrested, accused of the murder and tortured. All IAM workers were immediately withdrawn from the country until April 1981, when they began gradually to return.

In 1988 the Russians withdrew. For a time things got harder, as the Mujahedin were against all people working for the Government. Many IAM workers left, but its work continued in Afghanistan – at NOOR, at the Blind Institute, in Maternal and Child Health (MCH) and in orthopaedic rehabilitation projects following the almost continuous fighting. The Afghans suffered much: rockets continued to fly overhead and medical and food supplies remained scarce. Nearly every family was bereaved, and standards at the hospital suffered as a result. Senior Afghan doctors were not training up juniors and there was a great need for more expatriate workers, particularly those trained in ophthalmology. Slowly the IAM team built up again with enthusiasm and high morale, and with plans to move out into the provinces once more with an eye survey and eye camps.

IAM celebrated twenty-five years of service in 1991. In 1980 there were only a handful of known believers in Afghanistan. Eleven years later there were several hundred. Prolonged suffering had aroused interest in spiritual things. One way in which help, both material and spiritual, can be given is through outreach to the many refugees who leave Afghanistan for Pakistan and India, hoping eventually to reach the West. In Peshawar two Interservers from Malaysia, Koh Soo Choon and Lee Kok Joo were seconded to an evangelical organisation working among refugees, and Irwin and Rosalie Buchanan from the UK taught English to Afghan refugees in Islamabad. These, as Irwin pointed out, are people who have lost everything, but one of the small group of believers among them was able to write this:

> You are my hope, you are my desire;
> You are my salvation, you are my joy,
> You are my Jesus.
> My love you are, my comforter you are;
> My knowledge you are, my forgiver you are,
> My soul/body you are, my spirit you are.
> You are my hope, you are my desire;
> You are my Jesus.

In Delhi, too, an elderly Indian couple, Chandy and Mariamma Verghese, had a ministry teaching English to Afghan refugees on the top floor of their house. He, tall and distinguished in his Afghan hat and she, fine-featured, grey-haired, told me something of their story when I visited them in Delhi. Their links with Afghanistan began in the early 1970s, when Chandy was posted there by the Indian Government. They became involved with the Christian Community Church in Kabul, Chandy being on the Board. He told me some of the circumstances of the destruction of the new and beautiful church in 1973, including the Government's deception by which Christy Wilson was persuaded to leave the country voluntarily and then immediately banished: he was an influential and respected man, teacher of English to the King's children, and they would not have attempted the demolition while he was in the country. When Chandy heard that the demolition had begun, he opened his Bible and read Matthew 16:18, 'I will build my Church'. He and other church members went and watched, unresisting, while their church was totally destroyed, including the marble floor. Then kneeling down they committed themselves to God.

His government service there ended, in 1974 Chandy met Alan Norrish – at that time head of IAM – who invited him to join BMMF and work in Afghanistan. Ray Windsor, by then General Director of BMMF, arranged for him to have Bible training at the Indian Missionary Training Institute (IMTI) in Nasik, when it opened in 1976, and to go through the Indian Evangelical Mission, seconded via BMMF for work in Kabul. Here he worked as Stores Manager at NOOR, and at night used to visit secret believers in their homes, teaching and praying with them. As he put it, it was a very effective time.

With the arrival of Russian troops in 1980 many Christian nationals were arrested, probably because of connections with Westerners, rather than for religious reasons. Chandy and Mariamma were in Delhi at the time, and helped Ray to find temporary accommodation for the IAM team as they withdrew and went on to Landour. In 1983, after a spell of administrative work at IMTI, now at Chikaldara, it was becoming clear that there was need for ministry among the Afghan refugees who had fled to Delhi from the atrocities of the Russian invasion and subsequent bloodshed. Frances Iliff, a nurse who had worked with BMMF both in Iran and in Kabul, came to set this up, and Chandy and Mariamma came back to Delhi to work with her. Having made a survey among the refugees, they realised that a valuable point of contact would be Teaching English as a Second Language,

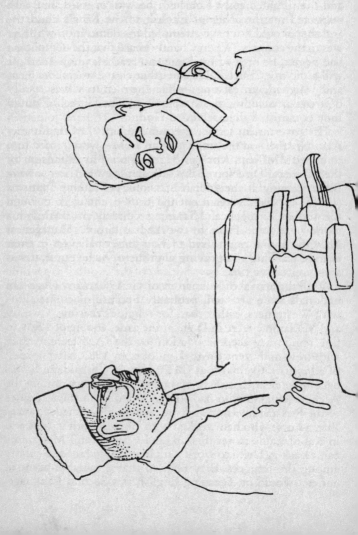

Chandi Verghese and Afghan student

as most of the refugees were hoping to make it to the West. As a result the Delhi Project for Displaced People was established in 1983, and run by BMMF jointly with IEM until 1984. Then Frances's visa was refused, but with support from the Indian Church and from TEAR Fund, the Vergheses continued the work. Fluent in Dari from their time in Afghanistan, they were ideally suited to helping these refugees. The visits they made to their homes and the practical as well as language help they gave was a lifeline to these people, and as a result some turned to Christ.

I was invited to sit in on two of the classes. Chandy himself took the class, and the young Afghans joined in with real interest. The spiritual ministry, with Sunday services on the top floor of the house, bore fruit too, with the first baptisms in 1985 and a rapid expansion of both language and spiritual work up till 1987. Later, owing to persecution by refugee Mujahedin, the rate of baptisms slowed down. The name of the project changed to Delhi Centre for Language and Training. Chandy and Mariamma carried on, ministering to the Afghan families in practical and spiritual ways, valuing fellowship and support from Interserve. The cry of the small group of believers scattered over Afghanistan and beyond, and of the country as a whole as it emerges from the horrors of civil war, is the age-old appeal: 'Come over and help us.' Who will go?

6

BMMF International

While Nepal and other new areas were unfolding excitingly 'on the field', or at the receiving end of BMMF's work, important changes too were taking place at the sending, initiating end. Jack Dain resigned from his position as General Secretary of BMMF in 1959. He had been invited to go to Australia to take over the administration of the Church Missionary Society there, a move which led to his ordination and eventually his consecration as bishop. His affection for BMMF was such that only the certainty that this was God's timing and call would have led him to leave.

Up till now London had been the administrative centre of BMMF's activities. It had always been a Commonwealth mission, with missionaries recruited from Australia, New Zealand and Canada as well as from Britain, but although recommended by their own national auxiliaries, recruits were all accepted and appointed by the London Committee. The appointment of Alan Norrish as Field Secretary in 1952 had been the first step in 'altering the centre of gravity', but now Jack felt that as BMMF moved towards internationalism, it was important for him to step aside to make it clear that London was no longer the nerve centre. This position became even more clear when in 1966 Alan, still then based at Edgehill in northern India, was appointed BMMF's International Secretary. Travelling widely in this capacity, dictating into a tape-recorder in the course of long train journeys, Alan became known as 'the one who shaped the future of BMMF from the top bunk of a third class railway carriage'. He would send off a shower of postcards, written in green ink, from wherever he happened to be: postcards travelled faster than letters; being open, they weren't slowed down by the censor.

In fact although the work of BMMF always moved forward in response to God's leading and the apparent needs at any particular time, its direction and policies were crystallised at its United Conferences which had been held quadrennially since 1950. At that first conference, held at Landour, the decision had been taken to open the doors of ZBMM to men workers and to work among both sexes; in 1954 the challenge was to the new field of work for a united mission in Nepal; 1958 launched the work of the mobile Caravan Hospital in Pakistan, and the conference of 1962 concentrated on student work in India and on the 'Tentmakers' scheme whereby Christians worked abroad in their professions or businesses, serving God as his witnesses and linked as 'Field Partners' with BMMF. Now in 1966, the keynote was internationalism. An International Council was established as the top policy-making body – to meet at the same time and place as the quadrennial United Conferences, to include the Directors of the various national councils and with the International Secretary as its Chief Executive. Jack Dain was the first International Chairman. At the same time the above-mentioned national auxiliaries became fully autonomous Councils and took full responsibility for appointing and supporting their own missionaries.

For Britain it meant stepping aside from international leadership. Arthur Pont was appointed as General Secretary of BMMF (UK) in 1967 – the first Director for Britain as a national Council on its own. Since 1959 when Jack Dain resigned, the UK Committee had been headed by his deputy Ron Hills as its Home Secretary, while Alan Norrish as Field Secretary led BMMF towards the fully international position which it embraced in 1966. Now Arthur took his new post with no international authority –

simply as General Secretary for the UK, one of an increasing number of member countries. Ray Windsor has paid tribute to Arthur as,

> a star, an entrepreneur, with magic in the words he uses; he brought flair, style and creativity to Interserve UK. What other person involved in mission would have advertised the need for young helpers by putting posters in the London Underground? Yet by doing just that he was letting young people know of a mission that was down to earth, with opportunities for helping needy people in the third world.

Arthur has done much to help the UK to adjust to its new role, to encourage new areas of work, notably that within the UK itself, to draw new countries in and to maintain prayer support and the flow of high-quality Partners from Britain.

During the 1970s the UK team of BMMF found itself in the forefront of several new endeavours that earned for it a reputation for innovation and risk-taking. This appealed particularly to students, large numbers of whom attended the special Students and Young Professionals Conference which was held in different parts of the country. The first student summer project team consisted entirely of members of the Executive Committee of the Cambridge Inter-Collegiate Christian Union. The team drove a land-rover and an ancient ambulance overland from London to Bombay. They then spent ten weeks working with the Union of Evangelical Students of India. So novel was the idea and so high the reputation of Cambridge that they found themselves addressing large audiences of 500 or more students, the majority of whom were Hindus. The more lasting work was probably done in the many Bible study groups they led and on practical issues of leadership on a one-to-one basis. From this original project in 1971 developed all the sets of initials such as HOP, SLOT and MEP described later, which eventually flowered as 'On

Track' and created opportunities for young people to serve overseas on short-term projects.

In 1969 the UK Council, led by the enthusiasm of its General Secretary, took the bold decision to charter two VC10 four-engine jets to take its missionaries to India. Support from other societies was immediate. This was the beginning of air travel for missionaries to the sub-continent, replacing the slow but more romantic sea voyages that had marked the first 120 years of the mission's history. Thus was born the Air Travel Association which has since helped thousands of missionaries and others to fly inexpensively to distant parts of the world. At the same time the UK introduced personalised support, or 'Team Support' as they called it. This was a virtually unknown concept on the British missionary scene when BMMF introduced it as a controversial measure in 1968. Since then it has become almost standard practice for interdenominational missionary societies, and the emphasis on linking individuals and churches to missionaries in a formal bond of voluntary commitment has widened missionary interest and responsibility.

The International Council authorised initiatives to respond to invitations from the Church in India and Pakistan to assist expository preaching. The UK Council took up the challenge enthusiastically and sent out a steady stream of Bible teachers to assist pastors to teach their congregations from the word of God, where the tendency to concentrate on exhortation had been resulting in a shallow level of faith. Equally the UK Council took initiatives in funding and bringing from Asia outstanding Christian leaders to minister to churches in Britain. And in the early '70s, too, the UK Council responded to requests from Pakistan and sent Joyce Chaplin to conduct writers' workshops, work which was continued by Paul Marsh, a member of the UK Council and former missionary.

In 1987 Bruce and Kathleen Nicholls were looking for help in developing the skills of Indian Christians in the visual and performing arts. Arthur Pont persuaded the UK

Council to sponsor a visit to India by the Riding Lights drama group to conduct drama workshops and present public performances – a major financial commitment on the part of the Council. The result was an enormously successful tour in several cities in India, following which the Indian Galilean Players Drama Group was established. This group has since been seen by millions on Indian television in the production of Christmas and Easter biblical and documentary plays which have earned high praise in the media. In these and other ways the UK Council continued its innovative role supporting its staff in their risk-taking ventures and funding projects outside its normal scope as an act of faith and a commitment to vision. In this they helped the International Fellowship to be in the forefront of change and on the cutting edge of mission.

The Australian auxiliary of ZBMM was for many years associated almost exclusively with the children's homes at Sholapur in India. When the work there began, back in 1907, it was 'adopted' by the Australian auxiliary, who supported it faithfully with money, recruits and prayer, support well illustrated by Miss Dora Barkla of ZBMM/BMMF (Australia), who worked at Sholapur for thirty years. Australia's involvement began to widen in the early 1960s when Jack Dain came to Australia and was on the International Council of BMMF. Australia became an autonomous Council, with state committees in New South Wales, Queensland, South Australia, West Australia, and Tasmania, as well as in Victoria where the National Office is based in Melbourne. BMMF (Australia)'s first graduate and medical doctor, Helen Murrell, went to India in the 1960s. She became Associate Professor of Obstetrics and Gynaecology at Ludhiana and then in 1971 went to Iran to investigate possibilities for possible future work of BMMF and CMS. She subsequently worked in Christian hospitals at Isfahan and Shiraz for some years.

In 1972 BMMF (Australia) was encouraged by the appointment of Howard Barclay as Director. Howard's parents had been involved in the Australian Nepalese

Mission which sent workers to the Indian border, hoping that Nepal itself would one day open to missionaries. His grandmother was still praying for Nepal when she died at the age of ninety-five, so it was perhaps not surprising that Howard (a teacher) and his wife Betty (a nurse), having worked for some years on the border with RBMU (Regions Beyond Missionary Union), found themselves at Amp Pipal in Nepal in 1960, where Howard became Director of the UMN education programme in Gorkha district. And as two other Australians who joined them in the Gorkha education project, Geoff and Eunice Reid, said, 'The input of Howard and Betty into the Gorkha region had already become mythology by the time we arrived there (1969)!'

Having worked with RBMU for twenty years, both in India and Nepal, in 1971 they decided they should return to Australia for their children's further education. It was then that Howard was approached by BMMF and asked to consider the position of Director of BMMF (Australia). So late in 1971 they transferred, within UMN, from RBMU to BMMF and came back to Australia where Howard headed up BMMF until the end of 1979, when they went back to Nepal to serve as personal counsellors; and then in 1984 Howard became Executive Director of UMN. Howard had made a particular point of visiting groups of Christian students in the colleges and universities of Australia, and this was crucial. With his wide smile, outgoing personality and robust attitude to life, Howard attracted young people to Christ and to his work. As a result of his visits many well-qualified young people applied to BMMF, and perhaps because of Howard's own links with Nepal, many of them went there. Medical students began going to mission hospitals to do their 'electives', and some subsequently became missionary doctors.

When the Barclays returned to Nepal, Keith Wilson became Director of BMMF (Australia) for six fruitful years, followed from 1986 until 1991 by Malcolm Macmillan, who had taught and been headmaster at Wynberg-Allen School, Mussoorie, India, and then by Brenton Wandke.

The chairman of the International Council of Interserve was for several years an Australian, Bishop John Reid; another outstanding Australian who served on the National Executive of BMMF in the 1970s was Dr David Penman, an adventurous missionary who became Archbishop of Melbourne. Beryl Coombe, Chairman of the International Finance Committee and Chairman of the Australian Council was another indefatigable and widely travelled 'Aussie' who added greatly to the Australian contribution.

For a country of little over three million, New Zealand has made an enormous contribution to the world of mission, Interserve included. First a branch of the Melbourne auxiliary, in 1918 New Zealand became an auxiliary of the London Council. In 1955, as we have seen, a big encouragement was the decision of Bruce and Kathleen Nicholls to join BMMF, soon to be followed by Ian and Elizabeth Kemp, Ian and Jenny McCleary, and Ray and Gwen Windsor, all in India. Ian Kemp had served for eight years as a Baptist minister in New Zealand when, through the preaching of a sermon of his own, he had a vision of God's ministry as something much wider than the local church. As a result, he and his family went to India, where Ian joined the staff of Union Biblical Seminary, Yavatmal in 1960. As he put it, 'I was happy to join BMMF because it was a service mission, seconding personnel to assist the Indian churches at points of felt need: in this case, the need was for the training of evangelical leadership for the churches: a strategic and challenging task.' It was exhilarating to be part of God's work of reaching out to the nations of the world. And as Ian commented too, 'BMMF, international, interdenominational, intercultural, is a beautiful and colourful mosaic of the Body of Christ. Its dedicated, loving, caring fellowship has shaped my life. Its biblical, sensible, co-operative and holistic policies have encouraged me through the years.'

The Kemps found that although people think of the missionary as someone who has given up everything, God gave them much too:

Because we went to India, travelling widely, we have
been scorched by India's sun, and felt the miracle of
its monsoons. We have scaled its snowy peaks and
walked through its green rice fields; boated on its
rivers and enjoyed its golden beaches. Our beds have
been on cow-dunged village floors, in city tenements, in
schools, guest houses, bungalows of government officers,
wealthy homes, and oh, so very often, the hard benches
of second-class railway coaches. Our multi-cultured
friends have introduced us to a kaleidoscope of Indian
singing, dancing, music and drama. Our journeys have
taken us to monuments a thousand years old . . . our
children have had an international education.

Ian found that as he discovered and used his gift of teaching
the word of God, 'Those years were the Lord's gift – the
best years of our lives.'

In 1962 the NZ Council became autonomous, and in the
same year Dr and Mrs Ray Windsor were accepted to serve
in India. The son of missionaries, gifted in music and sport,
Ray trained as a surgeon. After some years working with a
prestigious heart unit in Auckland, he and his wife Gwen
gradually felt drawn towards BMMF. As Ray recalls, they
knew Bruce and Kathleen Nicholls, also Ian Kemp; and
the visits to New Zealand of several key BMMF people
from Britain also inspired their confidence. All dedicated,
spiritual, highly professional, these people represented to
the Windsors the new era in BMMF. And with men as well
as women welcome, married couples could now apply. Ray
and Gwen made an open offer, prepared to meet whatever
need arose. They headed for India, where Ray continued
his medical work, first in the Landour Community Hospital, then at Chandigarh Post-graduate Institute and at
Herbertpur Christian Hospital. This move in obedience
to God's call meant giving up a promising future in the
rapidly developing field of cardio-thoracic surgery, which
did not have priority or the necessary funds in India. Over
the next few years Ray became deeply involved in setting

up a new Indian medical mission, the Emmanuel Hospital Association. He was also President of the United Mission to Nepal for a time and a member of the Executive Committee of the International Afghan (later Assistance) Mission of which he was President in 1980/81.

In 1970, when Alan Norrish 'ran out of green ink', Ray was appointed as the first non-British Executive Director of BMMF. The Fellowship took great strides forward in the 1970s, guided by his strategic and biblical thinking. When, in 1978 he and Gwen had to move back to New Zealand for family reasons, Ray tendered his resignation, but was asked to continue as General Director for four more years. This he did, spending five months of each year in Asia and the rest in New Zealand, and relying heavily on Hester Quirk, his Associate Director, and Michael Roemmele to manage things on the spot while he was away.

For many years the administration of the New Zealand Council was in the hands of Maud Spurgeon and Nellie Lamport, then from the early 1970s their place was taken by Carol Blight – now Assistant Director. During this time Margie Dennis (present Chair of Council) went to work in Pakistan and a general period of consolidation took place. Carol's organisational skills and sensitivity in handling people proved valuable assets in the growing work. Since its inception in 1962, the NZ Council had no national Director, then in 1972 Howard Barclay became Director for both Australia and New Zealand, making frequent trips to NZ till 1975. It was then realised that with a growing number of missionaries (twenty-five by the end of 1976), BMMF (NZ) should have its own full-time Director, and Alan Norrish with his wife Noel was invited to go to NZ in this capacity. They arrived in July 1976, with a visa for one year, so an important part of Alan's brief was the finding and appointing of his successor.

They found New Zealand to be a beautiful and prosperous country, with several congregations already deeply committed to mission. They travelled widely, visiting churches and small prayer groups often in remote farming communities, enthusing about the work of BMMF – its emphasis on Bible and medical work, evangelism and social caring, and the need for professional people to go out with a passion to serve those without Christ. And as Alan found, 'There is a growing realisation that Christians here are part of the world-wide church, a serving, suffering, martyr-witness, one-body people round the world.'

Then one day Alan was visited by a businessman from the South Island – David Graham. With energy and managerial experience, together with a Bible teaching ministry developed as an elder of a Brethren Assembly in Wellington, he was just the person to take over the Directorship of BMMF (NZ), so Alan and Noel were able to leave on the day their visas ran out with their mission accomplished, confident that the NZ wing of BMMF was in good hands. And indeed it was. David moved constantly among the churches, colleges and prayer groups of New Zealand, informing and challenging people about the work. As a result, the number of NZ missionaries – or Partners as they came to be called – grew. In particular, David was a strong advocate of the value of the 'tentmaking' ministry in mission – people serving God abroad in secular jobs; he was also on the South East Asia/Pacific Committee, an exciting development as South East Asian countries – Korea, Malaysia, Singapore, Hong Kong – themselves began sending out missionaries. David retired in 1992, and Chris Grantham became the new Director.

The Canadian auxiliary had been active for many years. It had taken particular responsibility for the Canada Hospital in Nasik since its inception at the beginning of the century, and was contributing key people to BMMF – for example the Rev and Mrs Eric Lowe who went to St Andrew's Church, Lahore in 1956. Eric later worked with Alan Norrish as Assistant Field Secretary of BMMF. Now the time seemed ripe to establish links with the USA. In 1963 the first American missionaries were recruited – the Rev and Mrs Ernest Arloff, who had already been working in India before becoming part of BMMF. At the same time,

after much prayer and deliberation, the Canadian Board felt
that God was clearly guiding them to establish a US Board
of BMMF, and this was inaugurated in February 1964, with
the Rev Dr Mario Di Gangi as President. He was a first class
theologian and Bible teacher and established BMMF's name
in the States. Among the Board members was C. Everett
Koop, former Surgeon General, and in these early years
BMMF (USA) owed a great deal to Ruth Rittler, a minister's
widow who first as Mario's secretary and then as Assistant
Director acted as 'anchor person', initially from a desk in a
corner of the Scripture Union office in Philadelphia where
BMMF (USA) began.

Seconded to Canada and North America at this time
to help with this extension of BMMF's work were the
Rev Dr Robert Brow and his wife Mollie. A theolo-
gian and creative thinker who had taught at Allahabad
Bible Seminary and worked with the Union of Evan-
gelical Students of India, he now transferred to Canada.
In 1967 the Canadian Board of BMMF invited Dr Di
Gangi to leave the historic pulpit of Tenth Presbyterian
Church, Philadelphia and to become Director of BMMF
North America, based in Toronto and dividing his time
between the USA and Canada. Then in 1976 the Rev
Laurence Wynne, a Presbyterian minister from Northern
Ireland who had emigrated first to Canada and then to the
States was appointed as US Director, and Mario Di Gangi
continued as Director of the Canadian Council, becoming
also Chairman of BMMF's International Council in 1978
in succession to Jack Dain. Professor of Pastoral Studies at
Ontario Theological Seminary, Mario travelled extensively
and people around the world benefited from his gifts of
preaching, writing and thinking.

Both Canada and the USA contributed many lively,
gifted and hard-working people to BMMF. Beryl Finch,
from Canada, served with the Fellowship from 1947 to
1988. From the day in 1947 when she first arrived at
Bombay docks, 'a scared, inexperienced young thing', she
did all she could to respond to what she heard as India's

call for help – especially that of the women. When she began pastoral and evangelistic work in the villages around Bulandshahr, she found very few Indian women in positions of leadership; when she left, having worked for the last ten of her forty-one years at Kalvari Bible School, Allahabad, she was glad to have witnessed the dawn of a new era in which 'Indian women take the lead, and the rest of us serve as helpers.'

Canada's first missionary to Nepal, who went out with the United Church of Canada in 1960 and became a Partner with Interserve in 1989, was Dr Helen Huston. She was also Nepal's longest serving Western doctor, and was the first recipient of the Sir Edmund Hillary Foundation Humanitarian Award in 1991, for 'dedicated commitment to the improvement of the quality of life for the people of the Himalayan regions of Nepal'. Lexy Cameron from Canada was involved in theological teaching at UBS Yeotmal until her death. Doris Bailey worked for thirty years in both India and Nepal, bringing care and rehabilitation to the destitute. She noticed that 'wherever I travelled my Canadian passport seemed to carry with it a sense of respect, liberty and welcome'. It was through Doris that John and Leona Garrison, of whom more later, were drawn into BMMF (Canada), meeting her in India in the 1960s. Naomi McGorman was a Canadian who worked for almost thirty years in India, notably in the women's side of the work of the Union of Evangelical Students of India, and George and Emmeline Bush were others, engaged in university teaching in the Middle East.

Another Canadian family to work with BMMF – this time in Nepal – were Dr Del and Bev Haug at Tansen. Del wrote while they were there, 'The darkness of Nepal, where less than one in 700 has yet heard and responded to the Good News, is especially visible at the annual festival when sacrifices are made to Kali, the goddess of destruction. The darkness stands in sharp contrast to the glorious light of God's creation, so readily apparent here.' The darkness almost engulfed the Haug family, as not only did Del come close to death with a severe attack of meningitis, but their daughter Anita went down with hepatitis. I met their other daughter, Erika, doing short-term work in India in 1992. She told me a little about the time when Anita, at the age of twelve, became delirious and was rushed to Patan hospital. Her liver was being destroyed by a rare complication of hepatitis and she was in a coma for two days with virtually no chance of recovery. Interservers all over the world began praying day and night, and a few days later she was better, sitting up reading in bed.

As remembered by Bob Morris, Canadian Executive Secretary:

> The guru, the creative urge of BMMF in Canada for forty years was Dennis Clark. Most Canadian Council members over the last thirty years credit Dennis with their involvement in the fellowship. The initial vision for BMMF (USA) was largely his as well. His extraordinary escapades in Afghanistan, China, Turkey were not only precedent-setting for Interserve as a tentmaking agency, but his creative ideas and motivating skills revitalised BMMF in Canada. His heart for missions and spirit of adventure flourished long after his body had begun to betray him, and two weeks before he died of leukaemia in 1991, six pages of notes arrived on my desk – a revolutionary strategy for the newly opened Central Asian republics. Urging Interserve to recruit gifted linguists, his thesis was that one of the biggest needs would be for translators and interpreters as the peoples of the former Soviet bloc emerged into the international family of nations.

Important too in the Canadian scene is Bob Morris himself, an enthusiastic and inspiring communicator, who with his wife Petie taught for six years at Woodstock School. Then after several key roles in Pakistan and India and a spell as Acting Executive Director in the International Office in

Cyprus he took over from Mario Di Gangi as Executive Director of BMMF (Canada) in 1987.

At the time of Laurence Wynne's appointment as Director of BMMF (USA), another important development took place: the merging of two closely related societies, both based in the United States and both working – initially amongst women only – in India and Pakistan. One of these was BMMF, the other was the United Fellowship for Christian Service (originally Women's Union Missionary Society – WUMS). Both owed their origin to a common source. Way back in 1833 the Rev David Abeel, the first American missionary to China, had fired both Mary (later Lady) Kinnaird in London and an equally remarkable lady, Mrs Sarah Doremus in New York, with the vision of the crying needs of the women of India. The result was the founding of ZBMM (now BMMF) and WUMS (now UFCS) respectively, both of which set up hospitals, orphanages and schools in India and other countries. For years the two societies had worked side by side and in close co-operation in Asia, and now that BMMF had its own Board in North America, it began to appear reasonable for the two to merge.

In 1974, Alan Norrish was invited to leave Kabul and go to America as Director of UFCS for a limited period with a view to UFCS work in India and Pakistan merging with that of BMMF. Two streams coming together was how he saw it, and this merger, he was convinced, would result in more effective work for the Gospel in Asia, and would prove to be 'a historic act for a historic time'. Alan was in a good position to see this merger through as he had been closely linked with UFCS work already in India. Despite understandable fears from some at the beginning, so well did the process go, with the ready co-operation of the chairman of UFCS, Ray Herrick, that Alan and Noel who had been invited to stay for three years were able to leave after eighteen months. And Alan rejoiced to see how the Lord of history had initiated, and now a century and a half later dovetailed two streams of his work. The job

was completed, and the united Fellowship was ready for
Laurence Wynne to take over as Director in 1976.

While Mario Di Gangi had achieved a high profile
for BMMF(USA) by his teaching and conference work,
Laurence, together with his English wife Margaret, concentrated on underpinning the work at 'grass-roots' level and
with informed prayer support. It was surprisingly difficult,
they found, to get prayer support for their missionaries.
One way of informing them and encouraging them to pray
was through a BMMF magazine, but *Go*, the magazine of
BMMF(UK), wasn't quite right for American readers – it
had too much plain print. To meet this need Margaret
Wynne set up and edited an American alternative: *Goal*, an
amalgamation of *Go* and *Link* (the magazine of UFCS).

Every two years Laurence and Margaret did a tour of
different areas of BMMF's work. Their main task was not
so much to help Partners abroad to relate to the people they
were working amongst as to help Americans and British to
work together. Temperamentally and culturally they were
often very different, but having moved from the UK to the
USA the Wynnes were well suited to the task. At the end of
1985 Laurence was invited back to pastor the Presbyterian
church in Enniskillen, Northern Ireland, where he had been
ordained in 1947. After only ten months there he was killed
in a road accident. To members of the church it seemed
that he had achieved more in ten months than most people
would have achieved in ten years.

In 1986 Dr Ralph Eckardt became the first American
Director of InterServe (USA). (The US Council is unique
in using the capital S – a way of emphasising the truth
expressed in their motto: 'We take servanthood seriously'.)
Under his leadership the Board of Trustees changed from a
local to a national Board represented right across the USA,
and the number of American Partners overseas doubled.
His wife Joyce had a special ministry to the children of US
Partners. His secretary, Miss Sandi Iadarola, had worked for
WUMS since 1967, was secretary to Alan Norrish when he
helped to merge UFCS and BMMF, and as well as her office

work, taught a lively history of BMMF at the Candidate School.

Scotland, although part of the UK, had always had a particularly active auxiliary committee. Indeed, Scotland had been crucial to Interserve from the beginning, with both its founders, Lady Kinnaird and Mrs McKenzie, having strong Scottish connections. For many years the women of Scotland backed the work through two Scottish auxiliaries, one based in Edinburgh and one in Glasgow. Fund-raising sales of work were organised, returning missionaries addressed packed meetings and were supported by prayer and by the money raised. But all decisions relating to Scottish candidates were made in London. In 1965 after one or two notable miscalculations by the London committee in rejecting good Scottish candidates, it was decided that Scotland should follow Australia, New Zealand, Canada and the USA in forming an autonomous council, selecting its own candidates and being wholly responsible for their financial support. Understanding of the people, of local conditions and of the Scottish churches was important, and this the Scottish Council had. Miss Elsie Knox, previously chairman of the Glasgow auxiliary, was its hard-working General Secretary, Dr Charles Anderson was invited to be Chairman, and the Honorary Secretary was Lady Sloan who had previously been chairman of the Edinburgh auxiliary.

The new Council forged ahead, and the number of Scottish missionaries increased. Among those already serving was Dr Winifred Anderson, whom I met at her home in Glasgow in 1991, still vigorous in body and mind at eighty-seven, reflecting in a lilting Scottish accent and with genuine humility and warmth on her forty or so years of work. Interestingly, it was hearing Dr Marjorie Roemmele – the aunt of the third Executive Director of Interserve – speak of the need for women doctors in India which led Win, then training as a doctor, to offer herself to ZBMM. Her career showed many of the characteristic ZBMM virtues: tenacity, sensitivity, flexibility.

Starting in 1932 at Lucknow, scene of the famous siege of the previous century, she then spent twenty years at Patna doing gynaecology and obstetrics. When it became clear in the 1950s that there was no longer a need for BMMF hospitals in India, she transferred to Kathmandu in the vanguard of the new UMN work in Nepal. She told me of two delightful friendships: one with Gyani, a Nepali princess who came to Patna as a refugee from an arranged marriage, became a Christian and trained as a nurse. When BMMF transferred its medical work from India to Nepal, she went too, and became matron of the Amp Pipal hospital and a leader in the church. The other friendship was with the mother of another princess, whom she found sacrificing a goat on the palace roof and praying for her daughter's safe delivery. 'We became good friends and when, some years later, she came in for major surgery, she asked me to pray. As I finished, she added, "and the blood of Jesus Christ cleanses me from all sin." Remembering our first meeting, with the goat's blood still flowing on the roof, I was amazed and thanked God that she understood this so well.'

Other Scottish missionaries were Kay (Kathleen) Chattock, who began work with ZBMM in 1931. She worked at Bulandshahr and Varanasi in a Bible teaching ministry for many years, then in an administrative capacity at Queen Mary High School, Bombay and in Interserve's Scottish Office and as Chairman of its Council. Also Janette Cowan, a lively and outgoing teacher with a great gift with people, who became Personnel Secretary in the International Office based in India; Maureen Clarke who set up the Christian Writers' Institute in India; Doris Hamilton who also worked at Khristya Lekhan Sanstha, the Writers' Institute, and then as Librarian at Union Biblical Seminary for many years and later in the Yavatmal College for Leadership Training; and Margaret Ross who was nursing sister at Rajpur School for the Blind.

George Dolby, the agriculturalist who helped launch the Christian Caravan Mission, was instrumental in the development of BMMF (Scotland) as an autonomous Council,

and was Scottish Home Secretary and then Chairman.
Another Scotsman, Murray McGavin, extrovert, cheerful,
both he and his wife Ruth from strong missionary families,
was consultant ophthalmologist at the NOOR eye hospital
in Afghanistan. Afghan fellow workers at the hospital
responded to his friendliness, and wandering into his office
to chat would find something of Christ reflected in their
talk. Notable too among Scottish Partners of Interserve
were Michael and Betty Roemmele, two of the first to
be sent out by the independent Scottish Council. From
Bible college and student work in India they went on to be
involved in the establishment of Theological Education by
Extension in India (TAFTEE) and then into administration
based at BMMF's International Office. From 1982 to 1992
Michael was Executive Director of Interserve, based first in
Delhi and then in Nicosia, Cyprus. During the 1970s and
'80s he also represented BMMF on many boards, and was
Chairman of Woodstock School and the UMN, and Vice
Chairman of HEED Bangladesh. In the first twenty-one
years of their marriage he and Betty had as many homes,
and brought up three daughters. Their happiness in the girls
was a constant source of wonder to the people among whom
they worked. Once in Delhi when Betty and the girls piled
into a taxi, the driver expressed great concern that there was
no son. 'I'll pray for you,' he said, and taking his hand off
the steering wheel, proceeded to do so for two or three
heart-stopping moments. Betty had an important role in
hospitality and running BMMF's 'transit house' in Delhi
for several years.

The work of BMMF (Scotland) was greatly facilitated
since 1978 by the appointment of Brian Ringrose as General
Secretary. I met him, a tall, genial man with all the facts
about Interserve (Scotland) at his fingertips, and his wife
Margaret at Elm Avenue, Lenzie, their home and the
Interserve Scottish headquarters. Here Margaret dispensed
kindness and countless meals to the hundreds, like me, who
came to visit. Before their appointment, Brian and Margaret
had worked with BMMF in India. In 1962 they were invited

to Nasik, one of the four holy cities of India, to establish the Bible Fellowship Centre. This was housed in buildings, then still owned by BMMF, which had previously been a BMMF children's home. The centre was set up with the encouragement of the Anglican Church as a conference centre for Indian Christian groups and leaders, with Brian as Director. In 1963 he and Margaret were joined by Mr and Mrs P.T. Abraham, who eventually took over the work. When the Indian 'Christian Medical and Educational Fellowship' trust, CMEF, was formed in 1968, the Bible Fellowship Centre was one of the five BMMF institutions whose buildings were handed over and which came under its management.

In 1968 Brian was asked to become minister of the English-speaking church, All Saints, Malabar Hill, Bombay. It was an interesting church with a wide racial mix in one of the wealthier areas of Bombay. Much of the work was among Indians from nominally Christian backgrounds and many came to real faith. Two important developments while they were there were the beginning of TAFTEE courses in Bombay, with which Brian became involved as tutor and in the writing of study material; and the outreach work in which better-off members of the congregation were encouraged to get out and help the needy in practical ways: taking food to people sleeping on the streets, visiting an old people's home, organising children's play schemes. In 1975 the Ringroses had to leave India, and not long after, Brian was invited to become full-time Director of BMMF (Scotland). Since then, the number of Scottish Partners with Interserve has more than doubled, and there have been other interesting developments, such as the recently formed links with churches in Egypt, and Interserve (Korea).

Northern Ireland has remained an auxiliary Council of the UK, but has contributed several Partners to key areas of Interserve's work, as has the Republic of Ireland. Director of the NI Council was Tony McGall, while the Secretary of the Republic's Committee was Elaine Graham, a veteran missionary who worked for twenty-two years in Pakistan.

The work of various Irish Interservers will be described in the course of the narrative.

The background to the formation of a BMMF Council in Holland is well illustrated by the story of Adriaan Los, now working at UMN headquarters in Nepal:

> I was born in 1952. My family were members of the Dutch Reformed Church. In my student days, along with most of my contemporaries, I rebelled against the post-war values of the previous generation. I was involved in riots, but mercifully my Christian background saved me from drugs. I committed myself fully to the Lord at the age of eighteen at my grandmother's confirmation. I had held back from this step as it would mean keeping a promise I had made at the age of eight to become a missionary. I had heard that missionaries in China had their tongues cut out. I had also had a recurrent nightmare about a dark country between India and China, but the example of my grandmother, taking this big step at her age, gave me courage. After three years at Bible college I wanted to remain with the Dutch Reformed Church but it seemed to me that they did little to support missionaries apart from putting money in the bag. My wife and I prayed for two years that God would show us a way of being sent out by our own church but also receiving the personal support we admired in other churches.

This was where BMMF came in, and as so often in God's mysterious economy, he had been preparing for this situation for several years. In 1968 Arthur Pont visited Holland to investigate and if possible start a new work. In May 1969 a Committee was formed in the hope of becoming the support organisation for Dutch workers. Without candidates it was hard to make a start, but the Committee did what they could. A Dutch group of eight went to BMMF's Annual Prayer Conference at Swanwick, England in 1971. By 1972 all Committee members had

had to withdraw for various reasons, and only one person represented Holland at Swanwick: Annie Schouten, who was becoming increasingly drawn to BMMF and agreed to become Secretary of the Committee. Despite the lack of candidates, she refused to give up, and her faith was vindicated when in 1975 the vestigial Committee was approached by a Dutch couple, Ed and Annie Kramer, who were sure that God was calling them to Nepal. This was the turning point, as although the Kramers were actually accepted by BMMF (UK), the need to support them gave the Dutch Committee just the impetus it needed. In 1976, new members were found for the Committee, among them the Rev Wim Bouw of the Dutch Reformed Church, recently returned from missionary work in Kenya, who did much to encourage the conservative Reformed Church to accept new ways regarding mission.

In July 1977 the Kramers left for Nepal. And as Annie Schouten rejoiced, 'Through this, the vicious circle (no workers, no mission; no mission, no workers) was broken through, to the joy of all.' The Committee had started as an auxiliary of the London Council, and for several years the work and its missionaries received a financial subsidy from the UK. But in 1982 BMMF (Holland) was established as an autonomous Council, and ten years later fifty workers from Holland were overseas, many in Nepal, where it was relatively easy for them to obtain visas. For the Dutch Reformed Church too there was new life, as it slowly accepted the concept of releasing and supporting its members to serve abroad with 'faith missions' like Interserve. And for Adriaan and Josien Los, it meant heading for Nepal in 1979 – the country of Adriaan's dream, where years later as a result of prayer and the laying on of hands, he was freed, at last, from the fear which still oppressed him sometimes of the dark country to which God had called him to proclaim the Light of the world. Many Netherlanders hold key positions in UMN: Dr Tjerk Nap, for example as UMN Health Secretary, and Henk Chevalking as Assistant Education Secretary.

Now free to work with and through Interserve, Dutch Christians, backed by Director Piet Vreugdenhil and the Interserve (Holland) Council, are making an impressive contribution.

Arthur Pont visited Germany to start, like Holland, a UK auxiliary branch in 1972. Subsequently it made a more direct link with the International Office and in April 1992 created a new Committee to be responsible for the work in Germany. In Switzerland an Auxiliary Committee of the UK Council was similarly set up in 1981, with Rev Neil Britton as its Chairman. In 1992 there were two Swiss couples in Asia, and several more enquirers. Also an opportunity arose to establish a similar position in France, and Mr Maurice Harrison, teacher and Principal of a small language school at Sorgues, Avignon, was appointed as Interserve Representative for France, accountable to the UK Council.

Another aspect of the growing internationalism of BMMF/ Interserve was the development of Councils in various countries of East Asia. Initially the idea was to liaise with the Overseas Missionary Fellowship which had been working for many years in East Asian countries. Concerned to avoid duplication of effort or competition, the hope was, rather than setting up BMMF Councils, for the OMF Councils to accept and send candidates to areas in which BMMF was already at work. And at the quadrennial conference in New Delhi in 1970, BMMF invited OMF to liaise over the sending of Christian workers from these countries. Such candidates would be full members of OMF but loaned to BMMF on the field. Co-operation was envisaged also in the Western sending countries (conferences, literature etc.). What had traditionally been seen as part of the 'field' – i.e. East Asia – was becoming a sending area. And following on from this, another major decision: 'We resolved at New Delhi to welcome into BMMF as full members or as Field Partners, workers of any nationality. This significant decision accepts all the implications inherent in becoming truly international.'

Exciting though the concept of co-operation was, it was slow in getting off the ground, and it worked out rather differently from expectation. There were already two BMMF Partners from East Asia: Shoko Thomson from Japan, married to Robin since 1969, and Chae Ok Chun from Korea who taught at Karachi Institute of Theology. But only a small number of people were recruited for work with BMMF through the OMF Councils in Hong Kong, Malaysia and Singapore during the 1970s. As a result, in 1981 Ray Windsor wrote to the Director of OMF expressing a concern to increase the flow of Asian missionaries into BMMF (known, since 1978, as BMMF International), and specifically into ISA (International Service Associates). ISA was a new wing of BMMF, also set up in 1978, as a way of enabling help to reach people in countries where missionaries were not allowed visas but development workers were.

In this letter, Ray asked, 'Will OMF have objection if, in close consultation with OMF Councils in Asia, we seek other agencies to whom ISA might relate, as distinct to our exclusive OMF/BMMF relationship?' He suggested a possible link with a Christian group called Malaysian CARE. At the BMMF quadrennial conference of 1982, with Michael Roemmele now Executive Director of BMMF and with the Director of OMF invited to participate, there was more discussion about 'partnership in mission and Asian membership', and it was agreed to continue co-operating with Asian missions rather than setting up new BMMF Councils in Asia; also to seek to increase the Asian membership of BMMF by recruitment by Asian missionary societies, for service in other countries. However, when the Director of OMF returned to Singapore he found little enthusiasm in the OMF Councils of Malaysia and Singapore for this approach. They were too hard-pressed with their own expanding work, and later in 1982 it was decided to revoke the decision and encourage BMMF to set up its own Councils in Asia.

In 1983 BMMF International appointed Paul Spivey,

who had worked as a pharmacist and then as head of the UMN Health Services in Nepal, to serve part time as its South East Asia Liaison Officer (SEALO), and Paul, based now at BMMF's International Office in Delhi, began regular visits to Singapore, Malaysia and Hong Kong. In Singapore, Alan Pang, who had been working in Nepal, became BMMF Representative; Malaysian CARE agreed to represent BMMF in Malaysia; and in Hong Kong, the enthusiasm of the OMF Chairman the Rev Ken Lo provided positive support, with the OMF Council screening and sending Winnie Lau through BMMF International to Nepal, where she became Business Manager at the hospital at Amp Pipal.

Two former BMMF couples were by then living in Hong Kong, serving with the Bible Society, but with wide experience of work with BMMF in India, Pakistan and the Middle East. With Ruth Thorne as its Secretary, the Committee of BMMF (Hong Kong) was registered in 1986, and at once took over from OMF managing Winnie's church-based support, as well as making BMMF better known in Hong Kong churches. The chairman of Interserve's Hong Kong Committee was a dental surgeon, Bill Yan, an elder in Winnie's supporting church. The Committee has informal links with the Council of BMMF (Australia) which gives some support. Many young people are now going from Hong Kong and the other East Asian countries to do medical electives and other short-term projects with Interserve's On Track programme. Someone with longer-term hopes of service abroad is Becki Chung, who when I met her in Hong Kong in 1991 was hoping to study Hindi in an Indian university and witness to fellow students in that way. By 1992 she was working in the Interserve office in New Delhi, so seemed to be well on the way to fulfilling her vision.

Korea's links with Interserve started in the early 1970s, when Dr Chae Ok Chun was teaching in Pakistan and a Field Partner with BMMF. Back in Seoul in 1981, she invited a small group of Koreans interested in mission to meet Ray Windsor. Then in 1985 Paul Spivey met a young Korean studying in the Discipleship Training Centre in Singapore – Andrew Narm, who was a staff member of the IVF in Korea and interested in the possibility of work in Turkey, with which Korea has ethnic and linguistic links. At BMMF's United Conference in Kathmandu in 1986 he presented a paper on the advantages and disadvantages of Korean Christians being related to international and interdenominational missions. In April 1987, following a visit to Korea by Michael Roemmele, the then Executive Director, it was decided that Interserve should proceed with limited recruitment of Koreans, and in May 1988 Andrew Narm was appointed Interserve Representative in Korea. The hope was that OMF would assist in the recruiting, being on the spot, but in fact this arrangement never came into effect.

In 1989, visits by Michael Roemmele, Naomi McGorman and Brian and Margaret Ringrose all served to increase the profile of Interserve in Korea. Naomi, after many years' service in India, had been seconded by Interserve to the Canadian IVCF with a brief to create interest and understanding in universities concerning world mission. So successful were her two visits to Korea in 1989 and '90 that her secondment to IVCF was extended with the agreement that this would include spending two months a year in Korea. As Michael Roemmele comments, 'It was interesting to reflect on the high degree of acceptance received by Naomi, a woman, in a society which tends to accord all leadership positions to men. Naomi herself attributed this to her seniority, but it was also her evident experience of cross-cultural ministry which gained her the respect she received.' In December 1990, an Interserve national Committee was set up in Seoul. Its first meeting was encouraged by the testimony of its first candidates, Dr Gweon and his wife Young Jin Lee. In 1992 both the Gweons and Mr and Mrs Jeong were hoping to go to Pakistan. Another young Korean, Sung Hee Kwon, was working with Interserve among Asians in London.

An impressive number of students and others are going out on the short-term On Track programme.

Malaysia, working through Malaysian CARE, had three Interserve Partners in Peshawar, Pakistan, working among the many Afghan refugees. And in Singapore the Interserve Committee was registered in May 1989, but since then suffered tension and difficulties, and had no full-time staff.

India was on the verge of forming its own BMMF Committee in 1966, but with the Indian Evangelical Mission emerging just then, an international initiative could have undermined the national one and so the BMMF idea was shelved. Recently, however, despite some dissenting voices among Indian Christian leaders, it seemed that the time was right to establish an Indian 'sending' Interserve group. A key person in this initiative was Dr Tluanga, an educationalist from Mizoram (North East India) whose brother, Dr Nghakliana, worked with BMMF until his death in 1985. Tluanga came back to Delhi from missionary teaching in the Gilbert Islands with his family in 1986. He was concerned for the need to recruit young professional Indians in God's service, and was accepted as a Partner with Interserve. He became part of the Committee which worked to set up Interserve (India). In discussion with Margaret Parkinson, Robin Thomson and others, a constitution was drawn up, and Interserve (India) was registered with the Government in 1990.

There were already a fair number of Indian Partners in Interserve, the majority working in India. These had been recruited through the International Office and 'field committee'. Now they came under Interserve (India). Quite rapidly recruits began coming forward, to work either in cross-cultural situations within India or to go abroad as missionaries. This signals a new degree of merging between 'field structures' and 'sending structures', a situation which may become more widespread in that any particular country is not pure 'field' or pure 'sending' but a bit of both. Interestingly too, the other country in which this merging is most obvious is the UK, where with the development

Outside the Friday Mosque, Old Delhi

of Ministry among Asians in Britain (MAB) and its team of thirty-five staff, the UK too ceases to be only a sending country and becomes part of the 'field', as it reaches out to immigrants from the traditional fields of work. So with the UK as the first sending country now developing a field ministry, and with India as the first field of ZBMM's work now developing a sending ministry, we see two remarkable growth points of Interserve's work, and another facet of the richly variegated pattern which is Interserve International.

INDIA

Amritsar
Ludhiana
Herbertpur
Mussoorie
Rajpur
DELHI
Bulandshahr
Darjeeling
Agra
Kanpur
Lucknow
Jaipur
Allahabad
Patna
Jhansi
Varanasi
Satbarwa
Ahmedabad
Calcutta
Nagpur
Yavatmal
Manmad
Nasik
Bombay
Pune
Panchgani
Sholapur
Hyderabad
Bangalore
Vellore
Madras
Uthagamandalam
Valathi
Kodaikanal
Palavoor

7

Change in India

In 1968, shortly after his appointment as General Secretary of BMMF (UK), Arthur Pont went on the first of several tours to acquaint himself with the work. This tour was interesting in that it was made at something of a turning point between two eras in BMMF, particularly as far as India was concerned. Up till then, although there had been notable changes in policy since 1952, the actual profile of the work, apart from the closure of the hospitals, had not changed very much. As we go with Arthur, we get a bird's eye view of BMMF's work in India, but even as we go, we are aware that more change was on its way.

Twenty years after gaining independence, India was increasingly rejecting outside interference and any help which appeared paternalistic. In May 1967 the Indian Government had placed restrictions on Commonwealth missionaries. New missionaries would only be given visas if an Indian could not do the task. All missionaries had to register with the police as foreigners. For re-entry into India a 'no objection to return' certificate had to be acquired prior to leaving the country, and some would be refused if the Government felt no real contribution was being made. Their wish was to see the Indian Church and all Christian institutions led and governed by Indians. These developments were speeding up BMMF's policies of appointing Indian staff and of setting up management trusts composed of Indian Christians who would take responsibility for the institutions in the future. More than ever, the key role of the missionary lay in training.

As always, Arthur found himself captivated by India: 'The surprising blend of beauty and poverty, of hot dusty plains and majestic mountains, of impossibly crowded streets and incomparably quiet dawns, of beautiful saree-clad women and simple dhoti-ed rickshaw-wallahs . . . the hospitality extended to strangers and the slow courtesies of life expressed in extended greetings.' He was all too aware, too, of the appalling poverty; poverty such that 'a man may work from dawn till dusk, seven days a week, fifty-two weeks a year, and still be in the leech-like grip of the money-lender with nothing to show for his toil. For many, of course, the situation is even worse, as they cannot find any work to do.'

His first stop was Bombay, the gateway to India on the palm-fringed shore of the Arabian Sea. He himself had been born in Calcutta where his father was an engineer on the North East India Railway. Trained as a civil engineer, he was later appointed to the Inter-Varsity Fellowship staff to work among students in Britain and then to BMMF (UK). Back now in India after many years he noted the tired-looking offices built by the British, the contrast of tall office blocks and appalling slums, the narrow alleys, the people sleeping on the pavements or in any shade at all hours of the day, the crowds. Factories were springing up as part of India's 'industrial revolution', and in the 1960s five BMMF Field Partners with their families were working and witnessing in Bombay in various areas of industry. Arthur visited Queen Mary School, where Betty Shelton of BMMF, the Headmistress, 'took prayers magnificently and held the girls' attention for a good fifteen minutes with her Bible exposition'. There was utter hush when she entered the assembly hall. The school, with extensive buildings and facilities, had 1,200 day pupils and fifty members of staff.

From Pune, where he visited the Church of Scotland Wadia Hospital and Dr and Mrs Donald Clunas of BMMF (Canada) who worked there, he went on to Kimmins High

School, high in the hills at Panchgani: '1888 and all that, dull red buildings falling down a hillside.' Marian Yelland of BMMF was the Principal, with five other staff members from BMMF (UK) and about twenty Indian members of staff. The school had 160 boarders and sixty day pupils of various faiths. As well as the school curriculum, Scripture Union camps, Crusaders and Sunday schools were all given high priority. At Independence the European and Anglo-Indian girls for whom the school was founded mostly left the country, and the school almost closed. However, by 1956 more cosmopolitan Hindus and Muslims realised the benefits of an English education, and Kimmins began to flourish again. In 1963 the first of sixteen cheerful Tibetan children, known familiarly as the 'Tibs' and partly sponsored by the World Council of Churches, arrived. They were just a few of the thousands of Tibetans, including the young Dalai Lama, who fled to India when the Communists took over in 1959.

Arthur's next stop was Nasik, where he visited the Bible Fellowship Centre and KLS – Khristiya Lekhan Sanstha, the school for Indian Christian writing and media work founded by Maureen Clarke and now directed by Ethel Raddon. Founded in 1962 in response to growing literacy among the Indians and the resulting 'battle for the mind' as they were bombarded by persuasive literature of all sorts, its students had produced radio scripts, Bible notes, poetry and drama in their own languages – essential for indigenous outreach. There were times of high enthusiasm, such as the first residential course held in 1963 when the twenty-five students included a pastor in charge of fifty village churches in central India, a youth leader from Hyderabad, a group from Darjeeling producing literature for Nepalis, a writer and translator from Calcutta and even a student from Iran. Sadly, when Arthur arrived, he found it 'a choice property of BMMF's, but under-used, with only six students at present'. Even more sadly, not long afterwards Ethel Raddon resigned, saying she felt that BMMF was not interested enough in mass communications media; the

Indian appointed as Director proved unsuitable, and the Institute was finally closed. Arthur also saw the Leprosy Hospital, run by the Leprosy Mission but with BMMF member Ursula Burrows from Canada on the staff: 'The place was spotless and the epitome of order and cleanliness. Prayers in the chapel were taken by the patients who sang me a welcome. There have been several conversions recently, and the emphasis is clearly Christian.'

At Manmad a little to the north east of Nasik he visited Manoram Sadan – a school of 450 girls with an attached orphanage of 180: 'Radiant with spiritual life – what a splendid jewel set on the edge of Manmad!' Set up by ZBMM in a time of severe famine and plague at the beginning of the century when many children were left as orphans, there had been a movement of God's Spirit here the year before. Joan Newton of BMMF was the Superintendent of the children's homes. She had worked previously at the Harvey Babies' Home at Nasik but had left, convinced that orphanages were out of date and that expatriates should no longer be involved in such work. Since then the work of Harvey Babies' Home and the Paton Memorial School, Manmad, had been combined at Manoram Sadan and Indians were much more involved on the staff and on the Governing Board, among them Miss Venubai Joshi, the Assistant Superintendent. And Joan had come to feel that there was still great value, in the absence of welfare services in India, in providing loving care and Christian education to needy children, especially to those from impoverished Christian homes.

Similar work had also been done by BMMF, particularly by its Australian members, for many years at Sholapur. Margaret Parkinson remembers it in the 1960s, when two to three-day-old babies left at the gate would be taken in. Nancy Basaviah was Principal of the schools, and took over from Dora Barkla as the first Indian Superintendent, introducing the 'cottage system', very advanced at that time. Now known as Jyoti Niketan, the children here have been sponsored by Interserve (Australia) and by World Vision

who have also sponsored children at Manoram Sadan. Many
children from these homes grew up to be active and in some
cases leading Christians. Some girls after training come
back as teachers and house-mothers. Among Christian
leaders can be mentioned the Rev Lakshman Choudhari
who worked with CSSM and at eighty was still doing
Marathi translation work for TAFTEE, and the Rev Rama
Joshi, on the Managing Board of the homes and Pastor of
the Ramabai Mukti Mission.

At Yavatmal in the heart of India – 500 miles to the coast
either way – Arthur attended board meetings at the Union
Biblical Seminary. Then a long journey northwards brought
him to Rajpur and the Sharp Memorial School for the Blind.
This, the oldest school for the blind in India, had been
founded in 1887 by an English woman, Miss Annie Sharp,
and was taken over by ZBMM in 1932. Arthur found it
peaceful and purposeful in its quiet setting on the Mussoorie
Hill Road. Given love and security in a well-disciplined and
well-cared-for family hostel, he found the children learning
many practical skills as well as reading braille (including, of
course, the Bible), music, science, braille typewriting, the
use of the sewing machine and other skills. Once a week
they distributed gospels in the local bazaar.

The next day a breathtaking fifteen-mile bus trip took him
up a further 3,500 feet to Mussoorie. Then a twenty-minute
walk led through Landour and along a precipitous path to
the very hub – as it was then – of BMMF's work: Edgehill,
'Looking as if it had been slapped onto the side of the
mountain, and clinging on by faith like an eagle's eyrie, it
had magnificent views across to the plains of India below, as
well as northward up to the snowy Himalayan peaks.' The
missionary community in Landour was involved in several
projects: Woodstock and the Wynberg-Allen Schools, the
Landour Community Hospital and the Bible Institute, as
well as the guest-house at Edgehill and the missionary
language school. The BMMF Field Headquarters and later
for a while the International Office was based at Edgehill.

At Varanasi (Benares), the famous Hindu pilgrimage

centre, Arthur visited BMMF primary schools, managed
by Miss Mary Masih and soon to be incorporated into
the Diocese of Lucknow, and in Lucknow itself the now
disused Kinnaird Hospital and the Nur Manzil Psychiatric
Centre, opened in 1950 as the first Christian psychiatric
centre in India. At Ludhiana he spent time with BMMF
members on the staff of the huge Christian hospital and
medical school, and realised the difficulties which arose
when Hindu heads of departments and professors were
appointed who then chose staff under them who were not
Christians. Finally the girls' school at Bulandshahr, south
east of Delhi, under its Indian Principal Lilian Das, and the
boys' hostel at Khurja which provided a Christian home
for Indian and Tibetan boys attending the local government
primary school.

I met Lilian Das in 1992, now in her eighties, in her
cottage called 'Bethlehem' in the grounds of St James's
Church near Delhi's Kashmiri Gate. Wrapped up warmly
in dressing gown and shawl, for it was February, she
told me of her work at Bulandshahr with Dulcie Rowell,
also of BMMF: 'We became great friends.' During her
principalship the school was asked to take fifteen Tibetan
children, and so began the area of ministry which is possibly
dearest to Lilian's heart. She became mother to those girls,
guided them into avenues of training, arranged marriages,
and still keeps in touch. Many of them became Christians
and were baptised. After her retirement she set up a school
for the children of the Tibetan refugee camp in Delhi, with
some of her ex-Bulandshahr pupils as teachers.

By 1969 things were changing rapidly. Indianisation
was proceeding apace, and so was the training of Indian
leadership. An Indian business manager had replaced a
missionary at Queen Mary School, Bombay – the largest
BMMF institution – and an Indian, Mrs Rajhuns, was
invited to prepare to take over the principalship from
Betty Shelton, which she eventually did in 1972. An Indian
office secretary replaced a missionary at the BMMF Field
Headquarters at Edgehill, and Brian Ringrose moved into

Lilian Das

pastoral work in Bombay, leaving the ministry of the Bible Fellowship Centre at Nasik under the sole leadership of the Indian BMMF couple, P.T. and Annamma Abraham. An Indian principal was appointed to the BMMF schools in Sholapur, and a similar pattern pursued in other institutions with which BMMF was involved.

In 1969 the control of five BMMF institutions in western India was handed over to the Christian Medical and

Educational Fellowship – a new Trust related to the Evangelical Fellowship of India. The five were Queen Mary and Kimmins schools, the two orphanages at Manmad and Sholapur and the Bible Fellowship Centre at Nasik. As Arthur saw it, 'This was one of the most altruistic things we ever did, in that we handed over millions of pounds worth of property, a process not without its difficulties.' But the resulting freedom from responsibility for these large institutions released people and resources for other ventures. What BMMF was left with was a very flexible force of highly professional *people* who could be deployed where needed. Some, still allowed to work in India, continued to work in the institutions handed over, or went into co-operative ventures; others moved on to pioneer in various countries, usually in co-operative work, always as servants of the Church. The aim where possible was to identify projects of strategic importance and potential for the future, and to 'lend' well-qualified staff to them at no cost for as long as they were needed. As the projects prospered, gradually they would provide their own staff, and BMMF workers would move on elsewhere.

Many of these key Indian groups grew out of the Evangelical Fellowship of India (EFI). This arose as far back as 1951 at a conference chaired by Jack Dain at Yeotmal, from a deep desire for Indian evangelicals to draw together. As they prayed, God's Spirit moved and EFI was born. The new structure united them in fellowship as they co-operated in evangelism, in seeking spiritual renewal in the church, in theological training and in supporting Christian workers in medicine, nursing, education and in other fields. The first Indian Secretary of EFI was Ben Wati, a Naga Christian from Assam who had studied in America but steadfastly refused offers of work in the West, convinced that his calling was to serve the Indian Church.

BMMF also became involved in the Union of Evangelical Students of India (UESI), a highly strategic ministry at a time when India was looking more and more to her own people for leadership. UESI developed out of the Inter-Collegiate Evangelical Union which had been founded in the early 1950s by a group of lecturers and students at Madras University, with encouragement from the Inter-Varsity Fellowship and the International Fellowship of Evangelical Students. Key figures were Professor Enoch, David Watson and Dr Norton Sterrett, and the student President was a veterinary student, Tom Thurley, now ministering to the Anglo-Indian community in Madras. In 1954 UESI was established as part of IFES by the merger of this group with another student group started at Coimbatore by H.S. Ponnuraj. The first General Secretary was another impressive Indian leader from Kerala, P.T. Chandapilla. He too had studied in America, at Columbia Bible College, and on his way back by ship made the symbolic gesture of assuming again his Indian clothes, kneeling down in his cabin and saying, 'Lord, I promise that I will never be an expensive servant of yours.' He kept his promise, always keeping to a simple Indian lifestyle, refusing financial support from overseas, maintaining the highest standards of conduct and service, and putting God first in his life.

Over the years many BMMF workers became involved in UESI. At one stage nearly half the staff were BMMF missionaries. One of these was Basil Scott, who actually became a student at Varanasi Hindu University in 1963. For him it was a dream come true: the chance to live in an Indian hostel in Varanasi, the citadel of orthodox Hinduism; to study the Hindi language and Indian philosophy and religion; to witness among the 7,000 students to whom Christ was not known, and to strengthen the small Christian group in their midst. Enjoying fellowship with the eight or so Christians, mostly from South India, he longed to see them sharing the riches of Christ more and more with their fellow students, and eventually moving on to witness for Christ in every sphere of Indian public life. His studies completed, Basil and his wife Shirley were seconded by BMMF to work full time with UESI, as were Michael and Betty Roemmele, Bob Brow, Naomi McGorman, Elizabeth Clark and others. The work was never easy, the UESI groups in the colleges were often small and struggling, but gradually there was growth, so that by 1974 Basil was able to report that 'the UESI which began as a tiny trickle in 1954 and turned slowly into a stream is now flowing like an ever-widening river.' Particular encouragement came as Christian graduates formed Evangelical Graduates' Fellowships which began to back up the student work.

As UESI was developing its work among university students, Margaret Hall of BMMF began a similar work amongst nurses in 1961, setting up Nurses' Christian Fellowship groups in hospitals throughout India. Soon to work with her was Mariamma Chacko, who had first joined BMMF in 1956 as a village evangelist. As she wrote, 'I thought I would be working mostly among the staff and students at the Kinnaird Hospital. I was nervous of the modern girls in the government hospitals. But then the Kinnaird Hospital closed, so I said, "Lord, thy will be done." Now here I am working full time among government hospital nurses, and I know that I am here today not by chance but by divine appointment.' The result was the formation in 1969 of the Evangelical Nurses' Fellowship of India (ENFI) with the aim of providing pastoral care for ex-mission hospital nurses who had transferred to government hospitals for various reasons – more pay, a less strict regime or simply to be nearer home. Marg moved from Varanasi to Lucknow, and for six years she and Mariamma were based in the Kinnaird Hospital bungalow, no longer needed once the hospital closed. Then in 1971 the Kinnaird Hospital was taken over by the neuro-surgical department of King George Medical College, but as Marg recorded, 'Among the nurses who took up their duties there was one of our ENFI members. Though the name Kinnaird has gone, the hospital will continue to be part of our area of ENFI ministry.' Later, Mariamma was joined in her work by Kunjamma Koshy, another fine Indian Christian.

A particular problem relating to smaller hospitals of which Alan Norrish had become aware was tackled at his suggestion by Ray Windsor. These mission hospitals – whether run by BMMF or by other missions – faced difficulties with the clamp-down on staff from abroad. As Ray wrote, 'The most vulnerable seem to be the evangelicals, who characteristically are jealous of their identity and have sought to maintain one or two small hospitals with limited finances and at the expense of professional standards.' Young Indian graduates from the Christian medical colleges were reluctant to go to hospitals like these, and equally there was a shortage of senior Indian doctors, as those who had worked and trained there had not always been given enough responsibility and so had moved on elsewhere. Ray Windsor's brief was to set up an alliance which became known as the Emmanuel Hospital Association, which would enable these small hospitals to work together to improve their standards and attract staff.

He travelled hundreds of miles by train visiting all the small hospitals of northern India which were affiliated with the Evangelical Fellowship of India and found that because of the reduction in missionary staff, many hospital boards had transferred management to the national church. Each mission set up its own board composed mainly of local Christians, who, however dedicated, often had no expertise in the field of hospital administration. The Emmanuel Hospital Association was registered in 1970, and as a result of Ray's visits seventeen small hospitals joined within the first five years, glad to hand over responsibility for recruiting doctors and administrators to the Association, and realising that such an association had a better chance of obtaining well-qualified national staff. In the process, each hospital retained its own identity but improved the quality of the service it could offer, as EHA, an Indian medical mission and unique at that time in the Third World, began to take over the work which had been founded and run for so many years by foreign mission boards.

At the same time as the small missionary hospitals were being reorganised and strengthened by this association, important rethinking was taking place regarding medical missionary work, and Ray Windsor, always a strategist, kept BMMF well in the picture. He was aware that although missions had majored on hospital-based medicine, and national governments for reasons of prestige tended to do the same, the numbers of people reached by the hospitals, especially in rural areas, was small. The need was to promote community health care and preventative medicine: to change the emphasis from individual patients receiving curative treatment in hospital – although that will of course always be necessary – to health education and therefore the prevention of illness through primary health care where the people live. The hope was that the personal nature of this sort of work would allow a spiritual dimension too. As a result, many BMMF medical teams based at EHA hospitals became involved in community work: as one writer put it, 'getting down to village level, understanding local problems and viewpoints, and motivating lethargic, fatalistic communities to get interested in their own health instead of a handout ... training local people who don't know a bacterium from a grasshopper to be competent village health-workers.'

In the field of theological education, too, the training of Christian leaders was of paramount importance. For example, the interdenominational Hindustan Bible Institute (HBI) in Madras had been founded in 1952 by Dr Paul Gupta, its first Director, a Hindu convert turned evangelist, for the purpose of training Indian missionaries. BMMF was represented on its staff by Robin Thomson, son of BCMS missionaries and born in India, who went first for two years experience but stayed on for five. For a time he was what was known as a Field Partner with BMMF – i.e. he was employed by the Institute, but linked with and supported in prayer by BMMF; later he was employed by them. In 1970 Ian McCleary from New Zealand joined the staff as Dean of Faculty. Graduates of HBI were to be found in every state of India, involved in pastoral work, village evangelism, crusade teams and literature outreach. In the ancient princely state of Rajasthan, one graduate built his

Outside the EHA office, New Delhi

church on the spot where he had previously been stoned by fanatical opponents of his message. Five HBI graduates, all from established churches in South India, had become convinced that God was calling them to go as missionaries to Rajasthan nearly 2,000 miles away in North-West India – underdeveloped, physically and spiritually a desert, with people who spoke a different language from their own. Fifteen years later, there were twelve churches founded by these men.

Another example of the value of the training given in these colleges can be seen in the work of the Rev Pannalall, who accepted the call to Bhilai after graduating from Union Biblical Seminary, Yeotmal in 1957. He started work single-handed, and by 1970 his congregation had multiplied into five churches with a total membership of over 2,000. Another high-caste Hindu, converted in Madras, went after graduation at Yavatmal as Pastor to a most unlikely-seeming church with many problems where he ministered to a mixed congregation of Indians, Anglo-Indians and Europeans. Within a year the church was transformed. These stories could be multiplied again and again.

In the early 1970s the Principal of UBS, Dr Saphir Athyal, visited some Communist countries, a trip which impressed on him the importance of training the whole church, not just the pastors. He realised that under a totalitarian government the pastors may be removed and imprisoned, but if church members are trained, the church has a better chance of survival. He spoke to Robin Thomson and others of this idea, and as so often when the Spirit of God is at work, similar thoughts were coming to other people at the same time. One of these was Michael Roemmele – whose mother and aunt had served as doctors in Lucknow and Patna respectively in the 1920s with ZBBM. He and his wife Betty had gone out to India in 1965 to work among students. Seconded initially to the Bible Seminary at Allahabad, Michael was also involved in student work locally in association with UESI. After a few years he was invited to join the staff of UESI full time as a Bible teacher, and spent two years travelling round India teaching at student camps and conferences, or giving Bible teaching for a week of meetings. Gradually he began to feel that it was not right that students and graduates had to wait for an expert to come before they did any in-depth Bible learning – should they not be doing this study by themselves? This idea was not part of the normal Indian concept of education at that time – the students were used to accepting information from the teacher and writing it down. However, it led Michael to consider the possibility of preparing written material for self-study. At this point he went home on leave for a year (1970–71), and coming back hoping to develop his idea, was delighted to find that it was already starting in the form of TAFTEE.

TEE (Theological Education by Extension) began in Latin America in 1962 and spread rapidly. In September 1970 a workshop on TEE was held at the Union Biblical Seminary, Yavatmal. Forty-six delegates representing Bible schools and churches met to consider how the leaders of Indian churches could be given theological training without being uprooted from their places of witness and source of financial support. As a result, in January 1971, at the EFI Annual Conference, an association to co-ordinate this new approach was set up: TAFTEE, or The Association For Theological Extension Education. Ian McCleary, until recently Dean of Hindustan Bible Institute, was appointed Executive Director, and began work from a base at Bangalore. The idea was to supplement the existing residential courses by making provision for pastors needing refresher courses and for others in secular employment or with family responsibilities who could not easily leave their jobs and homes for full-time training. The Association grew rapidly, enrolling 150 students in its first year, 'eager and talkative, mostly graduates, and from many church backgrounds.' BMMF was involved from the start, not only with Ian McCleary but with others who were not only suited by training and experience for the work, but also – as has often occurred in the history of Interserve –

providentially freed from other responsibilities at just the right time.

Firstly, Michael Roemmele, who made an early return from his home leave in order to attend the Programmed Instruction Workshop organised by TAFTEE in July 1971. Following this, he was appointed Associate Director, TAFTEE, with special responsibility for developing the work in the north of India while still retaining his links with UESI student work. At the same time three remarkable ladies left positions of prestige and responsibility in BMMF institutions to join the TAFTEE staff. Betty Shelton, having handed over the principalship of Queen Mary School, Bombay, to Mrs Rajhuns, came to Madras to help with the development of programmed instruction material for degree-level students; Marian Yelland similarly moved from Kimmins High School and came on to the TAFTEE staff in an administrative capacity, and Joan Newton, having handed over her work at Manmad to Miss Venubai Joshi, was seconded to TAFTEE to help with the development of the Diploma ('grass-roots' level) Course using SEAN (Study by Extension for All Nations) material which was translated into several Indian languages, starting with Marathi. As Joan began trying to make SEAN known in Maharashtra, she found many of her girls from Manoram Sadan, or their husbands, and others of her many contacts over thirty-one years, showing interest.

Gradually more Indians came on to the staff of TAFTEE, and in 1973 the Rev Vinay Moses, trained at UBS Yavatmal and Pastor of a large church in Hyderabad where he was also Dean of TAFTEE, was released by the Methodist Church to become Assistant Director of TAFTEE based at Bangalore. Koshy Muthalaly also joined the staff. But as Joan Newton commented in 1976, when TAFTEE had been going for five years, 'Robin Thomson is currently writing a course on Romans and Jean Brand (another BMMFer) on Ethics while I am starting on yet another course. Mike Roemmele is responsible for the curriculum. In its earlier years, obviously, TAFTEE has been nurtured and guided quite considerably by BMMF!'

It wasn't easy to do all this with little money and a small staff. The courses were based on programmed self-teaching and a weekly seminar where the local groups met with voluntary teachers. They were popular, and students rose early and sat up late to complete their assignments before and after their daily work. Typical of many was Willie Soans, a nominal Christian and an engineer from Bombay. Converted at a crusade in the city, he studied through TAFTEE and through a correspondence course at Allahabad Bible Seminary and subsequently became a full-time youth worker at the New Life Fellowship in Bombay. With students commenting, 'I've been waiting for years for something like this', the courses were meeting a real need.

One of the stalwarts of the TEE team, Betty Shelton, told me a little of her story when I met her at her home in Madras. 'I was first turned down by BMMF in 1951', she told me proudly. This was because she was advised that an eye condition would lead to blindness if she went to India. Eventually, after three years teaching maths in Leicester and studying for a theological qualification without further deterioration of her eyes, she reapplied and was accepted. In the event, it turned out that the humid atmosphere of both Bombay and Madras where she worked was the best possible thing for her eyes. For about twenty years she worked at Queen Mary School, Bombay, building up the science department from scratch. Later, as Headmistress, she maintained the highest standards, based on biblical teaching, so that many students later thanked her for the change of world-view which the school had produced in their lives. In 1971 BMMF handed the school over to the Indian Christian Medical and Educational Fellowship Trust and Betty continued as Headmistress, while training Mrs Rajhuns to be her successor. One day she was visited by Ian McCleary, who, surprised to discover how much she seemed to know about the new system of teaching that was being planned in TAFTEE, suggested that she join the team. As soon as she could, she moved to Madras and began writing courses and tutoring. Even now, officially retired from Interserve, she was Dean of TAFTEE in Madras and taking ten classes a week in different places. As she travelled everywhere by bus, her TAFTEE work alone took up a lot of time.

I sat in on three classes at her home. Four students came for the first: Sarah, a student of English literature, Victor and Noah, both pastors, and Isaiah, a lecturer at Hindustan Bible Institute. The course was on 1 John in Greek. Betty's teaching was stimulating, her mind incisive. We all caught the intellectual excitement as she explained to us the different meanings of the Greek present tense from the English: it means *keeping on* doing something. And turning to Victor, a large, smiling young pastor of a Pentecostal church, she pointed out how valuable this understanding would be in his preaching. Again, over the different senses of 'if anyone sins' in 1 John 2:1: in the Greek two different tenses are used, which sound the same in English. If anyone sins (once, from time to time) he can be forgiven; if he sins continuously, it may indicate that his faith is not genuine. Each student had a course book which he worked through on his own during the week, and Betty made sure that they were launched on valuable lines of study before they met again. For four solid hours this indomitable lady taught: three classes one after the other, with students for the next class arriving while the previous one was still in progress. But this was not all: she also took ten classes a week at Madras Bible Seminary. And also, possibly most dear to her heart, there was Valathi.

The story of Valathi, although not directly a part of Interserve's work, is told briefly here as an example of how one thing leads to another in God's plans, and of the remarkable adaptability of his servants in Interserve. In 1973, when Robin Thomson was at Hindustan Bible Institute and Ian McCleary had moved to Bangalore, Betty was invited to come on to the Faculty to introduce TAFTEE. This she did for three years. Sadly, after that time the Principal,

Dr Paul Gupta, became ill, and while he was in hospital serious trouble broke out at the college. The whole Faculty was dismissed and the students, some with final exams imminent, did not know what to do. After a short time, possibilities began to emerge. The girls moved to Ranipet, and a group of men, as a result of a link already made during an evangelistic tour, moved to Valathi, a village five hours' bus journey from Madras, to complete their studies. Once they had taken their final exams, they dispersed all over India. But in God's eternal economy, more was to come. The transplanted college members – staff and students – had been forbidden by the village headman to evangelise, but nothing could prevent the villagers crowding in to listen to their prayers, which were soon translated into Tamil for their benefit. One day the headmaster had asked if some of the students could teach English to the pupils of his small Tamil-speaking school, and despite their own studies they had done so, giving some simple Bible lessons as well. When the students finally dispersed, some stayed on, developing evangelistic opportunities in the area and continuing their TAFTEE studies at the same time. Soon Betty was asked to set up an English/Tamil-speaking school.

So one thing led to another. Now some sixteen years later there was a flourishing and growing work in the area, known as Valathi Outreach Church Ministries. From the Bible Training Centre first set up in the emergency for the students, twelve students and three pastors and their wives were reaching out and working in twenty-six villages. In Valathi itself a school held in a new multi-purpose church building took ninety children up to grade 6; soon hopefully to matriculation level. There was also a rehabilitation department, where patchwork and other handicrafts are taught. Some were so crippled that they had to be carried to the Centre, but they came. At Valathi everyone contributes something: the rehab people help with the cooking, and so do the senior citizens. A start had also been made in building accommodation for elderly people, particularly for those who have been turned out of their homes for their faith.

As well as the work in Valathi itself, pastors and senior students live out in different villages: Pastor Jesudoss, for example, with his wife Florence, lived in Thayanur Malmalayanur, a village with four separate communities where they ran a little church, and Florence held rehabilitation sessions in their home for local victims of polio, leprosy and other crippling diseases. Other aspects of the outreach ministries include medical camps in the villages, literacy work and a farm out of the drought area which provides both food for the centres and work for the villagers. Betty also had her eyes on another farm nearer by, and was counting up all the benefits to local people which could accrue from planting it with coconut trees. But how to find the money to buy it? Betty herself had paid for various aspects of the work out of her own small salary and gifts received, and now although officially retired, continued her work on her pension just as before. The weekend after my visit she was going to Valathi for a special weekend which would include the dedication of the church and new rehabilitation building at Valathi, a 'mini-convention' with representatives of all twenty-six villages, and the first baptism of believers at Thayanur.

One of the key principles of Betty's work was delegation. She was determined that when eventually she herself was no longer at Valathi, the people she had trained would be ready to carry the work forward. She had applied for Indian citizenship and hoped to end her days in her adopted country. I drove away in a cycle rickshaw through the mild February evening, watching the pavement-dwelling families lighting their fires and thinking about the range of this remarkable lady's work: from teaching privileged girls in Bombay, through theological teaching, to church planting in one of the poorest parts of India. St Thomas is believed to have brought the Gospel to India and to have been buried in Madras. The torch that he lit is still burning, and the flame is being carried by hundreds of South Indians like those at Valathi to other parts of India and beyond.

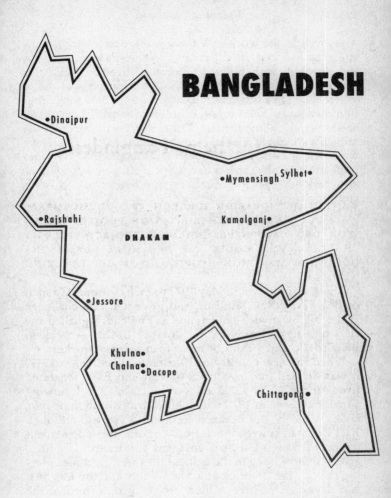

8

A cry for help: Bangladesh

WANTED ORTHOPAEDIC SURGEON TWO PHYSIOTHERA-
PISTS FOUR NURSES REHABILITATION PROJECT DHAKA
STOP TWO CARPENTERS BUILDING PROJECT VILLAGES
CHANDPUR STOP COULD USE TWO MORE NURSES ONE
DOCTOR MYMENSINGH HOSPITAL STOP GET CRACKING
WINDSOR

This telegram, sent in May 1972 to each National Council of BMMF by Ray Windsor, and presented as a challenge at the big Swanwick conference in England, signalled the start of a new chapter in the story of BMMF – work in Bangladesh, and a team of more than seventy workers.

When the new country of Pakistan was created in 1947, it was divided into two parts – West and East, separated from each other by 1,000 miles of India. In 1971, following a major cyclone in 1970 which killed half a million people, civil war broke out between East and West, and although East Pakistan emerged victorious to form the independent nation of Bangladesh, the cost was enormous. The lush, green country lying in the delta of the three great meandering rivers – the Brahmaputra, the Ganges and the Meghna, was devastated. Three million people died, a third of the country's homes were destroyed, farmland was ravaged and industry crippled. Bridges were blown up, schools destroyed and many thousands of people were injured.

The devastation was so great that the Bangladesh Government welcomed help from any source. BMMF soon became involved, together with TEAR Fund, under the auspices of the Evangelical Fellowship of India. As a BMMF commentator wrote, 'The refugees, the enormous camps for the homeless, the plight of widows savagely made so in the war that ravaged their country in its birth-pangs, the gaunt spectre of malnutrition stalking its victims to death in front of those who loved them but had no means to help – who in the name of Christ could resist the plea to "come over and help us"?'

The main needs were for rehabilitation of the war-wounded, care of children who had suffered, the supply of medical workers to hospitals lacking staff because of the war, and help with the food-growing programme. Much of the medical work was based in Christian hospitals which had been founded and run for many years by the Baptist Missionary Societies – notably of Australia, New Zealand and Britain. They needed extra help to meet the exceptional needs of this time, and BMMF was glad to be able to provide extra workers. At the same time an American orthopaedic surgeon, Dr Garst, who had worked at Ludhiana in the Christian Medical College for many years, approached the Minister of Health of the new Government and offered his services. They replied that they would indeed like the help, but had no suitable facilities. They did however take him to see a half-built hospital in Dhaka: 'If you can arrange the completion of the building,' Dr Garst was told, 'equip, staff and finance it, we would welcome you to work as a surgeon here.' Dr Garst at once approached the heads of various missions in India, including Ray Windsor of BMMF. It was this request for help which led to the telegram with which this chapter began.

So by July 1972, with TEAR Fund's generous help, BMMF medical teams flew in. With the agreement of UMN, Dr Bill Gould of BMMF, an orthopaedic surgeon working in Nepal, was transferred to Dhaka. One of BMMF's remarkably adaptable older workers came too. Dr Winifred Anderson, retired after her long service in India and Nepal, flew out to help: looking after the young nurses who arrived from Britain, New Zealand,

Australia and elsewhere, finding them somewhere to live, negotiating with landlords, acting as medical consultant to the missionary community around Dhaka. She also played a key role in 'building bridges' with the Baptist missionary groups already there.

The crisis in Bangladesh highlighted a new trend in missionary work – the use of short-term workers. Since its foundation in 1852, one of the conditions of acceptance as a worker with the Zenana Mission/BMMF had been commitment for life. However, in 1970 BMMF launched a programme to enable students to use their two to three months' summer break for short-term work. Some mission leaders saw this as tending towards lack of commitment – a sort of 'trial marriage' approach – but as the Bangladesh relief project got under way, with young people offering their help for an average six months to two years, Ray Windsor commented that this development was not just a gimmick, an attempt to show that BMMF was 'with it', and that it was more than the excitement of travel and the stimulus of working in another culture that drew youngsters to respond to the challenge. He wrote:

> My recent visit to Bangladesh has convinced me that these young people are making a thoroughly worthwhile contribution. Through their involvement they have seen the Spirit of God guiding their lives . . . already several have extended their term while others are returning home to enter Bible College or to gain more professional experience as preparation for their return, next time for long-term service.

Marcia Gagg, for example, was a young nurse who responded to Ray Windsor's telegram for help. She went for six months to work in a hospital in Dhaka. In the clamour and chaos of the city, milling masses spilt over into roads teeming with jangling rickshaws, and battered buses belching out acrid fumes over rickshaw pullers, loaded and unloaded clamouring passengers. She found the hastily-built hospital very inadequately equipped, but God's power was shown in remarkable ways, as with a child who had been wounded in the head by a land-mine. A large piece of bone was missing from his skull and the three-week-old wound was infected. He was conscious but unable to speak and deteriorating fast. The team prayed and wrote home to others to pray. After a skin graft and weeks of hospital care the boy was discharged.

As help began to arrive in Bangladesh in response to the desperate need, the various organisations involved formed yet another 'umbrella organisation' similar to UMN and IAM, and it was this united group which was invited by the Government to continue relief and development work in various parts of the country. The new group, arising out of the concept of holistic mission articulated at BMMF's quadrennial conference in 1974, was called HEED: Health, Education and Economic Development. The hope was not just to pour money and personnel into mopping up disasters, but to initiate longer-term projects – community health rather than just first aid in the camps, training of national staff, schemes to enable war widows to work and earn an income.

Rex and Jean Blumhagen, both very experienced in community health work, had by now had to leave Afghanistan, so they did a survey of Bangladesh, and as a result of this HEED was set up with Ray Windsor as Acting Director until Dr Malcolm Dunjey, from Perth, Australia, arrived to take over, seconded by BMMF. HEED was to work under protocol to the Government in the areas of Kamalganj and Dacope. BMMF and TEAR Fund were two of the participating missions. The symbol for HEED was two fish and five chapatis, signifying all that Jesus had been able to do with one boy's picnic lunch.

Work tackled by HEED included community health care in the hot, swampy, roadless and watery area of Dacope in the south, where people could be reached only by boat. Kamalganj to the north east within sight of the foothills of the mountains of Assam was the second major area, the work there including rural health care and preventative medicine, leprosy work, agriculture, and fish farming. Finally in Dhaka, and in Mymensingh in the north, medical care for thousands of refugees continued, as well as provision of low-cost housing, rebuilding of Christian schools demolished in the war, draining and restocking of huge ponds with fish for fish farming, and sanitation control. People responded either with profound gratitude or by taking the help for granted. Some were eager for Bible teaching, others were not. To reap in a disaster situation is to gather in both wheat and tares.

Another development under HEED was in handicrafts. Block-printed goods made up by the leprosy patients at Kamalganj, weaving by Manipuris, wood-carvings from Chalna and carpets from Mohammadpur, Dhaka: marketing these, taking care not to impose Western ideas – all helped the artists and craftsmen, women as well as men, to become more self-reliant and to support themselves.

One of those who came to help, originally in the short term, was Margaret Hurst, an English girl who had trained as a nurse in east London. Working amongst the many Bengali families in that part of London, she was ready to do a year's post-war relief work in Bangladesh – a year that left her convinced of one thing: 'I had no desire to return. Moses' desperate plea when commissioned by God to leave Egypt was mine: "O Lord, send, I pray, some other person."' But the Lord had other plans, and in 1978, having studied at Bible college, Marg went back to Bangladesh with BMMF to work in the HEED community health care project at Kamalganj. Following the tradition of BMMF from its inception as the Zenana Mission, Marg was particularly concerned for women. She recognised, ruefully, how strange she must seem to the women of Bangladesh, in this humorous account of a typical encounter:

I skidded clumsily across the yard of the rain-drenched homestead. Perhaps no-one would notice my frenzied moments of total immobility, as I was forced to unwrap my ankles, locked in the clinging, twisted hem of my sodden saree. Squatted in a huddle on the sheltered verandah, a group of women were engrossed in animated chatter. Enter this tall (*so* tall!) foreign . . . female – or is it male? (It's the height and the hairstyle that throws them.) Suddenly their thin figures stiffened into exclamations of curiosity, mingled with rising panic. Conversation trailed off into the sultry air as several pairs of eyes (some hidden behind slatted bamboo walls) turned to drill holes in my sunglasses. The inevitable ensued. A different kind of drilling, with a standard series of questions: 'No, I don't have any sons . . . no, nor daughters . . . well, actually, no, I don't have a husband here with me – I'm not married!'

'You're not married? Why? Haven't your parents made an arrangement for you?' And so on – *ad infinitum*. Act 1, Scene 1 of a thousand similar village visits. How odd and strange we must seem to rural women in this land. How odd and strange that God should send me here. But looking back, I can see solid evidence of his love – and sense of humour – in placing me in this 'man's world' of Bangladesh.

Indeed as she worked among them, providing preventative and curative health care and encouraging them in ways of earning their support, she was saddened to realise that the Bengali woman – especially in the remoter country parts – only achieves status and recognition as she takes on the primary role of wife and mother of sons. Even her name reflects this, as once married, she is chiefly known by terms related to her role: bou (wife), ma (mother), bhabi (brother's wife), and after the birth of her first son 'mother of so-and-so' – the name which stays with her till she dies. Marg grieved to see these women exploited sexually, socially and economically – up first in the morning, the last in the family to eat and the last to sleep at the end of a heavy day. While recognising that she had much to learn from them in their submissiveness, modesty and gracefulness, she nonetheless longed to see them freed from exploitation and injustice and from the drudgery and drain of too-frequent pregnancies. She longed for them to be recognised as persons, as Jesus recognised women as equals in another society which gave them a low place, and to find the true freedom which only he can give.

HEED moved away from its initial role in relief work, and with Colin Richardson of BMMF (NZ) as Associate Executive Director, became primarily a development agency, setting up small groups and training people in health, education, agriculture, handicrafts and small income-generating projects. It has a thirty-five-bed leprosy hospital and runs many clinics for leprosy and TB control. However, BMMF also continued to be involved in relief work, contributing, for example, together with TEAR Fund in 1987, to a project set up by Koinonia, the relief arm of the National Christian Fellowship of Bangladesh, to provide basic housing for the thousands of people rendered homeless by repeated floods.

The meeting of spiritual need was of course another area in which BMMF became involved in Bangladesh. In 1968, the College of Christian Theology of East Pakistan was founded, involving eleven affiliated churches and missions. The disasters of 1970 and 1971 robbed the already struggling college of nearly all its staff – they were out on relief work. By 1974 the college was at its lowest ebb, but then, with the arrival of new BMMF missionaries things changed dramatically for the better. When Dr Anderson left Bangladesh in 1973, her role as senior BMMF worker with HEED was taken by Hester Quirk (later to marry Jack Dain whose first wife Edith died in 1985). Hester had had a varied career with BMMF, as Principal of Kinnaird High School, Lahore; as Personnel Secretary in London; and then working with Ray Windsor in the International HQ in India for thirteen years as Associate Director for Personnel. Now in Bangladesh she felt it was important that BMMF should be involved in specifically spiritual ministry as well as relief work, so was delighted when an invitation came from the College of Christian Theology to provide staff.

She wrote round to all the different national Councils of BMMF: 'Answer to prayer. We've been invited by the CCTB to provide staff. Have you got anyone suitable?' And a prompt reply from the Canadian Council was yet another answer to prayer: 'We have a couple: Denzil and Iris Baker. Denzil was born in Bengal. He studied at Calcutta Bible College and then did further theological training in Canada. Iris was a missionary in Bengal and speaks Bengali.' This was clearly God's provision, and others followed. The Rev David Stuart-Smith joined the staff from the UK, and the Rev Peter and Dr Jenny Richardson came from Australia, Peter as Director of Theological Education by Extension (TEE), and Jenny with medical responsibilities in the college and in the community.

The college concentrates on training national church leaders, many of whom cannot afford full-time theological education or have family or church leadership responsibilities which they cannot leave for long. For such people short courses are arranged, and also theological teaching by extension. In 1977 Ian McCleary, who had set up TEE in India, was appointed Pastor of the Dhaka International Christian Church, where he not only ministered to an English-speaking multinational congregation but also worked part time with the college, developing teaching material.

In 1975 the Rev Robert Cutler came from Britain to Bangladesh, invited by the International Fellowship of Evangelical Students (IFES) to work among students. When Bangladesh became independent, UESI students and graduates had made contact with Bangladeshi students in the refugee camps in India, and again back in Bangladesh; in addition UESI staff worker Narayan Mitra had visited churches and missionaries – many of them Baptist – in Bangladesh. As a result of these contacts, it seemed that the time was ripe to start a ministry among students in Bangladesh and Bob Cutler, then on the staff of UCCF (Universities and Colleges Christian Fellowship) in the UK, was invited to go. He would have been pioneering totally alone, with little means of support or back-up, so readily took up an invitation from Arthur Pont to join BMMF and go with them, seconded to IFES who had invited him.

With the help of contacts already made by Narayan, Bob started work in Dhaka, where he also became a Presbyter of the Church of Bangladesh, attached to St Thomas's Church. As in Pakistan, there were churches in Bangladesh, founded during the previous almost two centuries by missionaries – many of them Baptist – going back to the pioneering work of William Carey. Because this work had been done originally among Hindus, special sensitivity was needed in helping people in the now predominantly Muslim countries to become believers: the cultural leaps they may be expected to make needed to be understood and carefully thought through. Also the churches had very few graduate Christian pastors, and as a result the students, mostly from nominal Christian families, needed much teaching – indeed many needed leading to Christ. Bob began inviting them to his home for Bible study, meetings which continued week by week. Slowly the student work grew, and eventually an independent national student movement was established and registered: the Bible Students' Fellowship of Bangladesh (BSFB), which was affiliated to IFES in the same way as UCCF, UESI and other national groups.

Together with other Christians, expatriate and Bangladeshi, BSFB ran an annual student camp and training conferences to strengthen Christian students and enable them to share their faith with others. Once a young man whose home was near the school where an annual camp was to be held, feeling excluded because he had not passed the school exam which would qualify him to count as a student and attend, took it out on Bob, tearing the shirt off his back. In retaliation, some Christian students from the camp and from the local church lay in wait for the young man and would undoubtedly have injured him, probably seriously, but for Bob's intervention. As a result, a great sense of repentance and the presence of the Lord came over the camp, and the episode proved a turning point in BSFB's ministry and the credibility of the work. As the young people saw how God had prevented them and saved the young man from harm, they had a practical illustration of what Bob was eager to teach: that God, the Lord, is real.

Sadly, some years later the faith of those associated with BSFB was sorely tested. The first national staff worker was Michael Mihir Sarker. He had worked with Bob for six years and then taken an honours degree in theology at the London Bible College. On January 1st 1991 he took over from Bob as General Secretary of BSFB, and for the next nine months they continued to work together, with Bob preparing to leave Bangladesh. In October 1991, three weeks before Bob was due to leave, Michael was killed: crushed when a bus pulled forward as he was getting into it in a traffic jam, on his way to the BSFB annual camp. Bob went back to the UK as planned, too shattered by the loss of such a friend and key BSFB worker to continue. A few months later he returned to Bangladesh to work alongside another Bangladeshi, Peter Mazumdar, already a member of staff of BSFB for a number of years, preparing him to take over as General Secretary. Soon a second and hopefully a third staff member were being appointed.

Wars and natural disasters can never be said to be good, but good can come out of them. In the case of Bangladesh they led not only to the arrival of short-term money and aid, but to the setting up of HEED and other schemes which helped to teach skills and get people on their feet. The attention of the world was drawn to Bangladesh. Christians were welcomed and were able to bring help and encouragement to the small and struggling church, and BMMF found an important new area of service. As time went on, Bangladesh introduced a tougher visa policy. The heady years of the 1970s when the doors were open wide for Western missionaries and relief agencies were over. But

Interservers are still helping where they can: some working
at the World Mission Prayer League's LAMB Hospital in
the north west of the country.

THE MIDDLE EAST
AND THE GULF

9

The Middle East

In 1965 Beirut, 'the Paris of the East', unspoilt then by the carnage of more recent years, had seven colleges and universities with students from over sixty countries. The population of Lebanon was divided almost equally between Christians and Muslims. The Christians were predominantly Maronite and other Catholics; Orthodox; and a much smaller proportion of Protestants. With its pleasant climate, cosmopolitan character and geographical position on the Mediterranean edge of the Arab world, Beirut, the capital, became a strategic centre, not only for commerce and tourism but also for Christian witness.

BMMF first became involved in a small way in Beirut through Dr and Mrs Robert Young, who were Field Partners, Bob being on the faculty of the American University. They held Friday evening meetings in their home and arranged student Christian conferences. Then in 1967 a Canadian, Dr George Bush and his wife Emmeline, arrived, George having been appointed to teach mathematics at Beirut College for Women. As he remembered,

It was largely Bob Brow's vision that moved us into Lebanon. We arrived a few months before the Six Day War, and had to leave the country for some months. Once back in Beirut we convened a monthly prayer meeting of workers who were interested in outreach to students. Out of the prayer group and the vision of Nate Mirza of the Navigators, a mission to students called

ICHTHUS was planned and eventually took place. There was also a student Bible study in our home.

In 1967 too, Mr and Mrs Raymond Joyce from Canada, already in Lebanon, joined BMMF, helping to co-ordinate the production and distribution of Arabic literature. Beirut was a good centre for this, and Raymond was soon receiving requests from places as far away as Indonesia, South Thailand and Nigeria as well as within Lebanon itself. Howard Norrish, son of Alan and Sylvia, also came to Beirut with his wife Nora, as Field Partners while Howard studied chemistry at the American University. The Bushes went home in 1971 expecting to return, but no suitable teaching job developed. Also in 1970-71 the fragile balance which had held for some years between the Christian and Muslim populations began to destabilise, armed Palestinian resistance organisations moved in to set up military bases, and the involvement of BMMF people in Lebanon, promising though it seemed, had to stop. The Joyces continued Muslim literature work based in Canada, and the Bushes moved to another Middle Eastern post equally full of possibilities – in Iran.

From early Christian times there had been a strong Christian church in Persia, but this had been largely suppressed by the growth of Islam. Of the one per cent of Christians in Iran in the 1970s, by far the largest numbers were from the Armenian Orthodox and the Church of the East (Assyrian). Roman Catholics and Protestants numbered only a few thousand. Protestant missionaries had been working in Iran for the last 150 years or so: the American Presbyterians had established hospitals and schools in the north, and the Church Missionary Society followed soon afterwards with similar work in the south. Both these missions, as well as the Assemblies of God and the Brethren, had established churches in Iran. The Bishop of the Anglican Church was an Iranian convert, Bishop Hassan Dehqani-Tafti. There continued, too, a small number of the Armenian and other Orthodox Christians whose churches pre-date the modern missionary movement, and whose membership now is estimated to total some 225,000.

In 1973 at the time of the oil boom thousands of Americans came to work in Iran at the Shah's invitation, and many British too. New towns were built to accommodate them. Schools and colleges with American teaching programmes grew. Churches multiplied. It was something of an American invasion, and not always welcome, especially as many Iranians felt the Shah was not wise in his exploitation of oil and that Islamic values were decreasing. The Rev Tateos Michaelian, a minister of the Presbyterian Church in Iran and General Director of the Iranian Bible Society, wrote an article in 1977 for BMMF's *Go* magazine in which he stated his conviction that the time for God to move in Iran had arrived. He called for a greater Christian presence in Iran, and for Western Christians to live there, either as missionary doctors, nurses and teachers or pursuing secular occupations.

Several members of BMMF were already there: Bob and Inga Young worked in student counselling; Dr Jennifer Nixon and then Dr Helen Murrell worked as gynaecologists at Shiraz Christian Hospital, and the Bushes moved to Pahlavi University, Shiraz, where George taught in the Department of Mathematics and Statistics. George was involved in a men's prayer breakfast and Emmeline in a children's summer day camp which attracted both Iranian and foreign children; Anne White worked as a nursing sister at the Christian hospital at Isfahan, Judy Manning was at the blind school, and Phyllis Tring taught English at the new Damavand College for Women in Tehran.

Converted as a student, Phyllis had taught English for nine years in the UK, 'waiting for her father to be converted', before she felt able to respond to God's call to work abroad. Converted he gloriously was, and Phyllis taught for ten years at Kinnaird High School, Lahore, after which, beginning to feel that God had something new in mind for her, she was asked by Ray Windsor if she would consider teaching in Iran. She went on to the staff of

Damavand College, a secular college for women which had developed from a small American Presbyterian school. It was now a liberal arts college offering a four-year degree course, with representatives of the local churches, business and the Government on its board. Once introduced to the Minister of Education as 'our only genuine English teacher', Phyllis taught English and communication skills; also an introduction to world literature and a course on ancient myth and epic, which gave scope for including the Bible. She was seconded and supported financially initially by BMMF, but later became a Field Partner, employed by the college. She always regarded the teaching itself as her main ministry, rejoicing to see young Iranian women opening up to new ideas, but she also ran a Bible study for Christian students who sometimes brought Muslim friends along, and managed to find time each morning to pray with the Christians – sometimes only one or two, at other times as many as could fit into her office.

Andy Dymond, a telecommunications engineer from Canada and his wife Pat also lived in Tehran as Field Partners, learning Persian and witnessing to Christ amongst friends and engineering colleagues, and Colin and Gladys Blair came in 1978 to work with Tateos Michaelian in the Bible Society. The BMMF staff members at Damavand College were joined by the Rev and Mrs Norman Friberg, and Marcia Sayre, all from the USA, who had had to leave Afghanistan. On her arrival in Tehran in 1976, Marcia began a strategy study for BMMF, researching what other missions were doing, where they overlapped and might co-operate, and the extent of Christianity in Iran. She travelled to many Iranian cities from her base at the Fribergs' home in Tehran. Norm and Jacque Friberg were full of enthusiasm about her discoveries as she returned from each trip, and around them a spirit of fellowship among the BMMF group grew. As Marcia saw it, many patterns were established at that time: the Middle East was on Interserve's map to stay; Interserve was seen to be a catalyst bringing other mission groups together; the 'tentmaking' pattern of secular work was established in the Middle East. And on the more personal level, the Fribergs developed gifts for building up a team; Marcia found a role as explorer and pioneer, while Phyllis Tring quietly got on with the work of the Kingdom.

The Fribergs were an outstanding couple – warm-hearted, extrovert. Norm taught English as a second language and was a great story teller, good company and also deeply spiritual. Young people loved him, and he and Jacque worked with the youth group of one of the Persian-speaking Presbyterian churches which grew rapidly. There was an increasing spirit of co-operation among widely varied mission groups. It appeared to be a time of great opportunity for the Gospel, with Iran, as President Carter of the United States described it, 'an island of stability'. Sadly, it was not to last. In 1978 the old order began breaking up, with unrest increasing as the people turned against the Shah and the pro-Western stance of his regime. In January 1979 the Shah left the country, never to return, and shortly afterwards the Ayatollah Khomeini reached Iran after fifteen years' exile in France and set up the Islamic Republic. Damavand College was closed by the Government for five months; the staff hung on, holding faculty meetings every month, but there was no future for them at the college, and one by one the BMMF staff members left. The Fribergs, Phyllis and Marcia all left in February 1979. In June the Christian hospital at Isfahan where Ronald Pont, Arthur's brother, was the Medical Superintendent, was taken over by the Iranian Revolutionary Council who demanded that all missionaries, including David and Helen Lyth of BMMF, leave or face imprisonment. In October there was an attempt on the life of Bishop Dehqani-Tafti, and in May the following year his son Bahram, who had taught at Damavand for two years, was shot dead. The new regime increased its grip on the people, and the small Christian Church was left to stand, trusting in Christ alone. As the Bishop said, 'Our numbers have become smaller, our earthly supports have gone, but we are learning the meaning of faith in a new and deeper way.' He himself had to leave the country, and now lives in exile in Britain.

Of the estimated three million Iranians who fled Iran at this time, some 10,000 came to the UK. The Christians among them continued to meet for worship and for fellowship – an Iranian service, for example, is held in a west London church once a month. In 1990 Sam Soloman, lecturer at Carey College of Islamic Studies, was released by Interserve to the Iranian Christian Fellowship in London to help prepare these Iranian exiles for outreach amongst their own people in Iran once they were able to return, and many Iranians in Europe and the US have come to believe in Christ.

For Phyllis Tring, many more adventures lay ahead as she followed God's lead into the 1980s. After a year's sabbatical obtaining an MA in England, it seemed that his call was to the Lebanon, still in the throes of civil war. She was not keen, neither were BMMF, but she was offered a job in a Christian school, and bravely she went. A year later, in 1981, she became Director of the teacher-training class attached to the Lebanon Evangelical School for Girls, a task which involved reopening the department which had closed during the fighting. For two years she ran the course and the department, doing much of the teaching and supervising of the Christian students herself. She was in Beirut at the time of the 1982 Israeli invasion of Lebanon and the siege of West Beirut. With twenty different factions fighting all around, she was caught in the cross-fire but not hit. And as she wrote at that time, 'I'm afraid that bullets and bombs will continue to be part of daily life here in Beirut. They hinder some things, but not the work of God's Holy Spirit.'

After two years that work came to an end, and Phyllis went to a sister school, the Lebanon Evangelical School in Tyre, where she was in charge of the pre-school classes, doing in-service training of the teachers. Ninety-seven per cent of the pupils in the school were Muslim, and one of her hopes was to encourage the teachers to give the children real joy in learning – not just to expect them to copy and learn by rote. Whatever job she did, and Phyllis did several more after that, she came more and more to realise the value of Christians working in secular jobs. As she put it, 'It gives one an identity – an understandable reason for being there. I feel that people need a secular job if they are to make contact with people.' This small, unassuming and rather frail lady had been in two of the world's toughest spots of the 1970s and '80s, following God's lead. She had certainly made contact with people for him.

Ten years or so earlier another way forward for the Gospel in the Middle East had been pioneered by Vivienne Stacey, then still Principal of the United Bible Training Centre at Gujranwala, Pakistan. Visiting the United Christian Hospital in Lahore for their twenty-fifth jubilee, she noticed a map showing where all their trained nurses had gone on to work. Over half of them were working in Libya, and in Saudi Arabia and other Gulf countries. This made her feel that if the Christian nurses she was training in Bible knowledge and evangelism were going to work in those countries, she should make an exploratory trip to the Middle East herself. In 1969 she asked BMMF for extra leave and visited Kuwait, Bahrain, the United Arab Emirates and the Sultanate of Oman.

Often she met people she knew from Pakistan – for example, a Pakistani laboratory technician she met in Muscat had attended lectures she had given for staff at the United Christian Hospital on 'How to share your faith with Muslims'. Now he gathered his friends together and asked Vivienne to lead a Bible study for them. As she travelled through the Gulf countries opportunities like this arose – invitations to Pakistani homes and through them to speak for Christ. In Bahrain she was welcomed by some of the 3,000 Pakistanis who had gone there for economic reasons, and was invited to speak at their monthly Urdu communion service.

Instead of bemoaning the fact that so many Pakistani Christians whom she had sought to train in evangelism had left Pakistan, this trip led Vivienne into completely new thinking about dispersions and the link between the spread of the Gospel and economics. After all, it was economic need which took Pakistanis to the Gulf, and Christians in particular. She compared this new situation with the dispersions of the Jews and of the Christian Church – the captivity in Babylon, the dispersion of Jews in the inter-testament period and in the early church. God used them. Her trip had showed her that the Pakistani Christians of this modern-day dispersion were forming worshipping groups in Muscat, Bahrain, Kuwait and Dubai. With encouragement, could not these Christians be used in God's purposes to witness for Christ to other Pakistanis, to other expatriates also working in the Gulf and to the Arabs themselves? Visiting the Gulf again in 1974, she found that the number of Pakistanis in Oman had increased ten-fold. Six hundred miles from Muscat where thousands of Pakistanis from the Punjab were living under canvas helping to build a new city, seventy Pakistani Christians attended a Bible study she led, showing marked interest and real spiritual hunger. She returned to Pakistan with gifts they had given for the work of the Gospel.

Colin Blair, too, of BMMF (Canada) and now working for the Bible Society in the Gulf, saw that among the 400,000 immigrants from South India in the Gulf, the 3,000 or so Pakistani sweepers keeping Riyadh clean, and the thousands of Europeans and Americans providing expertise, there were many Christians. As he put it:

They represent the largest single resource in the hands of the sovereign Lord, to communicate to the Muslim world. A new diaspora is upon us with all the possibilities the book of Acts describes, or the British Empire similarly provided. It is unplanned, uncoordinated, but nonetheless glorious and wonderful. What can the Fellowship do in this situation? As it has done in the past it can flow along the lines of natural advance. It can flow along these known paths of communication amongst communities of Indians and Pakistanis with

whom it has long-established contact. Strengthening
and encouraging these vigorous but needy groups is
the first priority. Helping them grow in their own faith
and then communicating to them the responsibility of
making disciples first among their own people, then for
a few of them gifted with cross-cultural ability to reach
out beyond to the others.

A few years earlier, Colin, one of BMMF's strategic
thinkers and visionaries, then working with the Bible
Society in Iran, had been appointed BMMF's Regional
Superintendent there. While the Revolution was building
up, he had been looking for openings in the Gulf – ways
of putting his and Vivienne's ideas into practice. The
first BMMF Partners to be posted to the Gulf with his
encouragement were Arif and Kathy Khan from the USA.
Arif had been pastoring an expatriate church in Tehran,
and when they had to leave, he went on to pastor the
Urdu church in Al Ain in the United Arab Emirates.
Colin himself became Regional Superintendent for the
Middle East, based in Bahrain and working part time as
an administrator at the American hospital. As Bob Morris,
Executive Director of Interserve (Canada) saw it,

> Colin and Gladys Blair's career in the early days tended
> to be following Dennis and Gladys Clark across Asia,
> picking up the pieces from Dennis's avalanche of ideas
> and giving them on-going viability. Overall they served
> in every region of the Fellowship except Nepal. They
> began with a Bible teaching and publishing house min-
> istry in Pakistan and later in India. They were administra-
> tive trouble-shooters and pioneers in Afghanistan and
> Bangladesh. They were the last people out of Iran, one
> year after the Khomeini Revolution, and spearheaded
> the Interserve presence in the Middle East through their
> secondment to the Bible Societies.

(When last seen, Colin was in Hong Kong, working for the

Bible Society, and married, after Gladys's death, to Janette Cowan.)

Vivienne Stacey visited the Gulf countries whenever possible, teaching the Christians, encouraging them to learn Arabic and to reach out for God in their new situation. She found many Indian and Pakistani Christian nurses in the hospitals, and many others in other secular jobs. As she saw it, 'The oil lands of the Middle East are the natural mission fields of the Pakistani Church. Urdu is heavily dependent on Arabic in vocabulary, and Pakistanis quickly learn to communicate in Arabic. Pakistani believers in secular jobs, like their Indian, Korean and Filipino brothers and sisters, are the Christian ambassadors of the oil age.' In 1975, after twenty years at Gujranwala, it became clear to Vivienne that God was calling her to leave UBTC and to devote half her time to writing and half to ministry among Pakistanis and others in the oil lands of the Middle East.

In 1977 Vivienne visited Salalah in the Sultanate of Oman and reported: 'A group of five keen Pakistani laymen take services in various Pakistani camps on different nights of the week. I joined their team for five days and held a series of four meetings at one camp and then held Christian services at two other camps . . . I was able to distribute thirteen sets of Urdu Bible study tapes in the peninsula.' In the same year she travelled across the whole of the coast of North Africa and found 'the wind of God blowing there . . . in Libya God has his "living stones" – Christians from East and West, helping to develop an oil-rich nation. Pakistani, Indian and Egyptian Christians are meeting in their homes for worship.' In Egypt at least 10% of the population was Christian, with encouraging signs of renewal in the ancient Coptic Church.

A rough overall picture of the state of the Christian Church among the Arabic-speaking peoples themselves during the 1980s might surprise us: approximately eight million Christians among the Arabic-speaking people of the Middle East. Of these, by far the largest group (66%) belonged to the ancient Orthodox churches, in parts of which renewal was taking place, and the next largest to the Catholic Church (27%). Only seven per cent of the total Christian population was reckoned to be Protestant, and they lived mostly in Egypt, Lebanon, Syria and Jordan. In Saudi Arabia and Qatar no known national Christians were to be found. The freedom given to Christians for worship varies from one country to another, with proselytism forbidden, and pressure on Christians varying from surveillance to outright persecution and prison. In some Gulf countries, notably Bahrain, Kuwait, UAE and Oman, the traditional Muslim toleration of other faiths is still maintained and several expatriate Christian congregations flourish; but in others, Islamic fundamentalism is still repressive.

The new awareness of the Muslim world among Christians in general created by the oil boom of 1973, and the explorations and studies of Vivienne Stacey in particular, led BMMF to consider in new depth the whole question of its outreach to the Muslim world. Its quadrennial conference in 1978 set up a commission to study the resurgence of Islam and to stimulate fresh efforts in its ministry to Muslims. The initial thought was to restrict the ministry primarily to the diaspora (dispersed) labour force from India and Pakistan, using Partners who had already been working in those countries, but in 1980 it was decided to recruit people specifically for ministry to the Arabic-speaking peoples of the Middle East, including Egypt.

Egypt, among Middle Eastern countries, has by far the highest proportion of Christians – particularly in the ancient Coptic community which goes back to the first century AD, but also in the Catholic and the Coptic Evangelical Church. Marcia Sayre was Interserve's first Partner to be located here, and she came in 1981, her task being to assess, in consultation with national and other Christian leaders, how best Interserve might serve God in Egypt and other nearby countries. Having been expelled from both Afghanistan and Iran at times of political upheaval, she expected the same to happen for a third time, when President Anwar

Sadat was assassinated two weeks after her arrival. But this time all was well, and she stayed for several years. Sadat's successor, President Hosni Mubarak, proved to be a shrewd political balancer. Gradually he brought the country back to stability which he managed to maintain despite Egypt's ostracism by the rest of the Arab world throughout the '80s, a vigorous Muslim fundamentalist movement and a hard-hitting recession.

Soon, with many BMMF Partners in India having their visas refused, some were posted to Arab countries to join Marcia. One of these was Moonyeen Littleton. From secretarial work in BMMF's London office, she had moved to its Field Headquarters at Mussoorie and then into Christian journalism based in Bombay. Now in 1983 she came to join a gifted team of national Christian writers and artists in the Arab world who produce the Arabic outreach magazine *Magalla*. Christians considering literature work in the Arab world had discovered a gap in the market – a real need for a young people's Arabic magazine which would be politically neutral, 'non-religious' in the Muslim propaganda sense, morally good and written lovingly for young people about things they were interested in. Including sport, fashion, interviews with famous people, each issue also covered a main theme: pollution, health, friendship or whatever, from various points of view: general, scientific, spiritual. Without feeling 'got at' in any way, the reader gradually sensed, 'These people know God – he is real to them.' For some, this would be the beginning of a search for him. *Magalla* is the most popular youth magazine in Egypt and the Sudan, with more than 60,000 copies being sold on the news-stands each month, and each copy being read on average by six to eight people, leading to a total readership of about 400,000. *Magalla* is one of the ministries of Middle East Media (MEM), an international fellowship of mainly Arab Christians of which Interserve is a corporate member.

Gradually more BMMF Partners arrived in Cairo, and by the late '80s there was a mixed group of people from the USA, Holland, New Zealand, Australia, and Britain.

Among them were David and Sally Teague from USA, who with theological training and Arabic studies behind them were hoping to develop TEE ministry in Egypt. This never materialised, and after patiently tackling any job he could find, from locum preaching to teaching Greek, David accepted the challenge of preparing study notes for the first ever Arabic Study Bible. By January 1992 the mammoth task of preparing the initial draft was completed and handed to the Director of the Bible Society of Egypt for editing and publication. David and Sally also taught Greek for five years in the Coptic Orthodox Seminary in Cairo. Together they produced a textbook, *New Testament Greek for Orthodox Christians*, and Sally has written a dictionary of Greek words used in the Coptic liturgy.

Other Interserve Partners in Egypt support themselves by teaching English, by a professorship in a university, through freelance journalism and so on. In their spare time they give strong support to Christian projects among the needy or assist in the production of Arabic Sunday school teaching materials. One Partner in particular set up a rehabilitation centre for mentally handicapped children, and was also hoping to start a magazine for those who care for such children. In all this, Interserve's strategy has included a strong emphasis on the spiritual renewal of the church in Egypt, which numbers over six million all told; also on improving relations between the Eastern and Western churches which have been estranged for centuries. Interserve Partners, notably David Teague and Alistair Wynne, pastor of the Nicosia Community Church in Cyprus, were part of a task group set up to explore the possibilities of Protestant missionary co-operation with Middle East Orthodox churches. The resulting book, *Turning Over a New Leaf*, was a handbook for Christians, especially Western evangelicals, to help them to understand the beliefs and customs of the ancient churches and to relate positively to this little known branch of the worldwide Church.

In other countries too there was scope for expatriate

Christians – some in secular jobs – to share their faith.
For instance in 1982 there were three BMMF couples
living in Bahrain. As Colin Blair reported, there were at
least thirty different fellowship groups meeting in Bahrain
at that time:

> I can go to an Urdu service among ditch-diggers on a
> Thursday evening and, on the following day, to a some-
> what more sophisticated group meeting for Bible study
> in English. These are mostly Europeans, with an admix-
> ture of Indian, Filipino and Sri Lankan membership. On
> Saturdays there meets a group of Arabic-speaking believ-
> ers from Bahrain, Lebanon, Syria and Egypt – mostly
> from long-established nominal Christian traditions in
> those countries. Then, on Sunday evenings I can go to
> a house church group meeting in Telugu-medium from
> India. This incredible variety of races and peoples is a
> new phenomenon in this region as a flood of migrant
> workers pours in to fill the labour force.

Today Interserve still has people in the Gulf. Maggie, for
example, a lively and energetic young woman, worked for
an oil company. Her call was to the Asians in the Arab
world. The Gulf War affected the Church in that many
Westerners left. It was a difficult and confusing time,
as Iraqi Christians and many others in the Middle East
supported Saddam Hussein against the West. The remaining
church was eighty per cent Asian. As well as her secular job,
Maggie was Pastoral Assistant at the Anglican church. The
congregation – largely Asian – grew from fifteen to
fifty in a year while she was there. She was amused when
an American work colleague commented, 'I think you'd be
a really good missionary!'

Interserve is also represented in North Africa as part
of a small 'umbrella' organisation of five member bodies
working under a protocol agreement between the Tunisian
and Swedish Governments on a community health programme and in vocational training. The first Interserve

Partners to work in North Africa on this project were
Arend and Grancien from Holland who arrived in 1986
and stayed for three-and-a-half years, Arend working as a
male nurse. And in another Middle Eastern country under
'Project Thanksgiving', one or two Partners teach English
as a second language.

There is still real scope for Christians to work in Middle
Eastern countries, pursuing their professions in a secular
capacity but also encouraging the Christians there with their
fellowship – for example through home groups. They are
needed to demonstrate, by the way they do their work and
in the quality of their lives and the relationships they form,
that real Christianity is a living faith, and quite different
from the decadent image of the West with which so many,
sadly, confuse it. The importance of the Middle East as part
of Interserve's outreach to the Muslim world is emphasised
too by the location of the International Office, which
directs the field operations of Interserve. In 1985 it was
moved from Delhi to Cyprus, a move made necessary by
visa restrictions. These had been introduced by the Indian
Government in 1984 after the outbreak of terrorism in
the Punjab which led to the assassination of Mrs Gandhi.
Although members of the team in Cyprus are conscious
of being placed in a slightly remote 'safe haven' which
is not officially a Region of Interserve, it is well located,
especially for the Middle East. And the fact that thirty
or so other Christian organisations are also based there
is conducive to co-operation, as together they enjoy the
freedom of working in the only relatively stable Christian
country in the area. This co-operation has occurred notably
in relief work in emergencies: missions based in Cyprus,
including Interserve, united to form ARC (Assist Refugee
Co-ordination) to help refugees in Iran in the aftermath of
the Gulf War. Dr Ray Pinneger of Interserve went out to
help in the refugee camps, in what she described as a hot and
chaotic but very rewarding assignment. ARC also facilitated
co-operative work by evangelical churches in Jordan among
the refugees from the Gulf War – the first time that such

co-operation had occurred – and in Cairo following the earthquake in 1992.

Cyprus is a happy place, with its sunshine, pine-clad mountains, unruffled blue sea and its friendly and extrovert people. The Gospel was first brought here by Paul and Barnabas in AD 45. Yet sadly it remains divided by a militarily guarded 'green line' between the Turkish north and the Greek and Orthodox Christian south. The line passes through the middle of the capital, Nicosia. Here, in the city centre, is Interserve's International Office, where I met several Interserve Partners, among them Margaret Parkinson, a tall and striking Australian whose quiet authority impressed me as it had impressed Dr Raju Abraham when Margaret was working in India. Trained as a nurse and with post-graduate studies in paediatrics, she was put in touch, while seeking God's will for her life in the 1960s, with BMMF's 'Ambassadors' meetings for young people in Melbourne. Here young professionals met in the home of Nell Pyvis, known affectionately as 'Auntie Nell', and here she met BMMF missionaries. As she prayed, the way opened for her to work among orphans at Manoram Sadan and Jyoti Niketan in western India, and eventually, having returned to Australia for a specialist course in the psychology of orphans, into training others in the essentials of residential child care. In 1975, having first carried out a feasibility study, she was involved in setting up an innovative Child Care Association – a co-operative venture for training people who were looking after children in Christian hostels and homes, including children with special needs.

In 1983, back in Australia, she was asked to return to India as BMMF's Regional Representative for India. This she did, having had her missionary visa renewed – essential if she was to be able to stay – and with a strong sense from God that things were going to change dramatically in India and that she was to be a bridge-builder. Her new work involved travelling all over India and providing pastoral care to the missionaries, as their numbers dropped rapidly after

1984. Great sensitivity was needed in helping enthusiastic young workers, newly conscious of God's call to India, to accept that they might have to leave; helping them to learn from their experience – a time that later they would see had been preparing and training them for their next area of work. It was equally important to encourage new Indian leaders, and to maintain relations with the various organisations to which BMMF people had been seconded. As people questioned, 'Where is God in all this?' it was essential to hold on to the unshakeable belief that he was sovereign and in control. As Raju Abraham observed, Margaret's role was crucial in holding BMMF together at a very difficult time.

Inevitably, the question was asked, 'Is there a viable future for BMMF in India now?' And Margaret, together with Bob Morris and Indian Christian leaders hammered out the answers at a consultation in Hyderabad in January 1986. As a result, Interserve (India) was born, with Margaret as its first Executive Secretary, working alongside and handing over to Dr Tluanga in 1989. Finally in 1991 she also handed over to Robin Thomson as Regional Representative for India. Her task there completed, she came to Cyprus as Area Director South with responsibility for India, Pakistan and Afghanistan.

Moonyeen Littleton worked in the Cyprus Office when I visited, having taken over from Phyllis Tring as Information Officer. Maggie Hobbs was there too. She had nursed at Kunri, Pakistan, for thirteen years, working with Dr Don Curry on the Government's Expanded Immunisation Programme, training Pakistani nurses to take over and then becoming Nursing Superintendent. Feeling eventually that her work at Kunri was done and that she should be open to the possibility of something new, she was invited to move to the International Office as Director of Services. This involved working with the three Area Directors on applications for placement of personnel, with responsibility for budgeting and the deployment of funds in the different areas, as well as routine administration: a big job for which her well-organised mind and her previous experience had equipped her.

Another couple based in Cyprus were Merrill and Lena Morrow, from Northern Ireland. Merrill, a burly bluff Irishman, was a photographer in an advertising agency in Belfast and Lena was a psychiatric doctor. Both wanted to serve God in their professions overseas, but wondered, 'How is the Lord going to work into his scheme a photographer and a psychiatrist in the same place?' At first it seemed as though, amazingly, he had – in Cairo. They had approached the Northern Ireland Director of Interserve, then David Porter, who inspired their confidence with his professionalism and told them of openings on *Magalla* magazine and on a drug rehabilitation programme. However, they had to go to Jordan first for language study, and while they were there both the Cairo jobs fell through. Then towards the end of their two-year period of study Merrill was asked to pastor the International Church in Amman, and found himself ministering to a mixed congregation of Irish Catholics, Armenian Orthodox, American Episcopalians and nine different kinds of Baptist. As he said, 'Pastoring the church gave me great freedom to be a Christian openly. As a "holy man" I was expected to talk about God.'

Lena, meanwhile, led Bible studies, particularly for Western women married to Muslims, who were able to visit people at home for coffee, but could not go to church. She also gave counselling and pastoral care to the many missionaries at the language school. They left Jordan the day before the start of the Gulf War. The congregation of the church had dwindled and hardly anyone was left. They moved to Cyprus, where Merrill was seconded to Youth for Christ and also served part time as Interserve's Regional Representative for Cyprus, Jordan and the Gulf, visiting and encouraging Interserve Partners in the Region. In particular he told me about two Indian Partners in the Gulf. Ernest Victor, an engineer, was in Muscat, with his wife Lalitha. He had left engineering and now had an itinerant ministry among Indian labourers. One Friday Merrill drove with him 1,100 kilometres, preaching six times to different groups meeting in homes. One place they visited was a copper mine – a self-contained community with many Filipino, Malaysian and Indian Christians. Ernest did journeys like this every week, teaching the Bible through TEE and preaching. Lalitha was teaching English in Oman, and her salary supported them both.

Similarly C. S. Dutt, also from India, had been seconded by the Indian Evangelical Mission to pastor an Indian congregation in Abu Dhabi. He too set up TAFTEE centres, and his wife, Roxana, had a special ministry to nurses in the hospitals. As IEM has no presence in the Gulf, Interserve helps with pastoral care and some financial support. It costs twelve to thirteen times as much to support a pastor in the Gulf as in India, and the Indian Church cannot provide this on its own, though the expatriate Indian community in Abu Dhabi contributes.

Finally in Cyprus I met Jim and Beth Tebbe. Jim had recently taken over from Michael Roemmele as Executive Director of Interserve. He was brought up in Pakistan, where his father was an American Presbyterian missionary and Principal of the prestigious Forman Christian College in Lahore. After theological studies in the United States, Jim returned to Pakistan with BMMF and studied Islamic history at Punjab University while also pastoring the International Christian Fellowship in Lahore. 'Being at Punjab University really established bonds because I came in as an equal and was treated as an equal,' he says. Then after spending the next three years pastoring the International Church in Dhaka, and further study for a master's degree in Near Eastern studies at Princeton, USA, he taught at the Ecumenical Study Centre at Rawalpindi, Pakistan before being invited to go to Cyprus, first as Area Director West for Interserve and more recently as Executive Director.

As he saw it,

The genius of Interserve is the grass-roots input into

our development, with resolutions from the United Conferences with the different National Councils represented being passed on to the International Council. We also have good internal structures which keep us functioning administratively and pastorally: local groups with a local group leader, Regional Representatives with pastoral responsibilities, and Area Directors who have time for the development of strategy and recruitment and placement of personnel as well as backing up Regional Reps.

And his vision for the future?

We are moving forward from our traditional mission structures, and we need to develop the corporate witness of Partners in secular jobs so that our ministry is greater than the sum of its parts. We must continue to pioneer, reaching out to the 'hard to reach people', co-operating in this aim with other groups. The torch of mission outreach is currently being passed from the West to the East, and we must do all we can to facilitate this, encouraging our fellow believers from the East to practise and witness as Christians.

To end this chapter on the diverse opportunities for Christian witness in the Gulf, let's visit Boota, a Pakistani Christian from near Gujranwala, now working as a cobbler in a small shop in a city in the Gulf. He has learnt Arabic and loves to surprise his Arabic customers by telling them that he is a Christian: 'They think all Pakistanis are Muslims and find it hard to believe that I am proud to be a Christian. But I tell them it is true!' After work, worshipping with others squeezed into a tiny room, he plays the dholuk – a small double-sided drum. The praise of God from the group of worshippers seems as though it will burst the walls, and the music revolves around the little drummer, eyes tight shut and voice clearly leading the singing.

In 1993 we celebrate the bicentenary of another cobbler, William Carey, who took the Gospel to India. Now Boota and many others like him tell the Good News to the Gulf.

10

Progress in Pakistan

With new areas of work opening up and BMMF involved in a multitude of co-operative ventures, how were the older fields of work developing during the 1970s and '80s? Pakistan, first of all. Here in 1970, in a moving ceremony in Lahore, the Church of Pakistan was founded by the union of Anglican, Methodist, and Lutheran Churches and the Sialkot Church Council (Presbyterian). The motif of the united Church is the Taxila cross – an ancient cross discovered by archaeologists in northern Pakistan, a vivid reminder that Christianity began in Asia and was not an 'implant' from the West. Christians in Pakistan come almost entirely from the poorest sections of the community, and national unity is more and more centred in Islam. Clearly the education and training of Christian leaders is of paramount importance.

In Lahore, Kinnaird High School was nationalised by the Government in 1972. Gradually the school had fewer Christians on the staff. Difficulties at the teacher-training college – Kinnaird Training Centre – on the next-door site led to its eventual closure, and the church and mission-sponsored Kinnaird College, the only Christian college of university status for women in West Pakistan, was nationalised too in 1972. Christian witness continued in both school and college, thanks largely to the efforts of two remarkable women, the Principals, both of whom I met in Lahore.

Kinnaird High School, near the railway station, was

founded in 1864 by the combined efforts of the American Presbyterian Church and a few local Indian Christian businessmen, to provide 'superior education' for Christian girls in the Punjab. Known first as Lahore Christian Girls' School, then as the Lady Dufferin School, it came under the auspices of ZBMM in 1871. Lady Kinnaird and her family helped and supported the school in many ways, and over the years a succession of dedicated ZBMM/BMMF Principals, together with their staff, worked to improve the facilities and curriculum. During this time the Kinnaird Training Centre and the College were both founded as offshoots of the school, to provide further opportunities for the girls.

In 1970 Miss Zeb Zaman, herself a graduate of Kinnaird College and a committed member of the Presbyterian Church, was appointed as the first Pakistani Principal, just two years before the nationalisation of the school. She showed me round when I visited in 1992: the pleasant red brick compound, modest in size for the number of girls (doubled since nationalisation to 1,600) with its shady brick-paved courtyard, old-fashioned classrooms and the Mainwaring-Burton science laboratory built in 1958. By 1972, although the number of pupils was increasing steadily, the number of boarders had decreased to twelve, so the boarding side of the school was gradually phased out and some dormitories converted into classrooms, while the major part of the boarders' hostel became a 'Christian Centre' – a hostel for Christian career women. This centre is run by a management committee appointed by the Society for Community Development (SCD) based at Gujranwala, an affiliation arranged by Interserve so that SCD could take over should the school be denationalised in the future. The property used both by School and Christian Centre belongs to the 'International Service Fellowship Trust Ltd'.

Known since nationalisation as Government Kinnaird High School (for girls), it has not been easy to continue to run the school on its old traditions. Members of staff are appointed by the Government, and less than one third are Christian. However, the teachers and Headmistress work hard to maintain its good name among other schools of the city. Christian girls are taught Scripture and the Muslim girls Islamic studies as part of a broad curriculum. At the back of the Christian Centre and looked after by its management committee is an area where the servants live, in mud and brick cottages – a small village community. The school laboratory technician has even converted an old well-head into a tiny chapel and leads services there. Some of the children of this community are given the opportunity of education in the school, and some do well, going on to nursing and other careers. Miss Zaman, an enthusiastic and independent-minded person, battled on in what appeared a very isolated position, maintaining as far as she could the highest standards of discipline and integrity in the school – the reason, no doubt, for its continuing popularity with parents and girls. In 1988 she was transferred to another school, but as a result of petitions from pupils, parents and teachers, she was reinstated in Kinnaird School, convinced that the prayers of Interserve, her church and others were keeping her where God wanted her to be.

Kinnaird College forms a peaceful oasis beside busy Jail Road. Dignified red brick buildings stand in spacious grounds, shaded by a variety of exotic trees planted by a diligent lady botanist formerly on the staff. Girls in brightly coloured shalwar kameez sit chatting on benches or in groups on the grass, or drift to their classes in twos and threes. Many are privileged Muslims from good homes and schools, for although fees at the college are nominal, entry is on merit and only the best-educated girls stand much chance. In 1991 500 girls were admitted out of the 5,000 who applied; the college is the first choice for young women in Lahore. However, if bright enough, poorer girls too can gain a place, including some Christian girls who often come from the less affluent section of the community.

Dr Mira Phailbus, elegant, dynamic, became Principal in 1972, the year when most schools and colleges were nationalised. Nationalisation, she said, was traumatic, as teachers and administrators who had been using well-tried methods of work for many years had to learn bureaucratic and often less productive ways. Along with nationalisation has come increasing Islamisation, but as in Kinnaird High School, Christian students receive teaching from the Bible, Muslim students from the Qu'ran, and all are encouraged to think about what they learn. Indeed in every area of life and study, Mrs Phailbus, working through faculty, aimed to see the girls' horizons widened as much as possible, and they were encouraged to think independently and to develop their potential to the full. Nothing could have pleased her more than when a girl's father, rather than complaining that his daughter was becoming rebellious, came specially to tell her how glad he was that she was arguing with him on politics. Dr Phailbus encouraged the girls in assemblies and at a more personal level; and through extra-curricular programmes – social work among the blind and handicapped, adult literacy work, an annual charity week and through the Christian Fellowship.

Although the position of women is on the whole a neglected issue in Pakistan, the girls are given instruction on women's rights and women's needs in the hope that they will go out and help others with fewer opportunities than themselves. Through the Pakistan Women's Institute, the college adopted a village where the women lacked health education and literacy and also wanted to learn to sew. The Association of Kinnaird College which represents the churches and the founding missions of the college, provided sewing machines, the girls visited and helped, and an outlet was arranged for the work produced through the 'Technical Services Association' which establishes cottage industries for women. Many of the girls graduating from the college make a valuable contribution, either through their jobs or in a voluntary capacity, supporting various projects for the needy.

As some of the students come from outside Lahore, or for some other reason cannot live at home, there have always been residential hostels on the campus, and these, not having been nationalised, are run by the parent body. This is the

side of the work where Christian staff members can make a
valuable contribution. Cathy Hine, an Australian and one
of three Interserve Partners involved in running the hostels,
was also assisting Mrs Phailbus with administration. She
told me,

> Mrs Phailbus is one of the outstanding women of
> Pakistan. She brought the college through nationalisation
> and martial law, and it is largely due to her that it has
> remained true to its principles and aims. She is a person
> of courage and vision, and she carries her vision through
> and conveys it to her staff. As a result the morale here
> is very high, and the staff maintain high standards and
> are dedicated to their work. Like Miss Zaman, she is
> convinced that only the power of prayer has enabled her
> to survive where she is.

Cathy herself first came out to Kinnaird College on October
2nd 1987. Four days later Mrs Phailbus was removed from
her post and told not to return. That same day, October
6th 1987, BMMF's prayer calendar focused on Lahore, and
Mrs Phailbus was allowed back after twenty-four hours. That
same day too, God gave Cathy a clear promise:

> When the Lord restored the fortunes of Zion,
> we were like those who dream . . .
> then they said among the nations,
> 'The Lord has done great things for them.'
> The Lord has done great things for us;
> we are glad (Psalm 126: 1–3, RSV).

These events came to Cathy as a clear call to commit
herself to the college, and in particular to the hostels. She
believes that in calling and keeping Mrs Phailbus, God has
kept the college as a pivotal place, with a unique opportunity
for work among women who would go on to have leading
roles in Pakistani society; a place for reaching out not only

to girls but through them to their families. For some years BMMF/Interserve had had people working short term at the hostels, but in 1989, partly as result of this vision, Interserve determined to contribute to a team of four people committed to longer-term work. Sue Aberdeen and Lyndal Dennis whom I met, recently arrived, were part of this team.

A growing work, also in Lahore, is the Christian Publishing House – Masihi Isha'at Khana or MIK. This was founded in 1946 by Dennis Clark, of the Brethren and later of BMMF (Canada). He described its beginning: 'A property was found and a few of us kneeled in faith to claim it for the Lord's work. The bathroom became a dark room, kitchens became the bindery and the garage a cutting room. Lacking the three kilowatt power for the arc lamps, we carried the vacuum frame with the plates and negatives out into the tropical sun for exposure.' The technology described here may be archaic, but the spirit of determination and improvisation has not changed. The work of MIK continues, under Brethren auspices, with the same aim of providing Christian literature in Urdu – books for all sorts and conditions of people: some for the newly literate, some for the women who still in many parts lead a sheltered and secluded life, some for Bible students who welcome various publications, including the first ever Bible dictionary in Urdu. A big step forward in distribution came in 1975 when MIK began adapting Suzuki pick-up vans as mobile bookshops which can drive into any bazaar, find a suitable spot and set up shop.

Closely linked with MIK, who print much of its material, is the Pakistan Bible Correspondence School (PBCS). This was established in 1957 as a joint form of outreach by several mission groups in Pakistan. For some years it was directed by James Mall, an enterprising and gifted Pakistani Christian from Sialkot. An Interserve Partner from Canada, Margaret Elias, was secretary to the Principal of the PBCS Faisalabad Centre. The correspondence courses aim to present the teaching of the Bible in such a way that no-one doing a course feels threatened if they belong to another faith. Follow-up is done through rallies, camps, nurture groups and through the PBCS Correspondence Club's Bulletin which is sent as a way of keeping in touch with interested students. PBCS also launched a Christian magazine called *Rahbar* ('guide' or 'way'), with Ruth Nicholls of Interserve (Australia) involved in its production.

The PBCS courses proved popular. Since the early 1980s student numbers stabilised at around 10,000 active students per month throughout the country, with less than half of them coming from the Christian community. Based in five regional centres, material is sent out in Urdu, Sindhi and English. Letters received show how valued the courses are: for example, 'I am very anxious to know the truth. My need and desire is not just to get certificates but to have real peace of heart. Who was Christ? Where did he come from? Why did he come, and where has he gone?' Yet another venture in the realm of communications is the Pakistan Christian Recording Ministries (PCRM), based in Faisalabad, where Ralph and Dagmar Baron of Interserve (UK) were seconded. Thousands of tapes are sent out to those who ask for them.

The Open Theological Seminary, Lahore, was under the directorship of Zafar Ismail, a member of the International Council and the International Executive Committee of Interserve. He had earlier been converted from Marxism by observing Christian love in action. He cared passionately that the Church in Pakistan – a small percentage of the population but numbering some three million people – should find its own identity and allow the Holy Spirit to reach out through its own people. Tim Green of Interserve worked here on Theological Education by Extension with an all-Pakistani team. I met Tim and Rachel and their small children in Lahore. Since they arrived in 1988, Tim had been helping to prepare self-study material and also training the Open Theological Seminary team, hoping gradually to work himself out of a job. Zafar, who selected him, appreciated Tim as 'unique; he demonstrates through his lifestyle that he is just like us. He is not like someone from an affluent culture.' Many Christians in Pakistan know very little about their faith, and so the TEE courses aim to meet the need for basic Christian education as well as providing training for lay leaders and pastors. Some 900 Christians all over Pakistan were doing these courses, backed up by sixty tutorial centres. Rachel Green, as well as looking after her lively children and making friends with neighbours and other young families, was doing part-time work with the Pakistan Fellowship of Evangelical Students under its Pakistani General Secretary, Irfan Jamil. Involved too in PFES was another Interserver, Carol Walker, who also worked for PBCS, particularly in follow-up work with women.

As Tim pointed out in 1990, 'In Pakistan Interserve runs no project of its own. Its Partners are seconded to work in different Pakistani organisations, usually under national leadership. In Lahore at the moment we have a medical couple and a sociologist working in community development, an artist in Christian publishing, a teacher in Scripture Union, and a hostel warden in a government

From one of Tim and Rachel Green's prayer letters.

college.' I met some of these people: the artist was Lois Rusbatch, who was doing layout, pasting up, editing and cover designs for the various publications of MIK. The sociologist working in community development was Wayne McClintock from New Zealand. He and his wife Avril, from Guernsey, were both called initially to work with the Church Missionary Society in Tanzania. While there, Wayne realised how little he and his colleagues understood about the world-view, customs and social organisation of the local tribal people, and concluded that this was the major reason why their rural development programme and evangelistic outreach was having so little impact on their way of life. So in 1980 he studied for a master's degree in sociology in New Zealand, and then, planning to return to East Africa, found that God had other plans.

Wayne and Avril went to Pakistan to meet a need for an anthropologist/sociologist to conduct field research among nomadic tribal people in the Punjab. They flew to Lahore as Partners with BMMF in 1984, seconded to the Association for Community Training Services (ACTS), which had been founded by a Presbyterian missionary. Its Board had decided to seek a study of the Mirasis, one of the twelve nomadic tribes of the Punjab, in order to understand and so help them better. The aims of Wayne's research were firstly to help ACTS do more to meet the felt needs of the Mirasis in a culturally sensitive way, and secondly to promote a greater understanding of the tribal peoples among the Punjabi Christian community by passing on the results of his researches to local churches, thus helping them in their evangelism and church-planting.

As a result of his research, Wayne produced an ethnography of the Mirasi people: 'A caste of genealogists, musicians, singers, dancers and comedians, who have a long tradition of entertaining guests at weddings and other celebrations in the Punjab. Quick-witted extroverts, who often have their audiences in convulsions of laughter or entranced by their music, they excel in extracting rupees from their hosts and guests alike.' He found that although most Mirasis continued as entertainers, some of them were taking up other forms of employment. Most of these jobs, however, were unskilled and provided meagre incomes, as their access to skilled work was hindered by poor education. Their literacy rate he found extremely low, although an increasing number were sending their children to ACTS centres for basic literacy and numeracy skills. They lived in tent-like dwellings made out of old pieces of cloth sewn together and stretched over a bamboo frame, and valued highly the freedom of their semi-nomadic way of life. They practised a folk-version of Islam, believing in the power of evil spirits and in the need of help from Allah through various intermediaries to save them from their power.

While working among them, Wayne and Avril witnessed among the Mirasis in practical ways – taking sick people to hospital and generally extending the hand of love and friendship. They found too that the death of their little boy, Thomas Edward, born prematurely in Lahore in 1985, painful though it had been to them, brought them closer to the Mirasi families, nearly all of whom had lost at least one child. As so often, in God's hands their vulnerability became a point of contact and an avenue of witness. They did not preach to the Mirasis, but were always ready to share their faith when asked questions – about the meaning of Christmas and Easter, life after death or their motives for working among the poor of Pakistan. They felt it essential to accept the people as they were, and to impose no conditions on their relationship. The headman several times told Avril, 'Wayne really loves us', and it was this unconditional love of God that they sought to convey. They left Lahore in 1991, and Wayne commented:

Missionaries need to invest a lot more time in seeking to understand the world-view and everyday life of the people among whom they minister before they can effectively communicate the Gospel. In Pakistan this means that a lot more attention must be focused on folk religion than has previously been the case . . . it appears to be the key to understanding how the people might be liberated from various kinds of oppression.

Supporting and supported by the various Christians working in Lahore is St Andrew's, 'the railway church', with which BMMF/Interserve has had links over many years. It was originally founded for railway workers who were mainly Anglo-Indians and then Anglo-Pakistanis. BMMF members have pastored the church, other missionaries have been members, girls from Kinnaird High School have attended services, and with Urdu-speaking as well as English-speaking congregations, the church has grown and reached out to railway workers, to prisoners in the nearby gaol and to many others. The church experienced a special movement of God's Spirit in the early 1970s and many young Pakistanis who were there then have gone on to become Christian leaders, among them Johnson Charles, now General Secretary of Scripture Union in Pakistan. Working under him was Anne de Reybekill, of Interserve, who concentrated on training SU's Pakistani field-workers, who then in turn trained others who work with children: camp leaders, Sunday school-teachers etc. Anne saw her role in SU as part of the emerging picture in Interserve of expatriates working under Pakistani leadership, as Tim Green and others were also doing: serving in a training or administrative role, helping in such a way as to encourage, not stifle the national leadership.

Particularly encouraging at the end of the 1970s was a work of God's Spirit in Sindh, in the south of Pakistan. As the Rev Bashir Jiwan, the Bishop's special Commissary for Evangelistic Outreach in Sindh and later himself Bishop of Hyderabad, wrote in 1976, 'It is increasingly clear to many that the wind of the Spirit is blowing among the tribal people of Hindu background. Several hundred a year have been baptised in recent years. As the medical, social and evangelistic work grows, tribal people are beginning to realise that there is a God in heaven who cares for them.'

The spiritual renewal was in part the result of a visit of

a man of God called Autar Singh, a convert from Sikhism who spent many months in Sindh at the invitation of the bishops of the Church of Pakistan and who encouraged the pastors and other Christians in the use of spiritual gifts. As a result the church was revitalised and grew. With Commonwealth missionaries at that time free to enter Pakistan without a visa, the Church of Pakistan called for twenty missionaries to come and work in Sindh in co-operation and partnership with local leaders, to teach and strengthen the new Christians in their faith.

Some BMMF workers were there already, working since 1975 on the Rural Health Care Project based at Kunri where the Caravan Hospital had come to rest, and seeking to serve the whole community in the desert town and its surrounding villages. And in response to the Bishop's call, several other BMMFers went to Sindh to work in the Church of Pakistan's Hyderabad Diocese. Amongst these in 1988 were John and Lilli Parsons from Australia who worked at the Diocesan Administrative Centre, John as consultant to Bishop Jiwan in the diocesan medical programmes and Lilli on the secretarial side. They also worked part time, together with other Interserve Partners, among tribal Hindus living in the Sanghar and Tharparkar districts of Sindh. Philip and Florence James moved from Kunri to tribal work at Khipro, and two more Interservers, the Rev Chris and Joanna Cant from UK, went to do similar work, developing a Christian centre and doing pastoral work amongst tribal people at Tando Mohammed Khan near Mirpur Khas.

Other medical projects in Pakistan besides Kunri to which BMMF workers contributed included the United Christian Hospital at Lahore, a Pakistani foundation formed after Partition, the only Christian hospital in Lahore and a training school for Christian nurses. The hospital was something of a show-piece for the new country of Pakistan, and it moved into a fine, well-equipped new building in 1965. Anne Cooper of BMMF worked there for many years as Nursing Superintendent, concentrating on the training of Pakistani village girls as nurses. Anne later became Director of the

Nursing Education Project, co-ordinating and improving training in the six Christian hospitals in Pakistan. She was also deeply involved in the Nurses' Christian Fellowship of Pakistan, running camps and seeking in other ways to help the young Christian nurses to Christian maturity.

Some 200 miles south west of Lahore is Multan, an ancient Islamic centre rich in beautifully decorated mosques and tombs. Here, in a broad street in the relatively affluent cantonment area, can be seen a surprising sign: 'Women's Christian Hospital' – surprising because neither women nor Christians usually have a very high profile. This hospital, for women and children, had been founded by the Church Missionary Society in 1899 and was taken over and run by the American WUMS/UFCS in 1957. It became an important area of BMMF work when the two societies merged, and, now an independent Christian hospital, provides a much-valued medical service for women, particularly for those in whose families purdah is still strictly kept.

A part-time doctor at the hospital, Dutch Interserver Agaath Bijl, told me a little of the history of a city that has always been a great religious centre, repeatedly conquered by different empires and faiths. A Chinese traveller, for example, visiting Multan in AD 641, found that Buddhism had been replaced by Hinduism, and that 'in the temple dedicated to the sun was the idol or image of the Sun-Deva – cast in yellow gold and ornamented with precious gems.' Long before this the Indus valley was part of the great empire of the Medes and Persians, and Alexander the Great had conquered, and been mortally wounded, here in 326 BC. Not long after the Chinese traveller's visit, in AD 712, Multan was conquered by the Arab Mohammed Qasim, and from then onwards Multan was the main outpost of Islam in India, the rest of the country being predominantly Hindu. In 1528 it came under the rule of Babur and successive Mogul emperors – a period of peace in which the system of canal irrigation was begun and large tracts of previously unusable land brought under cultivation, a process continued by the British. The Sikh Ranjit Singh

Multan

stormed Multan fort in 1818, and in 1848 the assassination of Patrick Vans-Agnew and Lieutenant William Anderson led to war with the British and the annexation of the Punjab to the British Empire in January 1849.

British rule lasted for almost a century, and during this time Christian work – that of the Presbyterians and others in the Punjab – led to large numbers of Hindu tribal people becoming Christians. As the Gazetteer of the Multan District 1923–4 recorded, 'The chief agency of the superintendence of the native Christian community was, for many years, the Church Missionary Society, which, beginning its work in 1855, founded educational and medical institutions of much value to all communities.' The Gazetteer commended too 'the women's hospital in cantonments and the congregation attached thereto . . . a monument to the devoted labours of the band of lady doctors and workers attached to it. The hospital is freely resorted to by women of all religions, and it is justly and widely known for its excellent work.'*

I spent two days staying in the pleasant shady compound of the seventy-five-bed hospital recently completely refurbished under Norman Norris's supervision, talking to various Interserve Partners who were seconded to work there. Mirjam Lukasse from Belgium (seconded through the Dutch Council) showed me the busy outpatients' clinics run by herself and two Pakistani nursing sisters. They had recently been joined by Jeanette Gan, a midwife originally from Malaysia but with Australian nationality, who after asking the Lord how he wanted her to serve him, was given a vision of a veiled woman, which led her, through Interserve, to Multan.

Other people I met included Dr Heather Carmichael of Interserve (Australia) who set up the Community Development Programme which reaches out into surrounding villages, and Aster Lal Din who worked with Heather

* *Gazetteer of the Multan District 1923–24* (compiled and published under the authority of the Punjab Government, Lahore, 1926).

and was now the Director of the Programme. Heather, although still Consultant for this programme, was now seconded to the Christian Hospital Association of Pakistan (CHAP) as Co-ordinator for Health Training in primary health care. This involves running workshops and visiting projects throughout the country. Agaath's husband, Leen Bijl, was also seconded to CHAP, with responsibility for the maintenance of hospital equipment in CHAP hospitals.

Another Interserve Partner who came to Multan in 1977, soon after BMMF became involved, was Dr Fiona Burslem, from the UK. When I asked her if she could give me a little time, she said the best would be if I sat in on a caesarian operation she would be doing that afternoon. So at 2.30, duly capped and gowned, there I was in the operating theatre, watching Fiona, barefoot, bright blue eyes twinkling, sew up a young woman who had just been delivered of a baby girl. With her Scottish colleague, Dr Marian Morrison, Fiona was the surgeon at WCH. Agaath helped too, relieving at weekends. The hospital still relies very much on expatriate doctors: it is hard to find Christian Pakistani lady doctors, as Christians tend to be discriminated against when it comes to training. WCH itself gives government-recognised midwifery training to girls from the Christian community, and is also recognised for post-graduate training in obstetrics and gynaecology. The operation over (the next patient had already walked in and climbed up on to the operating table), Fiona took me into a ward where a ward service was in progress. These are run by the Religious Services Department of the hospital, which also organises ward visiting and witness to outpatients. As I came in, the music group was just finishing singing and playing, and an elderly Pakistani lady, 'Auntie Ferozah' who has worked in the hospital for thirty-four years began to speak from the Bible, the patients all listening intently and nodding agreement.

The third Interserve Partner I met, who came to WCH at roughly the same time as Heather and Fiona, was Barbara Dyatt. She came first as a nursing sister in the hospital, but then moved into community development, becoming particularly involved in the development and testing of teaching aids and in an unusual 'child to child' health programme in which school children were used to conduct surveys and were also taught the rudiments of spotting ill health and looking after younger children. Often they learnt better than their mothers, and would relay vital health information to them. Eventually Barbara left community health work. She was ready for a change and was also keen for the village people to relate more to the Pakistani members of the team. She became the Interserve Regional Representative for Pakistan: a big job which involved pastoral responsibility for Interserve Partners throughout the country as well as liaising with the many projects and churches to which Interservers were seconded – making the necessary practical arrangements, drawing up secondment agreements and so on. In 1990 the Region was split into two, and Barbara became Regional Representative for Pakistan North. Jean Mullinger, Principal of the United Bible Training Centre, Gujranwala, was invited to become Regional Representative for Pakistan South based in Karachi. As she says, 'My job was to help the division process.' Quick, kindly and decisive, wearing her brightly coloured shalwar kamees with flair, Jean clearly enjoyed the task. (All expatriate women are advised to wear the tapered-in trousers, dress and scarf (doputa) in Pakistan, and to cover their heads with the chadar when out, as otherwise they are taken for loose women and may be treated accordingly.) Jean retired in May 1992, handing over to Sam and Janet Reeve from Australia. The Regional Reps. are the only two Interserve Partners in Pakistan who actually work for Interserve. All others are seconded to other projects.

Another couple also supporting their Interserve colleagues in essential practical ways were John and Jennifer Bowyer, who had run the staff house in Karachi since 1989. They felt it was important to maintain a good standard of comfort at the large, well-appointed house, so that people taking a much-needed break from pioneering work in tough

Street scene, Multan

places could enjoy rare luxuries like hot water. They would sometimes whisk weary Interservers to the beach, and with a sympathetic listening ear or with practical help as needed, help them to unwind. John, who previously worked for the St Ives local council in the UK, was Interserve Treasurer and was also appointed by the Church of Pakistan as Administrator to Holy Trinity Cathedral Church. He and Jennifer rejoiced in the work of the Cathedral, where Interservers Helen Irwin and Denise Boocock were also on the pastoral team. Helen had previously lectured in nursing at Kinnaird College. There were Urdu and English services, a drug addiction centre, work among the mentally handicapped where David Hanson, another Interserver worked, and other areas of outreach and pastoral work under Arne Rudvin, the Bishop of Karachi.

David described his work:

In the early '80s the wife of a local padre started a school for children with a mental handicap in her front room. Now, ten years later, there is a purpose-built school, Dar-ul-Khushnud, for one hundred children. The Principal, Miss B.K.Dass, administers the school as well as serving as Deaconess in the Diocese. I help with the programme of in-service staff training, encouraging the teachers to use play-based methods of learning. I also run a small project in a slum area of the city. Many disabled children living in these areas are not able to attend school or receive any help because these services are expensive. Our aim is to run a low-cost service which works alongside families and seeks to motivate the community to make its own resources available, perhaps enabling such children to go to school or to have access to special medication or equipment they may need.

One unusual project is DOOR Trust. Churches in Pakistan are often old garrison churches, too large for present day congregations. The same churches often own large blocks of land on which they are built, but they do not have the resources and skill necessary to develop these unused assets. Interserve assisted in launching DOOR Trust (Development of Overseas Resources). This has a revolving loan fund which raises capital from abroad for development on unused church land, which eventually produces income for the Church.

By 1990 Pakistan had become the second largest area of Interserve's work, with about one quarter of all Partners located there. In 1992 an advisory committee of Pakistani Christians was formed by Interserve, with the objective of promoting missionary interest in the churches, perhaps leading to the formation of a sending agency. Supporting many growing parachurch organisations as well as the churches in Pakistan in the various aspects of their work, Interserve's aim continues to be the making of disciples and the training of Christian leaders in a country where the spiritual warfare is very real and the Church far from strong.

11

Progress and freedom in Nepal

In Nepal, too, the work of UMN advanced excitingly if at times painfully, and BMMF, with by far the largest number of contributing missionaries, was in the vanguard of it all. Whereas visas for India were becoming steadily harder for expatriates to obtain, and from 1984 almost impossible; whereas for Pakistan it was still possible to obtain missionary visas for those whose work was clearly within the small Christian minority in the country; for Nepal visas continued to be readily available for all UMN workers on the understanding that they went out to do a job related to their professional expertise in some area of development, and not as church workers or evangelists.

In 1982 Shanta Bhawan Hospital, Kathmandu, where BMMF obstetrician Dr Mary Eldridge had been Medical Director since 1975, combined with the government hospital and moved from the former palace to a 140-bed purpose-built hospital on the edge of Patan. Known as 'the city of a thousand golden roofs', Patan is the twin city of Kathmandu, separated from it by the Bagmati River. The new hospital, carefully designed and built, was easier for people to get to and took many more patients. Much of the initiative in planning it had been taken by Paul Spivey of BMMF when he was Associate Health Services Secretary of UMN. His work was recognised in the Queen's honours list with an MBE. The new Medical Director, John Dickinson, was also seconded to UMN from BMMF. But the change was more than a change of premises: from now on, although

UMN still contributed finances and staff, the hospital came under the control of a Board which included members of the local community and Government as well as UMN. More than ever, Christians on the staff had to witness for Christ by the quality of their lives, their caring and their work.

Visiting the hospital in 1992 I was impressed: well equipped and run under a Nepali Administrator, B.B. Khawas, and the Medical Director, Dr Frank Garlick of Interserve (Australia), it is comparable to a hospital in the West, apart from the much greater involvement of relatives at the bedside, who wash, feed and generally tend the patients. Several Interserve Partners were on the staff: Dr Paul Johnson, in charge of outpatients, his wife Anna, the physiotherapist, Dr Val Garlick in the TB clinic, Stephen Cox the dentist and oral surgeon, Brigitte Alda seconded to Interserve from Germany as anaesthetist and Val Reid from Australia in the ultra-sound department. The work of the hospital is increasing all the time. A considerable part of the cost of treatment is borne by the patients, although the poorest are treated free of charge. But subsidies from donor agencies are decreasing, as they prefer to put money into preventative medicine and community health programmes.

I met Jo McKim of Interserve, a pharmacist from London. She told me how God had called her to work for him abroad, and how although at first reluctant to leave London, she had eventually gone to India, to Ludhiana. Here after less than two years her visa extension was refused and she was given two weeks' notice to leave the country. This was a painful and bewildering experience at the time, but now she was sure that Nepal was where God wanted her to be, and grateful for the experience she gained from her short time in India. There are difficulties: for example, in obtaining good quality drugs. Jo showed me with pride the hospital's new pill-counting machine for which money was raised back in England: 'I should be training the staff here as much as possible. Now I can, as they aren't spending all their time counting pills!'

Dr Charles Nankivell, a surgeon with Interserve (Australia), underlined some of the tensions of work in the hospital: 'The difficulty is for Christian people to say no. It's easy to become a door-mat and to consider it a virtue. When am I following Christ in going the extra mile, and when am I simply being made use of? Am I helping my Hindu colleague by doing his work, or would I help him more by saying "no", and forcing him to become more responsible?' These questions are more than academic for Charles. His superior is a Hindu, and in his culture, 'If you're at the top you do less work. This is proof of your success.' So Charles was doing six ward rounds a week and looking after fifty-five patients, and as a result he couldn't give his patients the attention he would like. And he was exhausted. 'I'm the door-mat, and the head of department gets the credit.'

The situation was graphically illustrated the day before I met Charles: it was his day off, but he came in to do an extra ward round. Frank Garlick – now sixty-two and officially retired from surgery, but on call as he so often was – needed to operate on a man with a bleeding ulcer. There was no blood for a transfusion, so Frank gave three pints of his own blood. As a result he was too faint to operate and Charles stepped in to do it. The man's life was saved while, as Charles somewhat cynically surmised, the third member of the team sat at home watching satellite TV. Charles suggested that this unsatisfactory situation had arisen from UMN's policy of Nepalisation – an excellent policy so long as it refers to Christian Nepalis. At the moment the best-qualified Nepali doctors came from wealthy high-caste Hindu families, as they had had the best education. But now that Christians are recognised in the country, would it not be better to wait till they were qualified, and then give them the headship of departments?

This is one Interserve Partner's view, but although Interserve provides twenty-five per cent of the total staff of UMN, it only has one Board member out of thirty-nine (i.e. each contributing mission has one Board member). Interserve, servant-like, keeps a low profile. 'Yes, salt dissolves, but beyond a certain point of dilution it ceases to taste', said Charles. 'Maybe we are overdoing being inconspicuous and should speak out.' He missed mutual support from other Interservers too, as they try (perhaps too hard?) not to be exclusive within UMN. Going the extra mile is exhausting, but Charles ended on a positive note. Opening a Bible at Proverbs 3:27–8 (NIV): 'Do not withhold good when it is in the power of your hand to do it', he pointed out that this is literally true for a surgeon. We must use our professionalism to serve others. And so Charles kept going, taking up the cross and following his Lord. An encouragement in the hospital is that since democracy, it has been possible to have Christian literature on display. I took a photograph of P.B.Rai, the Nepali head of outpatients, standing in front of this display. A faithful and long-standing member of the staff, the hospital relies on people like him.

Closely linked with Patan Hospital is the Lalitpur Community Health Project based at an ancient Newari village called Chapagaon not far away. Dr Graham Toohill, a humorous and determined Australian Interserve Partner in a supervisory role there showed me round. As he explained, health care and development go hand in hand. UMN is concerned for various aspects of development: drinking water supply, forestry, agriculture, income generation, non-formal adult education. At the health post itself there are weekly clinics for mother and child health, GP clinics, hygiene, dental care and nutrition teaching. This last is based in a 'nutrition centre' built to reproduce a typical Nepali house but with important improvements like a new-style stove with a chimney outlet for the smoke. There is even a model of a very simple toilet, with the aim of teaching the people to build them for themselves. If these were introduced and used, the reduction in illness would be enormous. So prevention and curative medicine are interlinked. Leprosy has been almost eradicated from this district, because of effective liaison between the health post and the hospital. As well as the clinics held at the health centre, midwives and health workers trained here go out

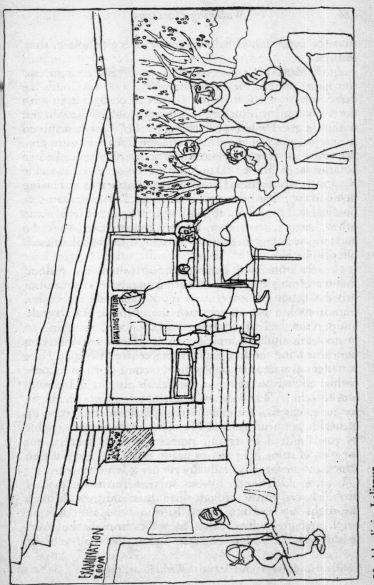

Health clinic, Lalipur

into the community, helping and teaching people in their homes.

At Tansen, 170 miles to the west of Kathmandu, the 'Hospital on the Hill' grew rapidly, and also built up public health services in the district in co-operation with the Government. Nursing sisters lived out in the villages, tramping over the hills and visiting the 20,000 or so scattered people with preventative medicine and TB eradication programmes, sharing the love of Christ. As Michael Cole comments, 'A brave girl from the West is prepared to tackle situations which would make a strong man wince. Having saved many lives she will return to Tansen exhausted, possibly suffering from amoebic dysentry, hepatitis or some other "nasty", then after a short recuperation, she'll be back to the life-saving task of love.'* In the hospital itself, Dr Bill Gould, a BMMF orthopaedic surgeon (who later took over from Pam Dodson as Superintendent) realised that many simple fractures turned gangrenous as a result of the application of home-made tourniquets and the several days it took a patient to reach the hospital. As a result, limbs often had to be amputated. As well as trying to prevent this situation arising, he developed a rehabilitation unit, including the first limb-fitting centre in Nepal. Here amputees as well as leprosy patients were helped to become mobile enough to return to normal life. It was Bill Gould, too, who in 1975 had the bold idea of using a hovercraft on the turbulent Kali Gandaki river to facilitate the setting up of health posts in parts of Nepal which were inaccessible by road. A trial hovercraft expedition was a success, but the plan of using it to service health posts was not put into effect, and new roads gradually render it less necessary.

Leaving Kathmandu by bus to visit Tansen in 1992, I travelled westwards through the sunset and then through the night, up and up, round hairpin bend after hairpin bend, arriving before dawn to walk through the town to the hospital under the stars. Below the road and the

---

* Michael Cole, *Journey to the Fourth World* (Lion, 1981).

hospital, daylight revealed the immense space of a deep terraced valley, while behind and to the north, the distant Himalayan peaks can be seen on clear days. I was shown round the busy hospital, with its new wing almost complete and its crowds of outpatients milling at the gate. Here, as at Patan, I met several Interserve Partners on the staff: John Watson, specialist physician, and his fiancée, Val Tuffin, nursing tutor; Malcolm Brook, surgeon – all from the UK; Mies Kooiman, also a surgeon, from Holland; Bruce Pipher, from Canada, GP and anaesthetist; and Valerie McKay, from New Zealand, pharmacist.

They told me a little of the joys and frustrations of their work: John, for instance, while rejoicing in the patients they could cure, was frustrated when treatment which he knew a patient needed was not available – such as dialysis; or when the equipment was too limited to make more difficult diagnoses; Val was saddened when she saw a poor woman with obstructed labour having to pay 2000–3000 rupees for a caesarian operation, the family taking out a loan at high interest or selling land or a buffalo to raise the money. Although fees are kept as low as possible and some patients are eligible for charity, costs at the hospital are increasing as more technology becomes available. Also the number of caesarians needed is increasing as small mothers, now better nourished, are producing larger babies. Another problem is persuading the patient's relatives to give blood for transfusion. They are usually reluctant, believing that the soul is in the blood, and that should the patient die, part of them will die too. 'We always try to find the reason for their fear, and encourage them,' Val said.

Malcolm Brook found his work as surgeon rewarding, though it was frightening at first, as he had to do operations he had never attempted before. Before an operation he would ask the patient if he could pray with him: 'They tend to regard us as gods, and I want them to see that God himself is in charge. The number of patients coming for surgery is increasing all the time. We are working flat out.' Indeed, as supper ended on the evening of our visit the phone rang, and Malcolm went out into the brilliant moonlight back to the hospital to do yet another operation. As well as his medical work, Malcolm and his wife Siobhan were active members of the local church. For some time the church was divided into two factions. Now reconciled, but in two congregations, the two churches were working well together, with the leadership – pastors and elders – all Nepali.

Mies, the Dutch surgeon, lived in a lovely wood-panelled house behind the hospital, one of the two originally built by Dr Friedricks. As well as her medical work, she was concerned about the poor status of women in Nepal, and keen to promote income-generating projects – sewing and embroidery – for them. She also used her creative gifts in organising the costumes for an unusual venture launched by Jim Dunn, a doctor and dentist with Interserve (Scotland), when at Christmas 1990 the Sunday school children of the two Tansen churches performed a nativity play in Tansen's Town Hall, and 700 people packed in to watch – something only possible since democracy.

Jim's description of a visit to a village across the valley from Tansen gives a vivid picture of what dentistry can do:

> I set out with a group of five Nepali Christian friends, one Finnish dentist and a visiting dental student from Glasgow to visit a village where the family of a Christian friend lives. I had been there recently and some of the village people had asked for Christians to come and explain to them about the Great God. On that visit I had met two people with toothache. Thus started the idea for a combined evangelism and dental camp. Everyone was invited to come in the evening either to have their painful teeth seen or to hear the Good News or both. About six thirty people began to arrive. Darkness fell but extractions continued by torchlight, the grass becoming littered with rotten teeth. Then oil lamps were brought and the programme of songs, puppets and drama began. The crowd grew to about eighty villagers, many of them

hearing about Jesus for the first time. With me were my very good friends Birkha and his wife Dhona who have a wonderful way of explaining the Gospel to their neighbours. The people quite forgot about their supper and were still asking for more stories and singing at ten o'clock. The result: a monthly fellowship group started in the village, led by visitors from the Tansen church.

The missionaries at Tansen also have an unusual link with a rapidly growing church at Nawalparasi in the flat terai in the south of Nepal. Once the pastor there, visiting Tansen with a sick family, invited a missionary to visit his people and teach the Bible. This she did, and from then onwards she would offer hospitality to the very poor people of the community in her home, when they had to stay in Tansen for visiting the hospital. This tradition has been kept by UMN team members living in that particular mission house – when I visited, Elly from Denmark and Val from New Zealand. The links continue too in other ways, as when Elly, Val and Mies visited Nawalparasi and enjoyed fellowship with the Christians there.

The pastor himself was converted as a young man through the witness of the Shining Hospital at Pokhara. As a result of his witness and the forced dispersion of Christians caused by a government tree-planting scheme, there are now about 3,500 Christians in the Nawalparasi area. Travelling between the small churches and house groups, the pastor is concerned for practical things: for the provision of good drinking water, for the women's sewing programme, for teaching about family planning, as well as for meeting the people's spiritual needs. And as Mies remembered, 'A few weeks before our visit, there was a patient at Tansen Hospital with inoperable cancer. When one of my colleagues told him the prognosis, the man took his hand and said comfortingly, "Doctor, do not worry about me. The pastor at Nawalparasi has told me everything about Jesus and I am ready to die."'

UMN's Palpa district Community Health Project, based

Outside Tansen hospital

in Tansen, was started in 1960 by Sister Ingebor, a Norwegian midwife. She set up a clinic for mothers and children in the town, and this was continuing, under the Nepali Director, Bhagat Bista. As he explained, the project had increased its scope and now encompassed four main areas of work, all of which relate ultimately to health: clinics for mothers and children, water supply, agriculture and non-formal education. Ten government health posts in Palpa district were being staffed as well as the one in Tansen itself, and work of all the four kinds mentioned above was pursued in seven other places in the district as well. Asked how the Christian emphasis of UMN's Palpa Project shows itself, Bhagat Bista replied, 'The Christian faith says that help should be given to the needy. I'm not a Christian, but I like this idea. I have learnt from UMN how to have respect and care for all.'

Two other places I visited in Tansen were the Tansen Tutorial Group, a small English language primary school, a life-line to the families of the little flaxen-haired Norwegian, British, Swiss and other expatriate children who attend; and HASP (the Horticulture and Agronomy Support Programme). The latter consists of a small burgeoning area of land on the hill behind the hospital where techniques for growing vegetables, bamboo and other trees and of disease and pest management are developed which are appropriate, organic and sustainable. A group of trained Nepalis then go out to the various rural areas passing on these techniques with the aim of getting the most out of the soil and at the same time improving its quality and that of the produce, and preventing soil erosion.

Another area of UMN involvement was Amp Pipal, a little to the north west of Gorkha and on the side of Liglig mountain. It is so inaccessible that, as Mies Kooiman, who worked there for a while before going to Tansen described, in order to reach Kathmandu she had, in the rainy season, to struggle four or five hours on steep, slippery narrow paths between sodden rice fields to reach the suspension bridge, 'high above a wild big river', and it was still several more hours to the nearest road. Yet this sort of journey was frequently undertaken by patients, or by their relatives carrying them long distances into the hospital in hammocks. Work here went back to 1956, when an American, Jonathan Lindell, who had been a missionary on the border of Nepal in the 1940s, set up, together with two Christian Nepali couples from Darjeeling, a 'Community Service Programme' or 'mountain project' with the agreement of the Government. The story of how they came to Amp Pipal is beautifully told in his book *Nepal and the Gospel of God* (UMN, 1979). In it he describes how a few days after their arrival, 'a dozen boys sat under a tree near the tent and the school began; and the next day a mother brought her burnt baby and medical work had its humble beginnings. From the first days team members held their simple worship meetings with Bible and songbook and curious villagers observing.'

Dr Helen Huston from Canada came out to Amp Pipal to help set up the small hospital, which eventually opened in 1969 and now has just over fifty beds. Here too in July 1970 came Dr Tom Hale and his wife Cynthia, BMMF members from America. Tom had worked as an army surgeon; Cynthia had been heading for a career as a concert pianist, but gave up that ambition when she became convinced that God was calling her to be a medical missionary. Tom has described their experiences at Amp Pipal – hilarious, frustrating, sometimes sad, in two delightful books.* The 'mountain project' involved a small team moving out into the villages and helping the people in various ways. Val Collett moved here from Bhaktapur, first running a small dispensary; then as a nurse at the hospital, 'teaching Tom Hale Nepali medicine', as he put it; then setting up a community health programme, walking one or two days to a place where a mobile clinic would be held. Val later worked for twelve years at Tansen, where she established

---

* Thomas Hale, *Don't Let the Goats Eat the Loquat Trees* (Zondervan, 1986; Marc/Monarch with Interserve, 1987) and *On the Far Side of Liglig Mountain* (Marshall Pickering, 1989).

ANM (Assistant Nurse Midwife Training), going round the villages on her newly acquired motor-bike as Director of the Community Health Programme. She then joined Mary Cundy at Paimey; and finally, instead of retiring, went on to obtain an M.Ed. in primary health care at Manchester, and to train nurses in community health care at the Institute of Medicine in Kathmandu.

Dr Tjerk Nap and his wife Corry, sponsored by BMMF (Holland), worked at Amp Pipal from 1982–84. While here, they adopted a little Nepali girl, Bimala. They became friendly with many needy Nepali families, and struggled to work out how best to help them: like the tailor's wife who made purses (not very well) from scraps of material and sold them to the missionaries. Soon the missionaries had more than enough purses. How best to go on helping this poor lady and her five children, as her husband is often not well enough to work? They also became friendly with a Nepali woman called Kamala, sadly oppressed in her family, whose life and that of her husband were transformed by coming to know Christ at Amp Pipal. Her life showed the destiny of many Nepali women, but not many show such a change. Tjerk and Corry went on to work for four years at Okhaldhunga, one of UMN's most isolated eastern outposts, due south of Mount Sagarmatha (Everest). Tjerk was Medical Director of the hospital, and they also became involved with the local church, concerned when local Christian leaders were imprisoned, impressed by those who remain faithful to their Lord. Dr Cleve Chevassut, with his wife Alison, and Dr Gary Parkes and his wife Debbie, all of Interserve (UK), as well as Dr John Padgett and his wife Sally from Australia worked too at Amp Pipal.

Other areas of Nepal where Interserve Partners are involved are INF's work based at Pokhara, including leprosy and TB control and rehabilitation; a development programme at Surkhet in the west of Nepal, and some interesting income generation projects which Robert and Denise Judge were involved in. They worked for six years in a very remote Gurung village called Thalajung, halfway up a mountain, getting a women's craft co-operative going, trying to help the poorest of the poor in addition to their teaching and medical work. They felt strongly that people must define their own problems and find their own solutions. The role of the missionary is simply to serve by helping them to get started. Robert and Denise eventually worked themselves out of a job; the projects they started in Thalajung continued under local leadership, and the church there saw considerable growth.

Quite different from anything else it attempted, UMN also gave a lead in technological development in Nepal – notably at the Technical Institute set up in 1963 at Butwal in the flat terai district bordering India, with the aim of providing apprenticeship training in mechanical, electrical and other skills. The Institute continues its work, with trainees, usually sponsored by the various industries also set up at Butwal, coming to learn the necessary mechanical skills. Here too under the leadership of Odd Hoftun, a Norwegian Lutheran, and with funding from 'Bread for the World' of Germany, a hydroelectric plant was constructed which made possible the introduction of electric light and power to the town. This and other projects were carried out by the Butwal Power Company, set up in 1966 as the development organisation for UMN's involvement in hydroelectric power. Hydroelectricity is clearly an ideal source of power in the mountainous terrain of Nepal, and the Government, aware of the rapid consumption of firewood, was needing to establish alternative sources of energy. The Butwal hydro-project was handed over to the Nepali Electricity Authority in 1978, but they did not maintain it and it ceased to operate. The Butwal Power Company may take it over again. Aart Stolk from Holland was supervising an electrical workshop with Nepal Hydro-electric at Butwal, while his wife Ineke found openings for friendship and Bible teaching with local lepers' families. And BPC has a consultancy division based in Kathmandu, where several Interserve Partners have been and are on the staff, among them Andrew Wilkins.

On Monday 28th September 1992 a PIA Airbus crashed into a mountain on its approach to Kathmandu airport, killing everyone on board. Among the passengers were Andrew and Helen Wilkins, Interserve Partners seconded to UMN, and their three children, Naomi, Hannah and Simeon. They were returning after a period of study in England for a second term of service in Nepal. Andy was a geological engineer, Helen a social worker. They first went out to Kathmandu in 1988, where Andy was a senior member of BPC's consultancy division. He was part of a team operating in conjunction with the Government of Nepal: designing, building, managing, and running a number of hydroelectric power stations so that the people in remote areas could have electricity. This meant much travelling, and as Andy moved around the country he went by public transport where possible, and would often take out his Nepali Bible and start reading it. Soon other passengers would become involved in an animated discussion of the Bible, helping him to understand some of the words! Sometimes he would walk for days to reach the more isolated projects. Helen was involved with the Nepal Women's Interest Group of UMN, teaching women to read and imparting other skills which would help raise their status, very low in Nepal. Both were concerned with a 'holistic' Gospel, which ministers to the whole person in his or her need. As Andy's tutor at All Nations Christian College said, 'They loved Nepal. They loved the people and they loved the work they were doing.' They were genuinely happy with the simple life they led in Nepal, and confident that their children's lives were greatly enriched by living there. Alas, not for long. The day after the crash their pictures were on the front of all the newspapers with their local vicar's comment: 'They were real Christians. They showed kindness and generosity in everything they did, and went out of their way to help people.' Their deaths were a great loss to many. Their achievements had been considerable. Also killed in the crash was Odd Hoftun's quadraplegic son Martin, an Oxford graduate who was studying for a PhD in Nepalese history.

At Baglung, near Pokhara, Ed and Annie Kramer, BMMFers from Holland, went to help set up another hydroelectric plant. As Ed described: 'Gone are the days when I just lifted a telephone or jumped into a car when I needed something urgently. Now the smallest thing involves an hour's walk and many conversations. I can't just show the Nepali labourers a drawing and expect them to do it, I need to explain to them how.' Similarly the Andhikhola hydroelectric project between Pokhara and Tansen, begun in 1981, brought clean drinking water, irrigation and other benefits to the villages in that area. Here a low ridge separates the Andhikhola river to the north and the Kali Gandaki to the south. The two rivers are only two kilometres apart, and there is a difference of 250 metres in the water levels: an ideal situation for the generation of hydroelectric power. The project involved two metres of tunnelling and a 250 metre vertical shaft five metres in diameter, all bored through solid rock. And at the Jhimruk River in Pyuthan District, Western Nepal, yet another major hydro-power scheme was launched, with UK Interservers Michael and Helen Francis on the team. Himal Hydro and General Construction Ltd, a company arising from the hydroelectric projects of the Butwal Technical Institute, specialises in tunnelling and has its headquarters in Kathmandu.

Also growing out of UMN's work at Butwal in 1970 was DCS (Development and Consulting Services). I met the Director, Mike Leane of Interserve (Australia). Trained as a mechanical engineer, he was impressed by Interserve's approach of sending people to developing countries to serve in their profession; and also by the calibre of people whom they sent. He applied, and arrived in Nepal in 1988. Already there when he and his wife Lyn arrived was Mike's university friend Tom Moncrieff, a civil engineer. Tom worked on material development, in particular with fibre-concrete roofing tiles, an adaptation of a Western type of tile incorporating coconut fibre. He also modified the process to use pedal power instead of electrical power.

The table with the mixture on it is made to vibrate by pedalling and this compacts the mixture. Tom had been training entrepreneurs to make these tiles, when on leave in Australia he was killed in a road accident. As his wife Elizabeth wrote, 'During his six years in Nepal, Tom was able to reach into people's lives by serving them in very practical ways within which the essential point was the ability to share with them the peace and joy of being in Christ.'

The aim of DCS is the development of appropriate technology. Once developed, a new idea is then promoted in the villages, installed and set in use. As well as the roofing tiles, other ideas being developed are small water-driven turbines for generating electricity and for turning small mills for husking rice, grinding flour, getting oil from mustard seed etc; the ram pump which pumps water to a high level using a greater volume of falling water as the energy source, a low wattage cooker which looks like two saucepans one inside the other; an apple crusher, and a fruit drier. Another unusual venture of DCS was biogas: gas for fuel made from cow dung. A key person in the development of biogas production was John Finlay, who went to Nepal from Northern Ireland with Interserve in 1973. John married Sheila Anderson, then teaching at Jaubari in Gorkha district, and they stayed on at Butwal for ten years before being posted to Jumla. In 1977 the Gobar (cow-dung) Gas Company was set up by UMN to promote the use of biogas plants throughout Nepal. This was highly successful, and UMN was eventually able to withdraw from active involvement. Mike Leane found great fulfilment in the work of DCS, commenting,

I don't see any dichotomy between service and proclamation, deeds and speech. In everything we do we aim to serve Christ. My work in a technical institution is an opportunity to witness to what motivates me. So too is my involvement in the local church, where opportunities for Westerners are increasing. The machines which we are

Vibrating tile-mix, Burwal

developing are mostly connected with the provision of the basic necessities of food and water. Similarly my work in the local church and in student Bible studies helps to meet spiritual needs.

In the cold, dry Jumla district in the north west of Nepal, UMN began work at the request of the Government in 1980 with the establishment of the Karnali Technical School (KTS). Adriaan Los, an engineer with BMZG (BMMF Holland), whose story has already partly been told, was appointed as site engineer for the buildings. It was not an easy task, as with no motorable roads within 100 miles of Jumla, all building materials apart from stone, wood, mud and sand had to be carried on men's backs for six days or else flown in by plane. The flights are for six months of the year; the other six months Jumla is deep in snow.

One day a local Hindu boy who had picked up a tract came to ask Adriaan if he knew about Jesus Christ. Addie gave him a Nepali Bible, which he at once began reading aloud in the village. Soon not only he but his whole village were professing faith. Sadly, this young man later came under attack. He was tortured and recanted, but with much prayer began eventually to come back. Several people have been baptised at Jumla, often following healings and deliverances. Some of the most primitive forms of Hinduism are practised in the area, and the resulting atmosphere can be spiritually very oppressive. The Loses stayed for nine years, with Adriaan eventually becoming Co-Principal with a Nepali colleague. Next, based in Kathmandu, he worked on curriculum and materials for KTS.

Another unusual area of work for Christians in Nepal is in forestry. Interserve Partner John Studley was surprised when God called him – then working for the Forestry Commission in Scotland – to work with UMN in Nepal. Seconded by Interserve to UMN in 1984, he became responsible for a community forestry programme based at KTS. The hope was to plant trees to replace those used for building, firewood etc. Progress was slow, but by liaising with local committees and also with local women as 'motivators', attitudes gradually changed, and as John put it after some years, 'Our measure of success in gaining co-operation and support has been possible through prayer, motivation, a commitment to understand the local people and a willingness to work with them.'

In education UMN has helped by establishing schools, all of which are now run by the Government, and by seconding teachers to other government schools. It is not easy work. In remoter places the pupils may have walked for up to two hours to get to school and they arrive at a ramshackle building raggedly dressed and sometimes soaked with rain. Equipment and teaching materials are often minimal. Other schools in Nepal, though, are very different. For example in Khatmandu UMN had established the Mahendra Bhawan Girls' School in 1957, providing the highest academic standards under the leadership of Miss Elizabeth Franklin of RBMU. Then early in the 1960s UMN was approached by a delegation of Nepalis about the possibility of opening a boys' boarding school in Pokhara. Working together with the International Nepal Fellowship, and with funding from the Dutch Government and churches, the school, known first as Pokhara Boys' Boarding School and then as Gandaki Boarding School (GBS), opened in June, 1966. Now, situated as it is below Machapuchhare (Fishtail Mountain) and the Annapurnas, it has a large campus of beautiful stone buildings, and having become a government school in 1971, continues, under its motto 'Knowledge, Character and Service', to educate some of Nepal's future leaders and professionals.

Many members of BMMF have worked here over the years, including Brian Wood from New Zealand who was Headmaster from 1977 until his premature death climbing Machapuchhare in 1980. He had previously taught music and PE at Hebron School in South India, where he was equally at home with a baton, conducting Handel's *Messiah*, or with a cricket bat. His humility was striking in view of his many talents, and he was much involved in Scripture Union rallies and various meetings for young people. In 1978 the staff also included Richard Clark and David McConkey, both teaching science and both subsequently to serve as UMN Education Secretaries. In 1983 the school won the King's award for results in the school leaving examinations. In 1985 it was designated by the Government as Nepal's first Regional School with the aim of providing students from all social and economic backgrounds with a high quality, all-round English-medium education to international standard. The headmaster selected to pioneer this important development was Dr David Bambach of Interserve (Australia). In 1986 the school opened its doors to girls, and in 1989 David was decorated in the King's Birthday Honours list, an award which he was conscious should be shared with many others who had made the school what it was. Sadly, the Bambachs had to leave in 1989 for health reasons. The new Principal John Barclay was another Interserve Partner from Australia.

In Gorkha district, the educational programme grew from the first small group of boys studying under the huge mango tree at Amp Pipal. Howard and Betty Barclay of Australia worked here from 1960, with Howard taking over from Jonathan Lindell as Director of the education programme. Gradually other schools were opened in the area: Luitel High School, where Geoff and Eunice Reid from BMMF (Australia) taught and which for many years led the nation in the highest average achievement in its school leaving certificate examinations, Jaubari where Sheila Anderson from Glasgow worked, and others – nine in all. None of these schools were owned or run by UMN, nor were they mission schools in the traditional sense – the teaching of Christianity had no place in the curriculum. However, teachers could give personal one-to-one witness where appropriate, and were free to hold Christian meetings in their own homes.

All this varied work of UMN in Nepal is supported from the UMN headquarters in Kathmandu, and here too many

Interservers work. In the quiet suburb of Thapatali in the south east of the city can be found the pleasant UMN guest house, run when I stayed there by an unflappable Interserver, Heather Hunt, who left her job teaching home economics in New Zealand to exercise her ministry of hospitality here. At meal times I had good opportunities to meet all sorts of people, including Eileen Warnock from Belfast, Counsellor with UMN and responsible for the pastoral care of mission staff; and twin brothers Ray and Glyn Mawson from Australia with their wives, who had both felt God calling them (separately) to use their gifts in retirement to serve him in Nepal. Ray was going to be the Administrator at Amp Pipal and Glyn to be Business Manager in Kathmandu: an example of an exciting trend for older people to be called to serve God abroad. I also met Sally and John Phillips. Converted in 1984, John gave up a good banking job in England and was now designated Assistant to the Treasurer/Controller for UMN. He and Sally were delighted with the schooling offered to their children in Kathmandu, with the British Primary School and KISC (Kathmandu International Study Centre) better, perhaps, than what was available at home.

Over the road from the guest house worked nurse Kerry Brown from Australia. From training auxiliary nurse midwives at Amp Pipal and at Tansen, she had come to run a clinic for UMN workers. She was also co-ordinating the programme for medical elective students, dealing with their applications and liaising with the hospitals. And a little way up the road are the pleasant modern buildings of UMN headquarters. As well as containing the offices of the Executive Director, Treasurer and Personnel Secretary, there are the four offices of the Education, Engineering and Industrial Development, Health Services and Rural Development Secretaries and their staff. Some of these are Interserve Partners, and some of them I met: Tjerk Nap, the UMN Health Services Secretary, and Henk Chevalking, Assistant Education Secretary, both from Holland. Working too in the education department on the administration of the adult literacy programme was Kath White of Interserve (Australia). She was particularly concerned to increase the literacy of Nepali women, currently only eighteen per cent, and told me how village women who may have been up since four or five in the morning would eagerly come together round a paraffin lamp for two hours six nights a week to learn.

Over the years many other Interserve Partners have held vital posts here: Richard Clark, as well as being Education Secretary was also President of UMN, and remembers the privilege of being able to give simple witness to the Lord before government officials in that capacity. Richard and his wife Janice recall the large debt they owe to their Nepali Christian friends who taught them much by word and example and gave them much by their love and acceptance. Richard's skill on the guitar opened the way to good friendships, and their close Nepali friends included Pastor Nicanor Tamang and his wife Elizabeth, Ramesh and Shanti Khatry and K.B. Rokaya (leader of Nepal's student work) and his wife Dranpati. Also in Kathmandu were Drs Tom and Cynthia Hale, Cynthia teaching in the Department of Community Medicine at the Tribhuvan University Institute of Medicine, and Tom teaching and translating Bible commentaries.

The story of UMN's work in Nepal is not all success. As seen at Patan, problems arose from increasing pressure to appoint Nepalis to senior posts in its work, and because there were still only a few qualified Christians, the alternative was to appoint Hindus. This raised uncomfortable questions for many. When is a hospital 'Christian', and when does it cease to be so? How did it deserve the title in the first place, and when does it forfeit it? Similarly development workers found themselves sometimes tempted to wonder why they were there at all. It's difficult for the people themselves to get food, and occasionally village people were heard to grumble, 'They come and go and nothing happens. Let these development people stay away. They come and eat our rice.' Not encouraging! Again, success in material realms – medicine, education – can lead to less interest in things spiritual, not more.

Christians suffer in various ways: sometimes they are thrown out of their homes, and girls face difficulties over arranged marriages to Hindus. If a man turns to Christ, he faces the hostility of the local community who are terrified because he will not appease the idol. At rice-planting time, no-one will help him or work with him. Similarly a Christian woman may not be able to draw water from the local spring, in case she contaminates it. Despite all these difficulties, the church continues to grow, under Nepali leadership; and in areas where there are no missionaries, people are turning to Christ in almost greater numbers than where there are. In 1982, for example, a new group of ninety-five believers was discovered near the Tibetan border in the far West. Some of their members had walked for twenty-seven days over the mountains to ask for Bibles, and up till then no-one else had known of their existence. In remote, fertile valleys, clinging to the sides of majestic mountains, in little mud and thatch villages, the church in Nepal is doubling and trebling in size. In Kathmandu, where in the late 1950s a handful of people met to worship, in 1992 I joined 450 people, members of the Gyaneshwar congregation, worshipping in their own purpose-built church under the leadership of Pastor Robert Karthak: joyfully singing, eagerly listening to an hour-long Bible exposition. This is but one of over a dozen flourishing congregations. These new Christians need solid Bible teaching, and 1981 saw the establishment of the Nepal Bible Institute founded by Ramesh Khatry, whose story is closely intertwined with BMMF.

Ramesh's family were strict and high-caste Hindus. After schooling at the Jesuit-run school of St Xavier's in Kathmandu where he first learnt of Jesus Christ, and having received healing from a serious illness whilst a student, he accepted Christ in the face of extreme family opposition and was baptised in 1972. His wife was baptised a year later. Hearing Ramesh preach at Tansen on Easter Sunday 1974, Bill Gould suggested Bible college training, and with encouragement from Robin Thomson, Paul Spivey and others, Ramesh went to Union Biblical Seminary at Yavatmal in India, for three years on a BMMF scholarship. The first Nepali graduate from UBS, his time there brought home to him the great need for good Bible teaching in Nepal, and so the idea of the Bible Institute was born. A Board was formed in 1980, comprising five Nepalis and two Western missionaries. The foundation stone was laid in March 1981, the Institute opened in temporary accommodation in May that year with Howard Barclay, Richard Clark and John Dickinson, all of BMMF, teaching part time, and in 1982 the building was complete – an attractive two-storey building on the side of a hill in Kathmandu. With Ramesh as Principal, the college began to fulfil his vision for training Christians to meet the needs of the many young Christians in Nepal. Suddenly in 1983 the Institute (now known as the Nepal Bible Ashram, NBA), was ordered to close, and moved temporarily over the border into India. At the same time one of the principal churches in Kathmandu was closed on Government orders and the pastors interrogated. It was all right to preach to Westerners, but the church was also full of Nepalis, and therein lay the 'crime'. In 1985 Ramesh Khatry was arrested whilst conducting a month-long Bible School in the far west of Nepal. He was eventually convicted of preaching to convert others (not true, as it was a school for believers), and sentenced to six years imprisonment.

Then in 1990 an amazing change took place in Nepal. On April 6th, the Friday before Good Friday, 50,000 protestors for democracy marched on the Royal Palace. Government troops and security forces killed 300 people, but the King was forced to give way. No longer would he head a virtual dictatorship, where democratic freedoms were denied. An interim coalition Government was set up preparatory to fully democratic multi-party elections. To celebrate, Christians held a two-hour Easter parade, marching through Kathmandu and stopping for twenty minutes of singing and prayer outside the palace, while police looked on unperturbed. Three months later a telegram

Church service, Kathmandu

reached Interserve's International Office from Ed Metzler, Executive Director of UMN: 'His Majesty the King, on the advice of the Prime Minister, has granted amnesty to all religious prisoners in accordance with the constitution of Nepal, and given instruction for dismissal of all cases against persons awaiting trial for religious activities.' In England, Ramesh Khatry, who was studying for a PhD in theology at Wycliffe Hall, Oxford, while on bail awaiting appeal against his sentence, said, 'It's wonderful news. The blood of the martyrs has brought democracy, but the blood of Jesus is more liberating. This is what I intend to preach, now that I can go back as a legitimate citizen of Nepal.'

He returned in August 1991 to a Church which had 'mushroomed' to more than 80,000 members, ready to serve the Church by writing and preaching. By 1992, leaders of the National Christian Fellowship of Nepal reported that the Church in Nepal numbered 120,000 of whom 80,000 were baptised. These believers were scattered among some 1,000 congregations. In Patan alone, a staunchly Hindu area of Kathmandu, twenty-five churches were meeting and worshipping. From its small beginning of some twenty believers in 1953, the Church in Nepal has doubled in size approximately every three years. Church leaders are praying and believing that the Church will number two million by the year 2000.

12

New initiatives in India

After much heart-searching, in 1987 BMMF changed its name. While the Bible and Mission, and to a considerable extent Medical work too remained the basis of its work, the name was changed to The International Service Fellowship, or Interserve, because the word 'missionary' was becoming more and more suspect in the eyes of national government officials. Different Councils adopted different schedules for the phasing in of the new name.

There were, and still are, many more developments in the work of BMMF/Interserve in India, and the more closely interwoven they become with the many indigenous Christian initiatives springing up, the more difficult they become to record. For those on the staff of the Union Biblical Seminary, Yavatmal, for example, there was change. Gradually, through the high quality of its teaching, the college which had been despised in some quarters for its strongly evangelical stance became widely respected. Its students gained distinctions in the nationwide examinations under its Principal, Dr Saphir Athyal, and the biblically-based ministry of its graduates was increasingly sought after by the larger denominations like the Church of South India.

In 1975, under Dr Athyal's leadership, it was decided to move the Seminary to Pune. The original founders had had a vision for rural India, so they had set up the college in the small town known then as Yeotmal in the central Indian jungle. However, as the college grew, there were students coming from all over India and even from other countries, speaking many different languages. Much course teaching and reading could be done in English or Hindi, but Yavatmal had only one church, with a Marathi-speaking congregation, so students who did not speak Marathi had no scope for practical work. Also staff coming from all over India had a problem with the education of their children, which made it hard to attract highly qualified staff. Eventually, after much thought, prayer and hard work, the college moved in 1983 to new buildings in Pune, a large city in the west with a population drawn from all over India and with churches of different denominations and languages. It seemed a far cry from the days when BMMF had endowed a chair at the seminary to facilitate the appointment of an Indian to replace an expatriate, an endowment funded from the proceeds of the sale of BMMF property in India, so that the money would be used for the strengthening of the Indian Church.

When UBS was relocated in Pune, its buildings at Yavatmal were taken over by the Yavatmal College for Leadership Training (YCLT), a college established in 1984 by a consortium of nine Indian societies and church groups. The aim was to train Indian Christians as cross-cultural evangelists and missionaries, and there was a strong emphasis on field work. A BMMF Partner, Doris Hamilton from Scotland, transferred from UBS to YCLT in 1986, continuing her work as tutor/librarian on the same premises. Things were not always easy at the new college. In March 1991 an armed mob invaded the campus shortly after forty-one members of the local Kolami tribe had been baptised. They rampaged through a Christian convention for local tribal leaders, armed with sticks, knives and swords, and did considerable damage. Sunil Sardar, a member of the college staff, was taken into custody, charged with forcibly baptising the Kolams, but they sang hymns in the police yard meanwhile and insisted that they were baptised by choice. Over 200 have now been baptised, and the first Christian marriage has taken place among them.

Dr Saphir Athyal retired as Principal in 1987, and his place was taken by Dr Brian Wintle, an Indian faculty member from Tamil Nadu who had been Dean of Students and was a specialist in New Testament studies. He had studied for a doctorate at Manchester University on a BMMF scholarship. One aspect of UBS's work was developing courses for Theological Education by Extension, and Robin Thomson and Mike Cleveland who were on the staff specialised in this, increasing its range by adding a higher level – Bachelor of Divinity. UBS also developed TAFTEE courses in Hindi and Marathi from a base in Nagpur. David Muir, who worked here with TAFTEE, described 'Nagpur, the orange city, famous for its twice yearly crop of something between a Jaffa and a tangerine. It stands in the very centre of India, at the crossing point of all the main rail-routes across the country. Its location would make it one of India's biggest commercial centres, but for one fact: it is one of the hottest places in India.'

Here in Nagpur, with its convenient access north to the Hindi speaking area and west into Maharashtra, David and others worked on through the heat, writing and administering TAFTEE courses. The students were very different from the residential students in Pune – mostly older, speaking less English, and already involved in Christian ministry. As a result of doing the TAFTEE courses, they were better equipped for their varied ministries – pastoring churches, teaching in schools and colleges, witnessing at their places of work, leading Christian organisations and promoting and tutoring TAFTEE courses in their own regional languages. Some Bible college trained pastors felt threatened by TAFTEE trained colleagues, but with ordained men frequently attempting to pastor ten or more small and scattered congregations, the only way forward for the Church in India is to make full use of this extra trained help.

Another exciting development in the Indian Church was the emergence of indigenous Indian missions. In 1965 the

Indian members of the Evangelical Fellowship of India, concerned to revive missionary interest among Indian Christians, set up the Indian Evangelical Mission (IEM) under the leadership of an Indian, Theodore Williams. Their hope was to send Indian missionaries to places where Westerners were not allowed to work.

The first missionary of IEM to be seconded to BMMF was T.M. John, who graduated from the South India Bible Institute and sensed a calling to Afghanistan. On learning that only medical workers would be accepted, he trained as a pharmacist at Vellore, and went as a missionary seconded by IEM to BMMF and from them to the International Assistance Mission (IAM) in 1968. He had a very effective ministry with many personal contacts with Afghans. He married Saramma, a nurse, and she joined him in 1970. They served in Afghanistan with IAM until 1972. The BMMF-IEM partnership continued from that time, the understanding being that IEM would function as the Indian Council of BMMF to recruit candidates and second them to work with BMMF outside India. Chandy and Mariamma Verghese (see ch.5) were seconded to Afghanistan in a similar way a few years later.

By 1985 IEM had about 190 workers in thirty-five locations in India itself, as well as people in Nepal, Papua New Guinea, Thailand and among Asians in the UK. This impressive growth was facilitated by the setting up in 1976 of the Indian Missionary Training Institute (IMTI).

IMTI was a venture in partnership between IEM and BMMF: one of the best examples, as Ray Windsor, who was involved, saw it, of partnership between an existing mission and an emerging indigenous mission. Its first course took place at the Bible Fellowship Centre, Nasik, in the summer of 1976, with eleven students. Its Principal was John Garrison who himself was born and bred in India and lived there altogether for forty-six years before continuing BMMF work in Canada. He and his wife Leona served in India for thirty-one years, engaging in village evangelism and literacy, city evangelism and student work. Now in 1976 they helped to set up IMTI, with short three-month courses. The aim was to train Indian Christians for cross-cultural ministry to Indian tribal peoples and others. Now under Indian leadership, IMTI changed its name to Outreach Training Institute (OTI) and moved first to Chikaldara, in the hills of north east Maharashtra, and then to Mugalapally, near Bangalore.

As well as theological training of different sorts, there is great need for training in other areas. Dennis Muldoon of Interserve, for example, an agronomist, and his wife Elizabeth were for some years on the staff of the Allahabad Agricultural Institute. Dennis was involved in planning courses for rural leaders and in teaching, including much practical field work: ploughing, sowing, silage-making; and Elizabeth taught short courses in child care to the women. There have also been valuable developments in India in provision for various groups of people with special needs. In many of these, Christians, and in particular Interserve Partners, are involved.

Marjory Foyle, whose path we have already followed from India to Nepal and back to India, was led in 1966 into a challenging new area of work. Having recovered from the period of severe overstrain and breakdown she suffered in the early 1960s, the suggestion was made at a BMMF conference at Mussoorie that BMMF needed a psychiatrist on its medical team and somebody proposed that Marjorie might be the person for the job. It seemed to her that this was indeed the right way forward, but on the principle that only the best is good enough for God, she insisted on becoming fully qualified, although by then well past the normal age for study. Emerging triumphantly from medical school with the Diploma of Psychiatric Medicine, she was seconded by BMMF in 1969 to the staff of the Nur Manzil Psychiatric Centre, Lucknow, where she had already been Medical Officer while at the Kinnaird.

Nur Manzil, 'Palace of Light', arose from the vision of Dr Stanley Jones, who as he counselled people in the course of his work began to dream of a Christian psychiatric centre which would combine professional expertise with individual care. Supported by the Methodist Church in the USA, and entrusted to the Methodist Church of South Asia, it opened in an old Muslim mansion in 1951. The work grew steadily, with successive Directors from Sweden, Switzerland, America and India. When Dr Ernest Chander, the first Indian Director, left in 1969, Marjory Foyle took his place. She continued and developed the fine tradition of the hospital, combining the normal work of a psychiatric unit with sensitive and unrushed individual counselling. Together with daily prayer in the chapel and the possibility of individual prayer for those who wanted it, the aim was to take time to hear the problem and to explore it in depth with the patient.

When Marjory retired at sixty, she was succeeded first by David Hickinbottom and then by Keith Bender, both from Australia. In 1985 Keith and Sally Bender were given fourteen days' notice to leave India, and after some months of uncertainty they transferred to Sialkot, Pakistan, where Keith provided a psychiatric clinic and consultation service at the Memorial Christian Hospital. From then onwards, Nur Manzil was staffed entirely by Indians. It was by now recognised for first year training of postgraduate doctors, so a stream of ambitious young doctors were applying. Marjory herself had been elected to a fellowship of the newly founded Royal College of Psychiatrists, a qualification which opened psychiatric doors to her all over the world, and after her retirement it became clear that she should launch out on a travelling ministry as a Partner with BMMF/Interserve, travelling initially in Bangladesh, Pakistan and Nepal as well as in India. She had become very conscious of all the needy thousands who had no opportunity of coming to Nur Manzil as patients, and was eager to disseminate basic psychiatric expertise as widely as possible. This she did, visiting small Christian hospitals and clinics, giving simple lectures in basic psychiatry to nurses, other hospital staff and to any other interested people.

Later still, from 1986, being acutely aware, partly through

her own experience, of the stress under which missionaries often work, she served with 'Interhealth', an organisation which looks after the physical and mental health of missionaries. When I visited her in her Ladbroke Grove flat, from the window of which as she proudly pointed out could be seen the weeping willow tree under which ZBMM prayer meetings were held in its faraway Ladbroke Grove days, she had just come back from the other side of the world where she had been counselling Christian workers on a missionary ship who had been traumatised by a grenade attack: an energetic and determined lady in the true Zenana/BMMF/Interserve tradition.

There are many people in India with special needs, as there are all over the world. Blindness is very prevalent in the subcontinent, with one person in seventy afflicted, and the Sharp Memorial School at Rajpur has been working to improve opportunities for the blind for many years. Jeanette Short of BMMF worked there in the 1960s and '70s, and was particularly involved with efforts to make the Bible available in Hindi braille. With the help of the blind people themselves, master copies were made of all the books of the New Testament by a laborious process over several years. The printing of John's Gospel alone took two years. This work has since been computerised, and a programme worked out so that if you type in Hindi script, you get back Hindi braille. I met Jeanette at the Interserve transit house in Delhi: kindly, friendly, a little blunt, prepared to criticise if she feels things aren't being done as they should. Knowing India so well, she now comes back to India frequently on temporary visas to meet short-term needs as they arise: running the transit house for a time or helping at Rajpur. When we met her, she was arranging projects for seven young 'On Track' volunteers on short-term programmes.

Some years earlier, Jeanette had been instrumental in getting four blind girls accepted at a BMMF 'Ambassador Camp' in the UK, with the result that three of the four turned to Christ and went on to become active

Christians serving God overseas. One of these was Rona Gibb, blind from birth, who later with her husband Tony became concerned at the attitude common in Hinduism that handicap of any kind is a punishment from God. As a result blind people are often shut away in their homes, as their families are ashamed of them. Rona and Tony realised that Christians were uniquely able to challenge this view and to show true love in action. They also felt that any work done should be indigenous, and with the help and encouragement of P.T. Chandapilla they acted as facilitators for Indian Christians who established the India Fellowship for the Visually Handicapped. There are now Fellowship Centres in Madras, Bombay, Calcutta and Dehra Dun – places of Christian friendship and fellowship for sighted and non-sighted, and bridges into the local churches which are slowly beginning to welcome the blind, as are Christian houseparties. Rona and Tony went back to England, where from a base in Devon they began producing the computer-printed braille Scriptures described above.

As with the blind, so with the deaf: often very little is done for them in India, but in July 1975 a young art graduate came to help. He arrived in India on a motor-bike, at the end of a 7,000 mile journey overland from England. Ian Stillman was profoundly deaf, and he was on his way to pioneer a project that would bring hope to hundreds of young deaf Indians. For India's deaf, especially those living in the villages, prospects of earning a decent livelihood are minimal. Many deaf children are rejected by their families, or are kept away from school and not given the special education they need. The incidence of deafness in southern India is particularly high, and increased by close intermarriage. Ian, whose family gave him every encouragement, first came to India to set up an art department in a Church of South India school for the deaf in Mylapore, a suburb of Madras. While there, he became aware of the acute shortage of opportunities for these children when they left school, and with encouragement from Basil Scott of BMMF, returned to India to see how he could help. He married an Indian teacher of the deaf, Sue

Rubin, and helped by her and by his growing awareness of God's call, headed for the southern tip of India.

Here, after a short time in Kottaram village, they found a suitable plot of land at Palavoor. They prayed, and felt that they should go ahead: an act of faith, as they had no money. Funds to buy the land came just in time from TEAR Fund, and with the help of local deaf people, whom they involved right from the beginning, the land was cleared, mud blocks were made, and buildings for a deaf centre, 'Nambikkai', began to go up. Sue and Ian were supported by their local church in England, and have been closely involved with Interserve, which had members on the Board from the start.

I visited Nambikkai in 1992: just a short distance from India's southern tip, a shady garden of Eden at the foot of the blue, hump-backed Western Ghats. We were met off the train by a jeep-driver who gave us a note. Slowly, as he drove us through the hot, quiet countryside, it dawned on us that he was deaf. We turned off the road at a sign 'Nambikkai Training Centre for the Adult Deaf', and soon became aware of an atmosphere of silence and concentrated activity: farming, planting, watering, building, learning. The word 'Nambikkai' means 'hope' or 'confidence' in Tamil.

The house where we stayed was remarkable: circular, modern and yet vernacular, built with the help of the well-known British architect, resident in India, Laurie Baker. Here we met an innovative, stimulating group of people: Ian, visionary, tireless in his enthusiasm, giving himself totally to the community he has built up; Sue: fiery, practical, determined, the perfect helper yet leader too with Ian, and Geraldine Dunlop from England, a Partner with Interserve, and, like Ian, totally deaf. I tended to speak loudly, which was pointless. As Sue spoke with Ian and Geraldine, moving her lips but making no sound, and using sign-language, I saw that silence is the medium of communication at Nambikkai.

Ian took us round, along gravelled paths lined with carefully tended flowers in the shade of craning palm trees, between coconut leaf-thatched buildings. Tending the garden is an important activity here. The buildings, together with an outdoor stage area for acting – basic for the deaf – are grouped around the circular prayer house, its thatched roof swathed in pink and purple bougainvillea. The work was growing rapidly, and with financial help from TEAR Fund, new buildings were going up, built of brick this time, instead of mud. We saw the training section: girls being helped with speech, sewing and other skills; and the farm where young deaf people from surrounding villages come for a few years to learn farming methods. Ian took a keen interest in the technical aspects of running the farm, and was determined to make it as productive as possible. Water storage and irrigation are particularly important. For the first few years of its existence, drought in southern India made successful agriculture very difficult, but they pulled through. Ian aimed to develop Nambikkai more and more into a community based on working on the land, where everyone makes a contribution of some sort: to provide an environment where damaged personalities could find healing. Geraldine worked particularly among the girls, gently welding these isolated individuals into the 'family'.

Spiritual development is an integral part of the life here, and at daily prayers in the round church the service was led by a deaf Indian using sign language. Mohan, another deaf evangelist gave a talk based on Matthew 7:11: 'If you then, though you are evil, know how to give good gifts to your children, how much more will your Father in heaven give good gifts to those who ask him!' In sign language, interpreted, it was so vivid that it had us all gripped with the excitement of God answering prayer. We sang together, we prayed together (strange but joyful sounds), and at the end the community forgave and welcomed a former one of their number who confessed to stealing, lying and setting fire to one of the buildings. Ian had spent the whole Christmas period counselling this man. Sue too spent much time and effort in counselling and arranging marriages for young deaf Christians. Yet as Ian pointed out, 'In Nambikkai we are

New buildings, Nambikkai

trying to bring deaf people together. If I have done my work in such a way that Nambikkai would be able to go on and develop without me, that would be the best possible achievement.' The story of Nambikkai has been captured on film and was shown on television in Britain and Holland in 1991.

Another Indian couple who became aware of special needs which Christians should be helping to meet in the name of Christ are M.C. and Anna Mathew, whom I visited in Madras. A couple in whom the love and light of Jesus are clearly visible, they both trained as doctors at Vellore. Although both from Christian backgrounds, as a young man M.C.'s concern about poverty and the maldistribution of resources in India led him through a brief Communist phase, which ended when he saw how much violence and confrontation that path involved. Reading John's Gospel, he saw a different approach: the realisation that there is more to life than the merely physical dimension was the start of his gradually turning to God. After a spell of work as a paediatrician at Nagpur, when with Dr Garlick of BMMF (Australia) he travelled widely, helping to establish the Evangelical Medical Fellowship of India, M.C. and Anna moved back to the Christian Medical College at Vellore, where M.C. lectured in paediatrics. Then the birth and death after a few months of their little handicapped daughter came to them as God's call to try to help such children; for at that time the thinking at Vellore and elsewhere was that nothing could be done for handicapped children before the age of six, by which time it was almost too late.

When M.C. approached the medical college about the possibilities of developing work with young children with special needs, he received little understanding. Only Ray Windsor of BMMF gave them the encouragement they needed at that time, saying, 'If God is calling you to this, then we'll support you.' Indeed, as Anna told me,

If it hadn't been for BMMF, we wouldn't be where we are now, because everyone else laughed at us. It was only

BMMF who said, 'Yes, you are talking about something important and worth developing.' And through the years when we've sometimes been despondent, they have continued to give us the support we have needed, including small grants for equipment and recently a large grant from a fund-raising event called Christmas Cracker which we will use towards fulfilling our hope of buying premises. Now we are beginning to see some fruit from our work, but the first three years were very difficult.

Once accepted as Partners of Interserve, they started work in a small room in Madras in 1983, writing and reading, hoping to establish a link with an existing institution, but nothing worked out. So BMMF encouraged them to start up on their own, and after a year's study in the UK and close involvement with the Fellowship there, which confirmed them in the conviction that early diagnosis and care was the way to help these children, they found the spacious house in Madras which they now rent as premises for their own foundation, 'Ashirvad' (blessing). Visiting them, I was impressed with the bright, welcoming and professional look of the place, the children's pictures on the walls and the thought-provoking posters. Like this one: 'You call me retarded. You speak about me as handicapped. You write about me as disabled. But I just have some special needs.'

I was privileged to sit in on two of M.C.'s consultations: gentle, slow-speaking, thoughtful, above all he is a doctor who *listens*. As he explained to me, 'First of all we listen to the story of the child. To me each child's life is a story and an adventure. We don't hurry. We ask questions. We try to understand.' With the first family, who brought in a floppy three-year-old with poor concentration and manipulative skills, not yet able to walk unaided, he asked the parents many questions and tested the little girl's reactions. When they had gone, he told me that nothing could be done to alter the child's cerebral palsy, but that the hope would be to promote her development with play-based learning, still a very new concept in India. The parents' resources being limited, M.C. gave the consultation free: 'We have a heavenly Father who provides,' M.C. explained. He told me that the future prospects for such a child were bleak, and that community and voluntary support would be vital.

The second consultation was with a family with a few-weeks-old Downs Syndrome baby, and I listened as M.C. tried gently to explain to them what was wrong. As he told me,

> I have come to realise that every family is in a stage of coming to terms with the reality of the disability of their child. This journey takes a long or a short time, depending on the type of information they are given – about the child and about the future – and the extent of the help they receive from the community, the immediate family and surrounding friends. To me, the spiritual dimension in this process is tremendously important, and I ask them, 'How are you coping with this? What is it that holds you, as you go through this state of grief and sorrow? What is your hope for the future?' Often they say, 'Well, we are shattered. We don't know what to do.' And I am ready, then, to enter into some personal dialogue with them in the spiritual realm – perhaps to pray with them, and to help them to see that there can be a purpose in suffering, that there is meaning beyond grief, there is hope beyond the present difficulty. Sometimes I have even been able to introduce Hindu families to the concept of the personal love of a personal God, shown in Christ; but with any family I can only go as far as they come with me in the dialogue. I move with those who move.

> During the consultation I keep things very informal and want to help the parents to feel that we are together with them in the pursuit of finding help for the child. But when they go away, they are faced with harsh reality, and then they are very much on their own. I can function at three levels: either simply as the professional doctor, or making myself wholly available to the family during the

consultation but then entrusting them to God, or thirdly, in certain cases, entering with the family and joining them on their journey, being available to them whenever they need. We are involved with some thirty-five families in this fully committed way.

I was shown over Ashirvad by Katy Hill from the UK, who was doing a six month 'On Track' stint between getting her degree in psychology and starting training in clinical psychology. Her parents, Peter and Christine Hill, had worked with BMMF at the Christian Medical College, Vellore, so she was not new to India. She explained that at the playgroup here, the mothers see how they can help their children through play-therapy, and also learn the importance of praising these children for what they can do and achieve, instead of thinking only of their weaknesses. As another poster put it, 'I heard you discuss my disability. That is only one side. I have many abilities that you forget to see.' The mothers can relax a little here, and talking to others with similar problems they give each other mutual support.

It is in this area of follow-up and support of families that the local churches can become involved, and Anna took me to visit an impressive project that has arisen in this way: ASHA ('hope'), the Johnny Samuel Memorial Project for the Disabled in the broad compound of St Andrew's Scottish Kirk in Madras. As she told me, St Andrew's, where she and M.C. worship, has been concerned for people in nearby slum areas for some time, and had set up ASHA with various programmes for children on the premises already. Then Anna and M.C. began to get the church people interested in children with special needs, and trained ten volunteers from the church to work with them. A special playgroup was opened in existing church premises two days a week, and run by M.C. and Anna with the volunteers. The church wanted M.C. and Anna to move Ashirvad there, but they felt no: 'This should be the church's work, not ours – something they can carry

on without us, though we still help in any way we can.'
The church continued the project with enthusiasm. They
raised money and built the special premises in their grounds
and employed a trained psychiatric social worker and three
teachers to run it. The children's medical needs were referred
to M.C. and Anna when necessary.

This is a success story in terms of co-operation between
the specialist work of Ashirvad and the support of a local
church. Ideally other churches should start similar projects
in their localities. Hard though it is to find the extra time to
spread their ideas, the Mathews are beginning to concentrate
more on training and equipping others to begin programmes
similar to theirs elsewhere. And M.C. made a final plea:

> The church, including Interserve, has been slow to
> respond to children with special needs worldwide. They
> need professional help in overcoming their disabilities
> as far as possible; they are also people who need Jesus,
> just like everyone else. It is high time that Interserve, as
> an international Christian service organisation, began to
> do more to focus prayer and concern on these children,
> and to meet not only their physical but also their spir-
> itual needs. Jesus said, 'Let the children come to me.'
> Undoubtedly he includes children like these.

In Delhi, too, God's work continues through various
initiatives in which BMMF/Interserve has been vitally
involved. I met, for example, Lalchuangliana, Executive
Secretary of the Emmanuel Hospital Association which was
set up in 1970 by Ray Windsor and others. Lalchuangliana
came from Mizoram, an area in the north east of India
sandwiched between Bangladesh and Burma, which is very
largely Christian. Having done well academically, he was
selected to join the elite Indian Administrative Service. As
a student at the Administrative Staff College in Mussoorie
he was already witnessing as a Christian, testifying in Union
Church with his wife Sangi. A promising junior officer, he
was posted as Sub-Divisional Magistrate in Madhya Pradesh

Playgroup for 'special needs' children, ASHA, Madras

State in central India. He was promoted several times in the Districts and finally to New Delhi where he was appointed, still very young, as an Under-Secretary in the Ministry of Defence. The 'perks' of the post included an official house, a jeep and a driver, as well as a good salary. By this time he and his family were strongly involved in the Delhi Bible Fellowship, which still continues its powerful preaching ministry in the centre of Delhi. In 1973, in obedience to God's call, Lalchuangliana resigned his government career with its bright prospects, took a fifty per cent cut in salary and accepted the invitation to use his administrative gifts with EHA. I talked to him in the EHA office in Nehru Place, where the Interserve office used to be until recently. Approached through a maze of dingy corridors and lifts, it seemed like a run-down version of 1960s London office blocks: Paternoster Square, perhaps. But the piazza outside was more fun than a London square, even on a cold grey Delhi winter day, with food-stalls, people milling round, and a central group apparently made up of meditative cows and men squatting over an absorbing game.

Lalchuangliana, kindly, his broad Mizo features beaming, had facts and figures at his finger-tips. He told me a little about the work of EHA, explaining that it is an Indian medical missionary society with the stated aim of providing 'comprehensive health care to people in rural areas of India in the Name and Spirit of Jesus Christ.' Rural areas are emphasised because the need there is greatest, but EHA has projects for the urban poor as well. It continues to provide a vital link between the fifteen member hospitals, which were originally founded by a variety of missions with widely differing ways of working; six partner hospitals (of which Ashirvad in Madras is one), and six community health and development projects. In particular, it helps these small, sometimes struggling hospitals to find Christian staff, by sponsoring students at Ludhiana and Vellore medical colleges; and by encouraging Christian students in government medical colleges to consider serving in the smaller rural hospitals. It also runs orientation and training courses, covering many aspects of Christian medical work. Over the years many BMMF doctors and nurses have worked in EHA hospitals, but since 1984 very few expatriates have been able to obtain visas to continue. The only expatriate medical Interservers left in India in 1992 were Colin and Wendy Binks (UK) at Nav Jivan Hospital, Satbarwa, Peter and Barbara Deutschmann (Australia) at Landour Community Hospital and Estere Guza (USA) who served for many years first with UFCS and then with BMMF as Director of Nursing Education at Jhansi. Through the 'On Track' programme, however, Interserve sends students out to do their medical electives at these hospitals, and they can make a valuable contribution in short-staffed hospitals.

Nav Jivan Hospital is in the heart of India's poorest state, Bihar. After a hot twenty-four-hour train journey from Delhi, the visitor arrives at a small dusty station called Daltonganj. Then after a drive by jeep through the flat dry landscape dotted with mud hut villages and buffalo carts, the hospital complex looms into view: wards, nurses' home, guest-house, church and a small area for patients' families to sleep and cook. The hospital hums with the usual chaotic mass of people milling around, sitting on floors, lying on or under the beds. Colin Binks was surgeon and Medical Superintendent with special responsibility for training and discipling doctors; Wendy ran TAFTEE classes in the local church. This is just one of the small hospitals still continuing to serve needy people in rural India.

Another small hospital with long links with Interserve is Herbertpur, not far from Dehra Dun. Driving the 140 hot, dry miles over the flat plain northwards from Delhi, suddenly through the haze the outline of the Shivalik hills is seen. On up a winding narrow road through the sandstone hills, the traveller comes upon the green Doon valley, with the Himalayas rearing up behind. Here, in the middle of the valley, is the village of Herbertpur. The hospital was founded by Dr Geoffrey Lehmann and his wife Monica. Her family had lived in India for generations and had made distinguished contributions in various fields. They also had a family link with BMMF/Interserve: her sister was Rosalind Broomhall, a key Committee member. Geoffrey, a member of the Brethren, trained as an engineer and then as a doctor. He designed the hospital and supervised its construction. From their arrival at Herbertpur in 1935, Geoffrey and Monica worked initially on their own. The hospital was independent and they financed it themselves. Gradually the team grew and the work and outreach of the hospital increased. The hill people came pouring in, regarding it as their hospital. In ones and twos some turned to Christ, but for many years no church met to worship.

Eventually in 1970 the Emmanuel Hospital Association was established and Herbertpur became one of its associated hospitals. Geoffrey stipulated just two things: first, no patient should leave the hospital without hearing the Gospel; second, no patient should be turned away through inability to pay. A Japanese-American doctor, Cy Satow, became Medical Superintendent and Geoffrey and Monica retired. In 1973 the work was greatly strengthened with the arrival of Paul East, seconded by Interserve, as Administrator. He was newly married to Su' Lehmann, Geoffrey and Monica's strikingly pretty youngest daughter, who had been brought up in India and trained as a nurse. God's mysterious ways had led them to Interserve, to each other (they first met at an Interserve 'Swanwick' conference), to the EHA and so back to Herbertpur. As well as administering the hospital, Paul set up a training programme for hospital administrators, some of whom went on to work in EHA hospitals. Su' worked at various times in every department apart from X-ray. Particularly exciting for Paul and Su' was the privilege of working under their Indian 'Boss', Lalchuangliana, seeing in him and his wife not only close friends but also valued national colleagues in the task of mission to which Interserve is called.

In 1985 Paul was suddenly ordered to leave the country, and in 1986 after appealing and receiving short-term extensions they left India and moved to Cyprus where Paul became Interserve's Area Director (South) until moving to

the UK for family reasons in 1992. And Geoffrey had the joy
in old age of knowing that at last several congregations were
worshipping regularly in the hill country of Herbertpur. A
young boy with cancer was converted and healed. A team of
Indian Christians started going out to his village and week
by week people were converted – first the boy's family, then
others. As the team preached, one old man exclaimed, 'This
is the same message I heard as a boy from Dr Lehmann!'
And so years of faithful work is reaping its reward as a small
church has been born and is growing.

As well as running the hospitals, EHA places strong
emphasis on community health with the aim of bringing
low-cost health care to villagers in their own communities.
Crucial to implementing this is the training of a woman
from each community as a village health-worker (VHW).
Dr Patricia Wakeham of Interserve was Community Health
Consultant to the EHA, and she has recorded how village
people reached through the Doon Medical Project found
new life in Christ as well as healing for their medical
problems. One elderly couple heard the Gospel and were
given a New Testament when they visited the village clinic
in the bazaar near their home. They turned to Christ after
the husband saw him in a vision. Their neighbours beat them
up and threatened to damage their crops and their home, but
they persisted in their faith and their home became a beacon
of faith in that mountain place.

EHA's aim to be a trail-blazer in new ventures to provide medical care for the most needy inevitably includes
the urban poor. When the British left India in 1947, the
population of Delhi was less than a million. By 1992 it was
ten million. A considerable cause of this huge increase is
the large number of people who have left the countryside
and moved to the city, hoping to find a livelihood. These
people have tended to settle on areas of waste ground
and build themselves small one-roomed shelters. As time
has gone on they have become established in the resulting
slums, but living conditions have remained extremely poor,
with no sanitation or services of any sort. It is in areas like

this that EHA has set up an impressive project known as ASHA (Action for Securing Health for All, with 'Asha' also meaning 'hope').

The project was headed by one of India's dynamic Christian women, Dr Kiran Martin, from a Hindu family, who came to Christ through a 'Youth for Christ' camp. As she told me, 'God put it into our hearts to do something for these people. We began in 1988 with one clinic as God opened up the doors. Slum land belongs to the Government, so we had to have their permission for anything we did, but God gave us favour with them and we went ahead.' They now had an office and health centre in extraordinary and unusual buildings designed by students of Laurie Baker, the architect also involved at Nambikkai, next to one of Delhi's extensive slums. The buildings, combining innovative low-technology with traditional construction techniques, taught builders forgotten skills and gave them a framework for personal creativity. We saw small decorative details introduced by the builders, not unlike those in mediaeval European cathedrals: the result, delightful and surprisingly low-cost buildings. This health centre was the joint responsibility of ASHA and the slum wing of the Delhi Development Authority who were extending the slum work.

Dr Martin showed me round three of the slums. I saw clinics where the varied activities all relate ultimately to health: ante-natal and post-natal care, under-fives clinics, immunisation programmes, doctors' surgery, supplementary feeding programmes, health education, literacy, training of community health-workers and midwives and much more. There are dispensaries, playgroups, women's groups and women's income-generating projects, and a considerable amount of work has also been done in improving the environment in the slums: building paths, gutters, installing water supply, taps, and communal toilets which are looked after by the people of the community. The slums are democratically run, with a slum leader who takes a pride in seeing that things get done. The women, too, are finding their voice, and as we visited, they all gathered round Dr Martin, vociferously

Slum-project clinic, New Delhi

insisting that they must have electricity in the slum. Indeed, in the hot weather fans are desperately needed as not only is the heat unbearable, but flies collect in myriads and spread disease. At the moment the problem seems intractable, as it is too dangerous to introduce electrical wiring into mud-brick huts.

Although many of the huts were still made of mud-brick, plastic sheeting and cocunut palm thatch, a start had been made in rebuilding some of the slums, much of the labour being provided by the residents themselves. Capital expenditure was provided by the government, running expenses for medicines, salaries etc., by TEAR Fund and similar groups. Dr Martin battled on, but it wasn't easy. As she said, 'The love of God makes you long to help these poor people, but many obstacles stand in the way. Sometimes the people themselves can be very aggressive if I don't seem to give them what they want, but I tell them, "God is the creator. He loves you. Trust him."' Raju Abraham, the doctor with whom this book began, hopes to see the same energy and determination in Indian women as he saw in the founding women of ZBMM. Nowhere is it better personified than in Dr Martin, taking on the Delhi slums for God.

I met other impressive people in Delhi: one was Harriet Sankaradas, who was not only running the Interserve transit house, but also with Mr Masih running the Delhi office as PA to Dr Tluanga, the head of Interserve (India). A real servant of God, she never seemed to stop working, and assured me that she loved it. Certainly her face was radiant with the knowledge that God is with her. She told me a little of her story: Tamil speaking, from the Nilgiri Hills in southern India, she was brought up as a Roman Catholic but rebelled against it. At fifteen she married a Hindu, with whom she was very happy. In 1966, after work as a clerk in a government office, she heard that an American wanted someone to help in his office. This was Dr Norton Sterrett of the Union of Evangelical Students of India (UESI), who 'put no pressure on his non-Christian secretary, but prayed me into the kingdom.' After a time when both Harriet and her

husband worked at Union Biblical Seminary, Yavatmal, he
on maintenance and she in the office, Ray Windsor invited
Harriet to work in the BMMF office which had moved from
Edgehill to Delhi as BMMF's work expanded. After much
prayer, the whole family came to Delhi in 1975. The children
went to the Wynberg-Allen School, Mussoorie. Harriet's
husband found it difficult to get a job, and then suffered a
heart attack and increasing ill health until his death in 1984.
It was a testing and difficult time, but Harriet testified to
the support she received from her many friends in BMMF,
and to God's never-failing love through it all.

She remembered too the good times when the International Office of BMMF was in Delhi:

> Each day was different – always busy but great fun. In
> our coffee breaks we would laugh and talk, people made
> a big thing about the football teams they supported, there
> were cricket matches and we would go out for ice-creams
> and cake. We used to go for picnics, prayer meetings and
> services together. There was a great deal of work, but lots
> of fun too. There were people from all over the world.
> Every Christmas all BMMF, EHA and EFI people with
> their families would go down into the square and sing
> carols. In 1984 all that changed as expatriates had to
> leave. It was traumatic for us. Mr Masih worked in the
> office before I came: we still talk together about those
> good old days.

Recently the transit house and the office – now the office
of Interserve (India) – moved to Janakpuri, a suburb in the
south west of Delhi. Also based in Janakpuri were Robin
and Shoko Thomson. Robin was the Interserve Regional
Representative in India, doing innumerable things unob-
trusively, in true servant style: working with Dr Tluanga,
the Executive Secretary of Interserve (India), and with
Lalchuangliana as 'Member-at-large' of EHA. Shoko, from
Japan, was one of BMMF's first recruits from East Asia.
I met Dr Tluanga and his wife Biaki, from Mizoram in

north-eastern India. He had a PhD in mathematics and was for some years the Director of Education in the Mizoram Government. Then, called by God to full-time work, he taught for a while in a mission school on Gilbert Island in the central Pacific. When they had to give this up, they were introduced by his brother, Dr R. K. Nghakliana, to BMMF. Dr Nghakliana had himself joined BMMF's Evangelism and Bible Ministry Department in 1972 and worked first among college students, seconded to UESI, and then among doctors and medical students with the Evangelical Medical Fellowship of India. As a result the Tluangas joined BMMF and he became Staff Consultant with the Evangelical Teachers' Fellowship of India. When Interserve (India) was launched, he was clearly the right person to lead it.

A valuable and enjoyable occasion in New Delhi is the monthly Interserve prayer breakfast, and the one I attended was held in the home of John and Janet Reynolds from Canada. They had opened an Indian branch of the family business in the vulcanisation of rubber and the manufacture of conveyor belts: a business set up by Janet's grandfather, a strong Christian and a brilliant inventor. Conducting the business in Delhi was not easy: there were many frustrations, but they felt that this is where they should be, serving God in a tentmaker capacity, employing and training Indian Christians and setting the highest standards in the way the business was run. Giving a lot to Interservers in India in the way of hospitality and encouragement, they also greatly valued the emotional and spiritual support that Interserve gave them. Bruce and Kathleen Nicholls, the Thomsons, and several 'short-termers' were also present on this occasion, and I was delighted too to meet Becki Chung again, having first met her in Hong Kong. She told me then that the Lord was calling her to India. Now here she was – helping in the Interserve office until she was able to start her studies in Hindi.

Others I met were Dr Lalchungnunga, the Assistant Secretary for Development of Interserve (India): a job which involves visiting churches and challenging to mission, making the work of Interserve known and contacting and encouraging new workers. He was previously the Vice-Principal of a government college in Mizoram; also David Mally from Andhra Pradesh: grey-haired, voluble, the Treasurer of Interserve (India) and Deputy Director of Employment in the Indian Government's Ministry of Labour. Looking for ways of serving God more fully while remaining in his secular occupation, David was applying to become a tentmaking Partner with Interserve. Jeff and Ruth Auty were at the prayer breakfast, too. They have been on the staff of Woodstock School since 1981. As Jeff put it, 'I originally came for a year, but I haven't left yet!'

One of the biggest changes to affect BMMF/Interserve's work in India came in June 1984, when the Indian Government clamped down on issuing residential visas to foreigners. From that time, visas for 'missionaries' have been unavailable, and few other long-term visas are given. The expatriates I met in Delhi were exceptions: either because, like the Nicholls and Robin Thomson, they had long-standing residents' visas, or because they were teaching at Woodstock, which with other international schools has a special allocation, or because they were in business – India welcomes businessmen but not missionaries – or because they were students or short-termers on tourist visas. It was hard to have to cut down on expatriate workers, but BMMF's policy of training indigenous leadership is being vindicated in the formation of Interserve (India) with its strong national leadership.

At the gathering, I saw Interserve Partners' mutual support in action as they prayed for each other. It was a moving occasion and a privilege to be there with such an enthusiastic, dedicated and international group. Although fewer and fewer of the old-style missionaries can be found in Delhi now, God's Church is clearly alive and well, and his people there are eager to reach out for him within India and wherever else he may lead.

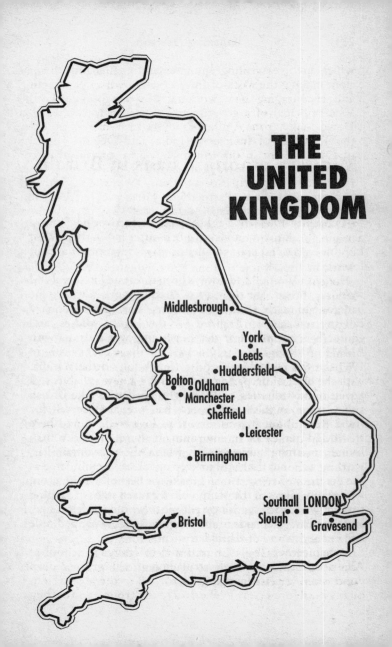

THE UNITED KINGDOM

Middlesbrough

York
Leeds
Huddersfield
Bolton Oldham
Manchester
Sheffield
Leicester

Birmingham

Southall LONDON
Slough
Bristol
Gravesend

13

Ministry among Asians in Britain

In February 1968 an English woman recovering from a nervous breakdown moved to a bed-sitter in Southall, West London: a modest start to what is now a significant area of Interserve's work.

Margaret Wardell had always been interested in travel and working abroad. She turned to Christ in Jamaica where she had gone to teach, seeking adventure. Sensing a missionary call she returned to England for theological studies, and gradually it became clear that her calling was to India with BMMF. Although strongly drawn to village evangelism, in 1963 she was posted to Woodstock School, northern India, with the brief of preparing and teaching a new syllabus to a group of missionaries' children who needed to take British and Commonwealth exams. She had prepared herself for India, read about it, was almost in love with it, and here she found herself in an environment more American than Indian, teaching subjects with which she was unfamiliar, working late into the night to keep up. Stress accumulated as she determined to submit and make the best of the situation, while daily views of the plains below caused stabs of longing to be down among the village people to whom she felt called, and the heavy demands of the teaching syllabus sapped time and energy from her Christian witness.

In September 1964 she returned to language school at Allahabad to find herself struggling in the grip of deep depression, 'a black clinging horror, an intolerable weight on my head forcing my eyes down to the ground and cutting me off from those around. I seemed to have nothing to say to anyone, and try as I would, I could not fight my way out.' In December Margaret turned in desperation to the Nur Manzil Psychiatric centre in Lucknow, where she received invaluable professional help from Dr Jim Stringham and his wife. Although greatly helped, it was not until February 1966, through a Christian friend's prayer for deliverance, that she was fully freed from the oppression.

Having already paid one or two visits to the district town of Bulandshahr in the plains below Mussoorie, she had started work there at the end of 1965, a happy, gentle life ideal for her after her breakdown. This was the work started by 'Granny' Pollen years before, after her husband, who had been District Officer in the area, had died. Margaret taught English to Tibetan refugees in the BMMF school under Lilian Das, accompanied Beryl Finch on visits to Kwarsi village, or went with Dulcie Rowell on three-week camping trips evangelising and teaching in other surrounding villages. The women's concentration span was short – their gaze would readily wander during a Bible story, leading to delightfully unrelated remarks, 'Where did you get that bangle?', and so on, but Margaret loved them, and they recognised and appreciated the missionaries' love. The work was everything Margaret had hoped for.

In June 1967 she went back to England on leave, and Arthur Pont suggested that as she was excused deputation work on health grounds, she do a short spell in a multi-racial area of Britain. She arrived in Southall in February 1968, seconded temporarily to the staff of St John's Church, her brief to prepare for a children's holiday Bible club to be run at Easter. Ten years earlier, a rubber factory in Southall had been short of workers. The Assistant Manager who had been posted to India during the war had suggested, 'Let's send for some Sikhs – they're the hardest workers I know.' So the firm recruited a number of Sikhs from the Punjab who soon encouraged relatives and friends to come too. As a result, as is well known, Southall, a pleasant west London suburb of small Victorian terraced houses beside the Grand Union

Canal, has become an outpost of the Punjab, as have several other industrial areas of Britain.

Margaret set about door-to-door visiting, where her knowledge of Hindi was invaluable, with the result that 130 children – many Asian, some British, poured in for the holiday club. Her visits and the club for their children were appreciated by the Asian families and formed the basis of contacts and friendships in many homes. Then, after a prolonged period of uncertainty, it was decided that for health reasons Margaret should not return to India. She was invited instead to join the staff of St John's as parish worker, with the result that her 'temporary placement' stretched out to seventeen years. BMMF bought a house in Southall where she lived, seconded to St John's and continuing her ministry among Asian families, befriending and helping them, running week-night children's clubs, and showing church members how they too could reach out to their Asian neighbours. Although no-one fully realised it at the time, BMMF's work among Asians in Britain had been born.

Margaret retired in 1985, but her work was continued by Richard Christopher, who came from an Indian Christian family but had lived in England since he was thirteen. He did door-to-door visiting and was involved in various 'bridge-building' clubs for young people, some of them part of the youth programme of the church, others in schools. The fact that he was Punjabi-speaking was a great asset, especially with the older people whom he visited who never really mastered English. His wife Kelly, from a Sikh family in the Punjab, came to England in 1978 and turned to Christ through the witness of her Christian aunt. As she said, 'In doing this the important thing for me was that Jesus is alive, whereas the gurus lived and died. Before I had felt miserable, but once I had made the commitment I felt happy inside.' The vicar of St John's, David Bronnert, was proud to be ministering to a multi-racial church. He reckoned the congregation was roughly one third African and West Indian, one third European and one third Asian.

Although the majority of the Asians in the church came from Christian families, there were conversions and baptisms. A racially-mixed young people's music and drama group helped with leading the services.

As time went on, outreach ministries to Asians were established in various industrial cities in Britain. The first of these to involve BMMF was in Bolton. Cradled in the low green Lancashire hills, the sky pierced with the red brick chimneys of its Victorian cotton mills, Bolton contains a sizeable Asian population. Wandering its streets, one finds shops like the Bombay Bazaar offering sarees; and the Shree Swaminarayan Temple advertising its carnival (star attractions elephants, Indian dancers and pipe band). In 1974 a Hindu boy riding his bicycle in Bolton was killed in an accident. There was no Hindu temple, so the family came to the church for help. As a result of this and similar situations, a small group of people met in the hall of Emmanuel Church, Bolton, to discuss the nature and needs of the Asian community. There had already been efforts to reach out to the Asian community from Emmanuel Church, and a Bible college student called Patrick Sookhdeo had led a student witness team to Bolton. Patrick's family were originally Pathans from the north-west frontier of Pakistan. He had come to Britain from Guyana in 1960 and turned to Christ soon afterwards. Eager to reach out to fellow Asians, he went to college and was ordained, a start to what proved to be an outstanding Asian ministry. He was one of those present at that seminal meeting in Bolton.

The student mission brought one or two to Christ and into Bible study groups. These people needed pastoring, and to meet needs like this the BMMF London Council were offering to help to bring Asian Christian pastors to work among immigrants in Britain. The first to come, following the Bolton meeting, was Wilfred Paul, pastor of a Pentecostal church at Dehra Dun in North India. A Bible college lecturer originally from Gujerat, the thought had come to him while still in India of the need for ministry among Asians who had left the country. Less bound abroad

by their own society, surely this was a Christian mission
field? Through BMMF the link was eventually made, and
Wilfred and his wife Mercy uprooted themselves from their
comfortable home and arrived in Bolton in June 1974.
They were well suited to the need, mature and experienced
Christian leaders who spoke Gujerati, Hindi and Urdu. It
was decided that they would be Partners with BMMF and
supported financially by the 'Bolton Council of Reference',
the group of local Christians described above.

The Pauls found things far from easy. The Asian Christians they had been asked to pastor failed to materialise, so
Wilfred began making links in any way he could: door-to-
door visiting, teaching Gujerati and English, and running
a children's 'Good News Club'. He visited nearby towns,
finding a few Christian families in Preston, Nelson, Burnley
and Huddersfield: the start of the Northern Area Asian
Christian Fellowship. In 1982 his support switched from
the Bolton Council of Reference to BMMF, as his work
was more outside Bolton than in it. He travelled from
town to town, evangelising, teaching and pastoring. It
was hard work and between November 1982 and March
1983 he suffered three severe heart attacks. Supported by
much prayer he made an excellent recovery, and after his
official retirement he continued his work freelance and by
faith. Soon after, Mercy died, but Wilfred soldiered on,
pastoring his Asian friends in and around Bolton. Keith
Wood, a BMMF Partner who first became involved at close
quarters with Asian work at about this time, held Wilfred
in the highest esteem, 'a very godly and gifted person – a
pioneer in Asian ministry across the north of England.'

In 1982 Richard Cook, who had arrived the previous
year as Curate of Emmanuel Church, made a survey of the
Asian population, their needs, languages and the response
to these needs being attempted by the churches in the North
West. The work in Bolton was extended to cover the whole
of Lancashire, and the Bolton Council of Reference was
superseded by the 'North West Committee of BMMF International (UK)', which took over Wilfred's support for two

years. Providentially, just when more people were needed to become involved in this extended work, George Skinner appeared on the scene. An RE teacher and Scripture Union staff worker, he was undertaking research at Manchester University into the educational needs of racial minority groups. Now in 1983 he was appointed by BMMF to follow up Richard Cook's work and extended his own research to study relations between Asians and the local churches.

At the same time, as a result of increasing prayer and concern to reach out to the Asian community, a move was made to set up a Resources Centre in Bolton, to include a wide range of literature about Asians in Britain, Christian books and posters in Asian languages and other audio-visual aids for use by various churches and groups. This was established in 1983, initially on the premises of St Paul's Church, Deansgate, where two sisters, Dorothy and Kathleen Fawell, had been praying for BMMF for many years. Later it moved to the Emmanuel Church Centre. Particularly active in producing audio-visual resource material for Asian work was Nishi Sharma. He had been converted from a Hindu background, and he and his English wife Ruth served in India, seconded by BMMF first to the Far East Broadcasting Association of India and then to UESI where they worked among Hindi-speaking students and in an audio-visual ministry. In 1980 they moved to England, and Nishi developed his audio-visual work first for Scripture Union and then in the Interserve office in London. He has produced many invaluable tools for Asian work, among them a teaching pack, 'Through Their Eyes'.

In 1983, too, another key couple arrived to work with BMMF in Bolton: Robin and Ros Holley. They had sensed a missionary call for many years, but even after a trip to Asia in 1982 the way forward was not clear. Then in August they heard Margaret Wardell speaking at a BMMF conference, and both independently sensed, 'This is it.' However, inspired though they were by her account of her work, they still did not know how to respond to their call – there was no framework within which to start. Writing to Arthur Pont of BMMF (UK), they were intrigued by his cryptic reply: 'Stay with us. We're interested.' Their letter had arrived on his desk at just the time that the BMMF Council was meeting to set up the framework that was needed. Indeed 1983 was a crucial year. With Wilfred Paul's pioneering work in and beyond Bolton supported by Richard Cook's and George Skinner's surveys, BMMF's North West Committee taking on the work of the Bolton Council of Reference, and the Resources Centre established, the name 'MAB' (Ministry among Asians in Britain) was devised by George and Wilfred and adopted by BMMF as part of its ministry. The aim, as always with BMMF, was to serve and enable the local churches to carry out this ministry as effectively as possible.

When Robin and Ros applied to BMMF, they did not fit the criteria for MAB workers, not having worked in Asia nor being Asians. The Personnel Committee also had reservations about a middle-aged couple with teenage children uprooting from the south of England, giving up their jobs and moving to Bolton. However, as they prayed on, the way opened for them to go as Field Partners with BMMF: Robin getting an unusually quick transfer in the Post Office, Ros miraculously landing a nursing job, not normally given to newcomers, in a health centre in a Gujerati area.

Ros moved north first, and found herself befriended by Asian neighbours who knew what it was like to be alone in a strange town. It was pioneering work, as they set about making friends. Ros gave a party for the children in the street, and the mothers collecting them afterwards said, 'Please visit us.' She began arranging outings and video afternoons. Often the door-bell would ring: 'Sister Ros, will you read this letter for me . . . take me to hospital . . . advise about my child's illness . . .'. Sometimes they were made use of; often they received as much love and support as they gave; always they were building bridges and establishing trust. By 1985 Ros had left her job and in 1986 Robin followed suit. Supported now by BMMF, they were free to concentrate fully on their Asian work which centred more and more around their church, St Luke's, and in the setting up of a multi-racial satellite church in a Punjabi/Gujerati area. Taking assemblies in local schools, running holiday ventures and Bible clubs, Ros was able to share the Gospel with large numbers of Asian children. They also supported the Asian Christian Fellowship in Bolton, helped by visits from Jim Hunter of BMMF who, having worked in Pakistan for many years, was fluent in Urdu. Over the years they saw some real conversions, and also encountered much opposition, including vandalism from the white community, demon possession and black magic.

Others to join the MAB team in Bolton were Arthur and Hilary Jones. After teaching in Birmingham, they had been Field Partners with BMMF, teaching first at Wynberg-Allen, then Gorakhpur, North India and then at Gandaki School, Pokhara in Nepal. They had hoped to join MAB in Bolton in 1984 when unable to return to India for visa reasons, but the urgent need for help at Gandaki School had postponed this, and they eventually arrived in 1987. Invited by the Diocese and seconded and supported by BMMF to help the local churches reach out to the local community, Arthur found himself taking over the running of the Resources Centre from George Skinner. Hilary worked in the local Council's 'speak-teach' project and later became a Citizens' Advice Bureau outreach worker, holding a clinic for parents in the school.

I visited Arthur in the Resources Centre in Emmanuel Church Centre and saw the specialist library with a large range of books and reports relating to racial issues in the inner cities. There are Bibles and audio-visual material for sale in Asian languages, and teaching material for church members. Arthur dealt with cataloguing, copying of tapes, arranging conferences, as well as writing. He reckoned that radical rethinking is needed in Asian outreach. Asians are barely being touched, and the reason, he said, is that they belong to close-knit communities and do not find a comparable sense of community if they turn to Christ: 'The danger is that if they become Christians they lose a

community and gain a meeting' – a frightening thought.
And yet it is the very closeness of the community which,
while it gives Asians their security, can also imprison them –
particularly the women. And the youngsters born, brought
up and educated in this country are torn between the two
cultures: the security and closed-in nature of their own
communities, and the materialistic freedoms of the West.
What a need for the Christian faith, which as Arthur pointed
out, is neither a Western nor a white religion, to be faithfully
proclaimed.

At about the same time as the Holleys went to Bolton,
another couple came to pioneer similar work in nearby
Oldham. George Whetham, a farmer, and his wife Karin
had been involved in the rehabilitation work in Bangladesh
following the war which led to Independence. They had
then transferred to Lahore in Pakistan, establishing schools
among a professional beggar tribe, the Lali Faqirs. In
Pakistan George became seriously ill and they were forced
to return to the UK. They had no idea what to do, still
hoping to work among Asians, but unable to return. It was
then that they were approached by George Skinner about
the possibility of working alongside the vicar of St Thomas's
Church, Werneth, to develop an Asian ministry. As Karin
put it, 'All our moving about suddenly made sense, and
the different languages we had learnt. In Oldham there
are such a variety of people, from India, from Pakistan,
from Bangladesh. Wherever they come from, we can say
we've been there!' George soon set up a second hand stall in
the 'Flea Market' in Oldham, selling bric-à-brac and clothes
as well as carrying a wide range of Bibles, cassettes and
videos in various languages which people could borrow.
In addition they ran a Saturday children's club and holiday
clubs, all of which were appreciated, and made links with
Asian families, and Karin taught Asian women English.

Also in Oldham were Steven and Margaret Masood,
Steven writing and directing a correspondence course for
Muslims called 'Word of Life'. He was brought up on the
northern frontier of Pakistan in an Ahmadiyya Muslim

family. Reading as a teenager what both the Qur'an and the Bible said about Jesus, he found that, 'There was a kind of enchantment and appeal in Jesus's personality. The love and affection he showed for children captivated me. Muhammad and Mirza Ahmad were my heroes but day by day the person of Jesus was overtaking them in every way. When I was eighteen I left my home and my people, to search for HIM. At the age of twenty-three I found him and surrendered my life to him.' More recently Jim Hunter, with experience as a missionary engineer to the former Caravan Hospital and then as Project Director of Kunri Hospital in Pakistan, was appointed Vicar of St Thomas's Church, Werneth. He believed it was God's hand that brought together this group of people dedicated to work among Asians there, and George and Karin, too, were encouraged and hoping for new growth after years of groundwork in Oldham. Others working with MAB in the north of England included Lee and Angela Burrows sharing the love of God with Muslims in Middlesbrough (Lee from Egypt and Angela a Bengali), and the Rev David Corfe, Asian Worker in Old Trafford, Manchester. David and his wife Rosemary had both worked in India with BMMF, and were invited by a group of ethnic churches – Chinese, Jamaican, and others – to help them to reach out to their Asian neighbours from a base at St Bride's Anglican Church.

In the Midlands, too, MAB is at work. In Birmingham Tim and Satpal Boyes, both teaching in a Muslim area of the city, were joined by Frances Iliff who previously nursed and did radio work in Afghanistan, India and Pakistan before embarking on a church-based ministry amongst the Asian community. The Rev John Ray, MAB's Chairman who had previously worked with CMS in India and Pakistan for many years, was ministering there as well. And in Leicester Basil Scott, based at an inner-city church, was the National Co-ordinator of MAB. Basil and his wife Shirley had lived and worked in India for many years, where Basil was on the staff of UESI and also BMMF's India Superintendent.

In 1983 they left India, and in 1984 Basil was appointed to lead the MAB team. In less than five years he saw it grow remarkably: between 1987 and 1989 the number of workers doubled from fifteen to thirty. He felt very strongly that, 'working in this country among the immigrant population is what gives us credibility. For years British Christians have crossed the seas to reach Asian people in their countries of origin. Now they are here on our doorstep, we must reach out to them with the love of Christ. We are in a missionary situation in this country.' He summarised the aims of MAB as follows: evangelism by Christians of all races among people of all faiths in Britain; education of the churches to reflect the multi-cultural body of Christ and to meet the needs of Asian people; co-operation amongst churches and missions working with Asians; and training of Asian Christians for ministry in churches in the UK and elsewhere.

Another leader of the MAB work was Keith Wood. A school-teacher, he became Home Secretary of BMMF (UK), based in the London Office, and then in 1984 he moved to York as Northern Secretary. He was closely involved with the setting up of the Bolton project, observing that 'it was done on a shoestring and remained on a shoestring: an example of the church at its weakest and poorest pioneering something vital.' Once there, he concentrated on the need for Christian workers in the multi-faith context of the North and the Midlands, bringing those concerned together in friendship and fellowship, aware of the lonely furrow they ploughed. In 1987 Keith helped to launch an 'Urban Ministries Training Scheme': a scheme for two-year placements in which, working with a church in a multi-racial area, people gain experience and learn on the job. The first UMTS trainee was Sally Morton who went straight from taking a degree in modern languages at Oxford to work in Bradford in 1987. Peter and Joan Bell also served under this scheme in an Islamic area of Huddersfield. Peter, a Lancashire textile designer preparing for Asian ministry, was approached through MAB by the Vicar of St Stephen's

Church, Rashcliffe to help the church reach out to its Asian neighbours. But they soon found that the family they befriended next door were forbidden to visit them by the community leaders; a holiday bus for children was vandalised and a church banner promoting a summer holiday club was ripped up. It was a struggle, and they very much needed support, but they battled on.

Looking back over his work, latterly as MAB's Administrative Secretary, Keith Wood highlighted the endeavour to be supportive and to give full recognition to Asian Christians, observing that their pastors, often not in the mainstream churches, tended to be bypassed and disregarded. He gave, for example, full support to Pastor Massey in Oxford, with the result that together they convened some conferences for Asian pastors. Keith was happy to have been a servant and enabler.

MAB is eager to train cross-cultural workers, whether of Asian origin or not. Usually Asian Christians are best suited to evangelism, while English Christians with cross-cultural experience are needed to train church members to reach out and welcome Asians into the churches. MAB provides an ideal opportunity for partnership between Western and Asian Christians in a multi-racial team. Its workers are attached to local churches – usually invited by a church which has become aware of the need for someone experienced in this work to help them.

Someone who felt strongly the importance of the church-based nature of MAB work was the evangelist Sukesh Pabari, based in Bristol. His Gujerati grandfather left India for Kenya early this century, and the family came to Britain in 1975. An accountant involved in the installation of computer terminals in British Aerospace factories, he was converted through the witness of a friend at work and through reading the Epistle to the Romans. He soon became burdened for his fellow Asians without Christ, and linked up with the Bristol Asian Ministry, visiting Asians, leading Bible studies and taking evangelistic meetings.

In 1989 a group of Bristol churches – Baptist and

Anglican – decided they needed a full-time Asian worker for the 15,000 Sikhs and Muslims living in the city. They approached Interserve who seconded Sukesh for this work. He studied theology part time at Trinity College, Bristol, and began his work as an evangelist. I met him in his book-lined study (the books mainly the works of the Puritan writers): 'The Asian community don't quite know what to make of me,' he said. 'I aim to help the churches to set things up – children's clubs and so on. I am not a children's worker myself. I belong to the local Baptist church – "Kensington Baptist" – and they have really caught the vision. They're eager to take up ideas and put them into practice.' There is an Asian Christian Fellowship, too, with about fifty people who meet on Sunday afternoons: a welcome opportunity for Asians to meet to worship and to talk about spiritual things in their own languages. This started with three or four Christian families who decided to meet, and grew as members invited friends and extended family, and as nominal Christians found Christ for themselves. Sukesh concentrated on giving them Bible teaching in their own languages, so that eventually some of them would take on leadership. Most of all, his concern was to lead his fellow Asians to Christ and then to help them to become established in multi-cultural churches.

Sukesh was wholeheartedly committed to the vision for a multi-cultural church that is also a missionary church: 'The people in Jerusalem at Pentecost spoke so many different languages. Empowered by the Holy Spirit, they later went back to their own countries. I hope the Sikhs and Muslims here in Bristol will eventually go back to the Punjab, taking the Gospel with them.' He aimed, too, to help people to come to Christ without breaking their own family ties which are so important to them: like the young believer he knew who still lived with his Muslim mother and sister and tried to show the reality of Christ's love to them at home. Sukesh hoped to help young people's families to see that they can become Christians without becoming totally westernised. Another unusual enterprise in Bristol was the shop called

'Basics' which was acquired by Kensington Baptist Church and which sold, not tracts or Bibles, but items of hardware, toiletries etc – the 'basic' things someone might need on moving into the area. Sukesh and others from the church took turns to serve in the shop on a voluntary basis. They found it an ideal neutral chatting ground; a good base for building bridges in the community.

MAB is also involved in inner-city work in London. Sung Hee Kwon, for example, came to England to study at All Nations Christian College, expecting to go straight back to work in South Korea. Instead God called her to stay for a time before returning to train missionaries in Korea. Becoming an Interserve Partner, she led a mission and ran a weekly Bible study group in Streatham, south London, with many nationalities represented and many turning to Christ. At one time the group included a Buddhist nun, Jehovah's Witnesses from Burma, Pakistanis, Malaysians and Kenyans: nine nationalities were represented, and eight people turned to Christ in just four months. 'I have noticed that foreigners in London open their minds to me and talk to me about their problems – maybe because I am a foreigner too,' she commented. And as the pastor of Streatham Baptist Church observed, 'She is governed by the heart, not the filofax. She is helping us to be a witness to the community.'

Also in London was Bobby Bose, for some years a full-time worker in Tower Hamlets, but joining MAB more recently for fellowship. Born in Calcutta, he was brought up in a strongly Christian home and committed his own life to Christ at the age of seven. He came to the UK in 1983 for theological studies, intending to return to India; was invited by the East London Tabernacle to help them in community and Gospel work in Tower Hamlets and has been there ever since. In 1990 he married Margie, who came to Britain as a missionary from the USA. The community is primarily Bengali and Muslim, and as Bobby said, 'From time to time one does see interest in the Gospel in ones and twos, but pretty soon it is squashed by community and family pressures.' The Association of Bengali Christians in the UK was started by Bobby to support those who turn to Christ. Also in the East End of London, Canon Patrick Sookhdeo directed his complementary organisation called In Contact Ministries. As well as ministering to the congregation of St Andrew's, Plaistow which is drawn from over twenty different ethnic groups in the area, he co-ordinated international outreach to Muslims. And two other Interserve Partners, Graham and Sabine Stockton, were appointed by a church in Gravesend to help it relate to the thousands of Asians there.

When Graham's wife was killed in the Philippines where they had been working with the Overseas Missionary Fellowship, he came back to England in 1987 with three small children and moved to Gravesend where he had a house and was a deacon of the local Baptist church. Church leaders there had been praying for someone to start work in the large Asian community, and Graham took up the challenge, seconded first to Interserve by OMF. He set to work in various ways, teaching English as a volunteer at the Adult Education Centre, chatting to fellow parents at his children's school, educating local churches about reaching out to Asians. In 1989 he married Sabine, from Germany, who had been working among Bangladeshis in London's East End. Graham left OMF and Sabine the Shaftesbury Society with whom she had been working, and both became Partners with Interserve. Sabine subsequently became aware through her own pregnancy of the needs of Asian women at such a time – often speaking little English, very isolated, needing help with transport as their husbands worked long hours. She was welcomed on to the chaplaincy team of the maternity hospital, where she helped with communication, trying to give Punjabi women the confidence that somebody cared, sometimes raising necessary equipment and help from the local church. Graham meantime developed links with a few local men, Punjabi and Cambodian, some of whom began coming for weekly Bible study – a real encouragement.

Besides factors already mentioned, such as the risk of loss of family and community for those who turn to Christ, various other things militate against success in MAB's work. One is the counter-productive effect of low secular moral standards in Britain and other Western countries, which Asians, used to culture and religion being closely linked, associate with Christianity. Another is the strength of Asian communities, which are now well organised to meet the needs of their members and keep them from following other faiths. Thirdly there is the sad fact that often the churches themselves appear to have no vision or interest in sharing the Gospel with Asians – either because they genuinely believe it is not possible or desirable for people of other faiths to be drawn to Christ, or because of lingering racial prejudice, or because they are unaware of simple changes in their behaviour which would make Asian people feel welcome.

These attitudes are slowly changing, and MAB workers are involved in educating church members in what can be done. Joan and Ruth Millson and Jan Clark had all worked in India. Back in the UK, Joan moved to Slough and Ruth and Jan to north London. As well as teaching English and reaching out to Asian women in various ways, they were concerned to show their fellow Christians simple steps they can take – obvious once you think of them, but easy to neglect – to make their Asian friends welcome: signs written in appropriate languages, church people dressing in ways that Asians find acceptable, offering appropriate food, respecting sex distinctions – providing separate clubs and so on for girls.

Joan Millson's links with Asian work in Britain went back a long way. Having gone out initially by ship to teach geography at Wynberg-Allen School in India, she flew back on leave in 1969, arriving at Heathrow. Seeing the crowds of Indians at the airport, almost as if she had never left India, she wondered why she had to go so far to minister to them: it seemed that there was a mission field at home. In fact she did go back and taught at Queen Mary School, Bombay, for

some years, and in TEE. More and more though, she became
certain that God wanted her in England, and eventually,
with an Indian TEE student qualified to take over her
work, the time seemed right and she came back, first to
work among international students, and then in 1983 to
Slough with MAB where she taught Asian women English,
befriending and reaching out to them in the community.

Ruth Millson and Jan Clark had also worked with TEE in
Bombay. Having to leave for visa reasons, they were invited
to join a church-based Asian ministry in north London.
They launched a new venture: TESL classes which were
church-based, recognised but not run by the local authority.
These were very popular and had the advantage that church
people could become involved – running creches, forming
friendships and so on. Ruth continued in this work and in
training Asian workers; Jan went on from TESL work into
training for the ministry in the Church of England where her
experience of Asian work was to stand her in good stead.

The UK Council have consistently supported the expensive pioneer programme of MAB. In this, as in all its work,
Interserve aims to make Christ known through evangelism
and service. New ground is being broken as a group which
began so long ago to serve people in India now finds
the people of the Indian sub-continent on its doorstep.
Britain, the first 'sending' country of ZBMM, is now well
and truly part of the 'field'. Similar developments will no
doubt occur in other 'sending' countries. There is already
an Ethnic Ministry Programme in America, where Moses
and Nancy Jesudass reach out to immigrants in southern
California through TEE and Bible correspondence courses;
and in Canada.

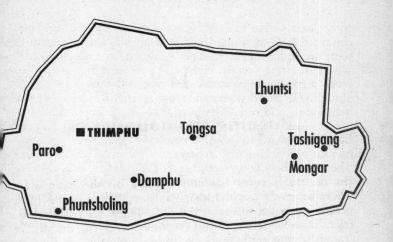

BHUTAN

14

Pushing the boundaries

So far this history has concentrated on the main areas of Interserve's work: India, Pakistan, Nepal, the Middle East, and more recently, the UK. There are other areas, too, where Interserve has become involved, usually in response to specific need. Notable among these is Bhutan, a small land-locked mountain kingdom to the east of Nepal: 'Land of the Thunder Dragon', a country with fabulous monasteries or dzongs clinging to vertical mountain-sides, enchanting trees, flowers, waterfalls and chalet-style houses. The major religion is Tibetan Buddhism, although in the south there are considerable numbers of Hindus, many of Nepali origin, and a few Christians, also mostly from Nepal or India. Until 1964 few Christians were allowed into the country, but in the 1960s Bhutan, like Nepal some ten years earlier, began to open up channels of communication with the outside world and to invite help with development.

The way this happened in God's providence was remarkable. Following Indian Independence in 1947, Bhutan remained isolated socially, linguistically and intellectually. It was the Chinese invasion of Tibet in 1959 which forced the Bhutanese to realise that unless they modernised their country and allowed themselves to be allied with India politically, they could well be swallowed by the Chinese dragon, too. But you can't bring a country into the twentieth century without relating to other people. Bhutan sent its brightest sons and daughters to the best available schools in India – which happened to be run by Christians. This meant that they not only heard the Christian message, but they also were educated in English, which opened Bhutan linguistically to the rest of the world. English became the second national language – a tremendous advantage for communication.

Indian blue-collar workers were invited into the country – teachers, nurses, engineers, secretaries, many of whom were Christians, especially those from Kerala and the South. Similarly Nepalis came – office workers and labourers, together with Nepali nurses from mission hospitals in Darjeeling – and so Nepali speakers, some of them Christians, were added to the mix. Roads were built – largely by the Indian Army – for defensive purposes against China. This improved communication again. Instead of taking a week or more to walk from the Indian border to Thimphu, it could be done in a day, by bus. Finally Western organisations, including missionary societies, were invited to provide various skills and services. In the east of Bhutan the Norwegian Santal Mission set up medical work, and the Swedish Blind Mission a school for the blind. The Jesuits contributed as well, and in 1964 three members of the Leprosy Mission were invited to the capital, Thimphu, to discuss the possibility of starting a programme of leprosy care. As a result, and with personal interest and support from the Bhutanese royal family, a small leprosy hospital was built at Gida Kom, fifteen miles from the capital, to be followed by another hospital at Mongar to the east.

The first BMMF member to be seconded to the Leprosy Mission's work in Bhutan was Barbara Burrett, a nursing specialist in community health from the UK, who started work at Mongar. She found the country peaceful, its small population of 600,000 or so people largely self-sufficient. Although TB and leprosy were prevalent, as were illnesses caused by lack of sanitation and hygiene, she found many people healthy and well fed. As she put it, 'a people untouched by television, radio or telephones, whose luxuries arrive in the form of soap and rubber flip-flops. Life is simple, but not unhappy.' To her, the all-important question was just how the love of Christ could be communicated across the cultural divide. Evangelism and preaching were forbidden, but Christian worship was allowed for staff within the hospital. Patients could not be invited to attend, but they did not have to be turned away, and balconies were public, after all . . .

Soon Barbara was joined by a young woman doctor who was destined to become one of BMMF's most intrepid and adventurous pioneers: Ray (Rachel) Pinniger from the UK. Ray's parents were enthusiastic supporters of missions, and their home was always full of missionaries coming and going. As a result, when the time came for her to do her elective as a medical student, she went to Tansen Hospital in Nepal. Then after further training in paediatrics and obstetrics and a further two-year spell at Tansen, she was seconded by BMMF to the Leprosy Mission's hospital at Mongar to do general medicine. She found the work less challenging than at Tansen. There were few patients as the hospital was remote and the people had little trust in Western medicine. After fifteen months she was invited to go to Thimphu for work in the paediatric unit of the 150-bed government hospital. The unit was being set up to mark the 'International Year of the Child' in 1979. When Ray arrived, the foundations were not yet laid; she watched it being built, mostly by female labour. Together with nurse Joy McConnell, who transferred with her, Ray set about establishing the first paediatric provision in Bhutan, also training and supervising community health auxiliaries to work among women and children. Joy became the hospital's Theatre Sister. She had brought a number of operating instruments into the country, and did what she could to improve equipment, procedures and training in the operating theatre.

Ray's work at Mongar had meanwhile been taken over by John Burslem, a surgeon with a special interest in leprosy whose sister Fiona was the doctor at Multan in Pakistan. John, a former marine commando from Yorkshire in the north of England, had been contemplating becoming a 'semi-professional mountaineer', doing medical locums and spending his salary on climbing expeditions, when during a trek in Nepal in 1977, he had to spend some time in a tiny clinic with a sick friend. While there he helped out temporarily as the clinic doctor and was shattered by the death of a young woman who was brought to him too late for help. She had had what could have been a trivial abdominal injury from a cow's horn while pregnant. By the time she had been carried three days to a clinic where the doctor was away, one day to a further clinic where she was given an injection and then aborted, and two more days to the clinic where John was, the horrendous journey back and forward over the mountains had led to gas gangrene, peritonitis, and as John watched helplessly, finally to death. As he saw it, 'This woman's death, or at least others like it, could be laid fairly on my doorstep. As I frittered away my time, money, and expertise on self-indulgent trivia, young mothers were suffering from want of a few pennyworth of care.' He went straight home and joined Interserve, fully prepared to commit the rest of his life to serving needy people like this wherever God might lead.

Three years later, having studied at All Nations Christian College where he met his wife Hilary, he flew to Bhutan, seconded to Mongar Hospital. Then, ironically, the tragedy that triggered his full commitment to Christ was mirrored when in 1987 Hilary died giving birth to their second child. Though suspecting that things were not going to be straightforward, they had decided against her returning to the UK for the birth. As John put it later, 'There's no way she was going to go racing off. What sort of witness is that? Childbirth is a major cause of death among Bhutanese women. You can't have Christian folk rushing back home for every bit and piece' – a practical application of Interserve's guideline that its Partners' life-style must give credibility to their ministry. Things did indeed go wrong, with a severe haemorrhage in the course of a caesarian section, and despite John's own intervention and a six-hour battle for her life, she died, although their baby daughter lived.*

As John wrote, the two funeral services which were held, one in Mongar and one in Thimphu, had large congregations of local people and government staff, and in Mongar the Gospel was preached in public for the first time. It was an opportunity to proclaim by word and life that the Christ of the Christians has truly overcome death. Interserve colleagues saluted John and Hilary's integrity, but continue to be concerned that their Partners, and especially pregnant mothers, have full medical support and care. Alone for a while and then with his second wife Helen who had previously worked in Nepal, John stayed on at Mongar.

In October 1981 another BMMF Partner arrived as medical specialist at the government hospital in Thimphu to join Ray and Joy: Dr John Sleggs from the UK with his wife Melody. John had previously looked after the medical ward and outpatients at Tansen, but back in England on home leave he had been asked by BMMF to transfer to Thimphu in response to a specific need. He found the new situation very different in various ways. For one thing, he now specialised in hospital medicine: 'anything you can treat with pills' – at Tansen his work had been more that of a hospital-based GP. Then this was a government hospital, whereas Tansen was run by UMN under government protocol. Here at Thimphu John and Ray were the only Christian doctors and the direction of the hospital was in the hands of the Bhutanese Medical Director. At Tansen all patients were treated equally, apart from a few private patients; here staff were expected to treat VIPs with special deference. At Tansen trust and efficiency were hall-marks; here John was grieved to see patients' treatment interrupted through inefficiency and delays in obtaining medical supplies. He did his best to change what he could and to live with what he could not, and to balance the required deference with care for the needy and poor. TB was endemic, and there

* See John Mayberry and Richard Mann, *God's Doctors Abroad* (Gooday, 1989).

was also much hypertension because of the high intake of (delicious) salted butter tea. On the other hand there was less night-blindness (caused by vitamin A deficiency) than in Nepal because of the widespread consumption of red chillies.

Spiritually the situation was encouraging – more so than in Tansen, where the church had always seemed to struggle. Here in Thimphu, as well as meetings which were primarily for English-speaking expatriates, there were three thriving Nepali-speaking churches: one, led by an Indian Christian from Kerala, had started with the miraculous healing of a thirteen-year-old girl whose family were then converted. The congregation, many of them Nepali road workers, were full of praise, if short on teaching. Then there was a 'Bhakt Singh' group, also led by an Indian Christian: anti-charismatic, rather like the Brethren, with a number of Nepali shop-keepers involved; and a third group which included several Nepali hospital workers, where John led Bible studies and sometimes preached as well as teaching with TAFTEE. Melody helped with a Sunday school, and Ray and Joy ran a social group for Bhutanese Health School boys. All three churches saw regular converts, possibly partly because these Nepalis were separated from their extended families and therefore free to choose their own life-style; also because they were very strong on prayer, having a day of prayer and fasting every week. However, life for the Christians is not easy. There are many pressures on them, and for Bhutanese of Nepali origin there are political pressures as well. Through it all Jigme Norbhu, who was suddenly removed from his post as Mayor of Thimphu and who was to suffer many more setbacks, was able to declare, 'If one views the situation from the worldly point of view, I am the greatest fool who lost position, prestige, respect, money and so on. But personally I feel the Lord has chosen me to be worthy of a crown of life in heaven.'

Among the original Bhutanese, or Drukpas, it is proving very difficult for a church to be established. A few have turned to Christ while abroad, but have mostly reverted to Buddhism on their return. Family links are strong, and it is hard for a Christian to be different. There seems to be strong spiritual as well as family opposition, and this affects expatriate workers too, who suffer many attacks upon their health. There is also a linguistic problem. Many Christian concepts like that of sin and of a personal God do not exist in Buddhism, so it is hard to explain them in Buddhist languages. So daunting is the task that it is not easy to find people to translate the Scriptures into Dzhongka. There are a few Drukpa Christians across the country, but they meet in Nepali churches, as Bhutan still struggles towards the planting of the first truly Bhutanese church.

Among others to work in Bhutan over the years have been Shelagh Wynne, daughter of Laurence and Margaret Wynne of the USA, who had previously used her nursing and midwifery training in Nepal and who became Assistant Matron at Thimphu, Dimity Compston from Australia teaching in the Health School, Sue Leathley (UK), pharmacist at Thimphu and Andrew and Muriel Schachtel from Australia and Northern Ireland respectively. Andrew was a nutritionist and the Interserve Regional Representative for Bhutan. At present several Interserve Partners, notably but not exclusively from Australia and Holland, are seconded to the Government of Bhutan to work in various areas of health, nutrition, agriculture, engineering and irrigation. Opportunities like this do arise, and the need is always for Interserve Partners with the particular expertise to respond promptly when they do.

As for Ray Pinniger, her frustration in the face of endless red tape did not diminish, and she eventually began to feel she had contributed as much as she could. Back in the UK, a new challenge was opening up. She was invited by Squadron Leader Mike Cole, leader of the previous hovercraft expedition on the Kali Gandaki river in Nepal, to lead the medical team in a new hovercraft exploration, up the Yangtze river in China in the summer of 1990. A description of the expedition falls outside the scope of this book, but when Ray, later described by a fellow team-member as 'a delightful, shrewd, unthreatening lady, whose fire for the missionary task has been tempered by many years work in the Third World to a strong blend of faith and patience', was asked how she felt about the discomforts she might experience on the trip, her reply was characteristically 'laid back' and worthy of ZBMM's early pioneers: 'So long as one is fit and reasonably relaxed about life, I see no reason why this expedition should be very different to what I am used to.'

Ray visited Mongolia too, at the invitation of John Gibbens, an Englishman married to a Mongolian who had many links there. He finally completed a translation of the New Testament into the traditional Mongolian vertical script – a task he had worked on for eighteen years. The Mongolian Republic was keen to build links with the West since the ending of its Comecon pact with Russia and Eastern Europe. John had been asked about the possibility of aid from Christians, and suggested that Ray be consulted. She took medicines and had a meeting with the Minister of Health who sought her advice on drawing up a list of essential drugs.

Already by 1991 it had been decided that Interserve, with more than thirty years' experience of work among Tibetan Buddhists in Nepal, India and Bhutan, would recognise Mongolia as a region of its work. The aim would be to supply people with professional skills, especially English teachers – viewed by the Mongolian authorities as the key to its economic future – to Mongolia by December 1992. On October 1st 1992 a united venture called Joint Christian Services (Mongolia) was formed by eight agencies including Interserve and the Overseas Missionary Fellowship with Richard Clark of Interserve Chairman of the Board. In 1992 two Partners were in Mongolia doing language study and teaching English as a second language – Hugh (son of Ian and Elizabeth) Kemp and his wife Karen, from New Zealand. This move followed the drafting of a resolution at Lausanne II Conference on World Evangelism in Manila in 1989 to help Mongol believers build their Church, without creating dependency. After sixty years of Communism a large proportion of the population was atheist, some Tibetan Buddhists, and the first small church was established in 1990.

Then, with the newly independent republics of Central Asia on the old 'Silk Road' between India and China eager for the help of doctors, technicians and those with entrepreneurial skills, Interserve's International Executive Committee decided in May 1992 to extend its work to them. Whereas the extension into Mongolia arose out of a general cmomitment to Tibetan Buddhists, this new response to the needs of the Central Asian Republics – Uzbekistan, Tajikistan, Kazakhstan, Kyrghyzstan, Turkmenistan and Azerbaijan – arose from Interserve's commitment and experience in the Muslim world and their previous experience in Afghanistan, Iran and Turkey. Straight away two or three couples began preparing for a location in one of the Central Asian republics. Similarly Interserve was working with others to place and support professionals in western China with a focus on those of the Muslim and Tibetan Buddhist faiths. In 1992 seven Interserve Partners were in China, meeting specific needs with their professional skills.

15

Young people

'We are willing to serve anywhere, provided we don't have to be separated from the children!' How often have parents told selection boards this. Schools for 'mish-kids' have been of the greatest importance in Interserve since 1952 when married couples began to be accepted, as without them many missionaries would not have been able to remain long term on the field. Many are boarding schools and inevitably do involve some degree of separation, but at least parents and children are on the same continent.

Murree Christian School, established on a former army hill station forty miles north of Rawalpindi in northern Pakistan, is set in a pine-clad circle of hills with majestic mountains behind. It was opened in 1956 in an ex-army church building and Sande's soldiers' home which were left when the British withdrew. Many of the children are American, their parents serving, for instance, with the United Presbyterian Church which has been active in Pakistan for many years. But pupils come from many other countries, and their parents work in other countries too. Over the years Interserve has provided teachers, and Interserve families' children have been educated here, as they have at Woodstock, an international school seven thousand feet up in the foothills of the Himalayas at Mussoorie, India.

Woodstock School was founded by missionaries in 1854. As Gavin McIntosh, of Interserve (NZ) and Vice-Principal described, 'Visitors are struck by the beauty of the place, and the coolness after the baking heat of the plain below. But beautiful though it is, living here is not always easy. To get anywhere means a steep climb up or down. Stone and cement walls shore up building sites and roadways, and the trees – cedars, rhododendrons, and evergreen oaks – help to keep the hill in place. Our only playing field is an irregular-shaped wedge between two hills, always harassed by monsoon deposit and subsidence.' The monsoon brings rain, mist, landslips and mildew. Wind and storms play havoc with the power supply, communication with Dehra Dun below is often obstructed. Health, too, of both pupils and teaching staff can suffer. Some people find the isolation and the spartan conditions all too much to bear. Others rejoice in the beauties of the hills. Pupils are approximately one third American, one third Indian and one third from other countries. Parents are missionaries, diplomats, businessmen, top government officials in neighbouring countries or serving perhaps with the United Nations, UNICEF, and other relief organisations. Nephews of Pandit Nehru and relatives of the King of Bhutan were educated here. Educational standards have always been high, with Interserve Partners well represented on the staff. The teaching syllabus is American, but many students are also prepared for English exams. Discipline and morale have at times been low, with drug problems and teenage rebellion getting out of hand. At other times there has been transformation and revival. One big bonus at Mussoorie is that one or both parents can easily make a temporary home near the school for some months – for example, at holiday time.

Teaching and other related work at international schools like Woodstock is almost the only exception to India's 'no visas for expatriates' rule, so some of the few expat. Interserve Partners in India are teaching in these schools. Two I met who were enthusiastic were Jeff and Ruth Auty, from New Zealand. They first met at Woodstock, and were the first couple of the three engagements for May 1982 and one of a total of five marriages in that year. Neither had come to Woodstock with BMMF, but they decided to join when they married for various reasons: for one thing, Ruth, doing residence work, had five BMMF children under her care. Also the mission impressed them particularly by the love and care shown to the children not only by parents but by older 'aunties' who, staying at Edgehill on holiday, looked after them as though they were their own. Ruth had seen slides of Woodstock shown at her church in New Zealand when she was young, and as she says, 'I remember thinking it would be a great place to go one day. Now, I cannot think of any greater place to be – except heaven!'

Also in Mussoorie is the Wynberg-Allen School, originally an orphanage for children of the neglected Anglo-Indian community which became the Wynberg School for Girls. In 1926 the Allen Memorial Boys' School was added – built as a memorial to Mr H.D. Allen, a dedicated Christian, businessman and Plymouth Brethren lay-preacher, the father of Rosalind Broomhall and Monica Lehmann. He had taken great interest in the children of the Wynberg School, but his hopes of seeing a boys' school added were forestalled by his early death. His widow provided funds for the new school, and now Wynberg, the girls' section, stands on a high rise of the ridge, directly below Mussoorie's clock-tower landmark, while Allen stands some three hundred feet below. Children move backwards and forwards, up and down the hillside, between classes – a necessity which keeps them fit. Wynberg-Allen caters for children from many countries, including India, and particularly for refugees from Tibet. Henry Allen's son-in-law, Dr Geoffrey Lehmann, served on the board of Wynberg-Allen School for over forty years.

Other international schools, in southern India, are Kodaikanal, which emphasises special educational needs, and Hebron, a co-educational boarding school in the hills at Ootacamund (now called Uthagamandalam) which caters particularly for the children of Christian workers, together with some from business families, and provides a Western-style education with GCSEs. The Vice-Principal,

Peter Hill, and his wife Annette who was the school doctor and taught music, were both Interserve Partners. For the staff, it is not easy to combine the Western way of raising young people, with its free social interaction between boys and girls, with the stricter expectations of Indian Christian families. The Principal, Rod Gilbert, saw that as one of his greatest challenges – to look at social attitudes not just from a cultural stand-point but to search out a biblical view.

This difficulty relates to the general one which faces all international schools: the different culturally-based expectations which must be catered for. But the bonuses are many, in the generally high standards of education and the broad horizons which such mixed communities inevitably open up. Children educated in these schools are well prepared to be citizens of the world. As Joan and Anthony Sinclair put it, having worked at Murree, 'Mishkids are often more mature than those from one culture and more aware of world issues. They are often good at discovering other people's needs and getting alongside them. They can be multi-lingual and adept at living and communicating multi-culturally.' Joan and Anthony were also aware of the considerable difficulty such youngsters often have in relating to their own culture and contemporaries when they return to their country of origin – perhaps for university – and back in the UK did all they could to help to meet this need, arranging special gatherings and offering friendship and support to such young people.

Another aspect of Interserve's involvement with young people lies in its efforts to educate them in the reality and possibilities of missionary work. The earliest effort in this direction, started in the late '50s, was known as 'Ambassadors': the vision of Barbara Spanner from the UK who directed it for several years. As well as an evangelistic programme staffed partly by new BMMF candidates, her idea was that if Interserve was to draw recruits well prepared for a long-term missionary career, they would benefit from learning and thinking about it early in life. There were summer houseparties when the young people could meet and get to know serving missionaries. Hundreds of young people came, and as a result many became friends and prayer supporters, and some eventually became missionaries themselves. Margaret Wilson, principal later of Kinnaird High School, Jeanette Short, Janette Cowan and Moonyeen Littleton were four people among many others who were introduced to BMMF through Ambassadors. Initially for girls only, soon Peter Bayes developed a boys' programme which included sailing holidays on the Norfolk Broads.

Ambassadors was succeeded by a varied programme of short-term missionary experience which Interserve has provided under various names for some years. Before 1970 the possibility of short-term work did not exist. People offering to BMMF were expected to commit themselves for life. But at the Quadrennial Conference in 1970, sensing a new concern for world mission among young people, it was decided to create a structure for short-term assignments which would give some insight into openings abroad. The first such scheme, was known as HOP (Holidays Overseas Project), and BMMF's original thinkers helping this forward were Anne Cooper, backed by Anne Yeardley, later supported by Yvonne Dorey, Gordon Scoble and Ken Wycherley.

Soon more students went out to make a vital contribution in the crisis situation in Bangladesh, helping with the combined TEAR Fund/BMMF relief project from 1972. Once the way was open to them, young people were eager to help in whatever ways they could. In the summer of 1973, for example, BMMF sent two students to Pakistan where they were involved in a student camp and in local churches, six to India where they lived alongside Indian students in colleges and hostels, linked with and supervised by UESI; five to Central Asia to work amongst 'world travellers', two to Lebanon where one stayed on to work with Lebanon Inter-Varsity Fellowship, and six nurses to Nepal and North India where they worked in rural hospitals. This, being a holiday project, involved just two to three months of a student's long vacation. Other short-term projects involved a period of one to three years – as for example when David Muir, a theological student, spent a year helping Bruce Nicholls establish TRACI or when Philippa Rann worked as secretary in Delhi for Ray Windsor and then for Dr Ben Wati, the Executive Secretary of the Evangelical Fellowship of India. But as Hester Quirk pointed out at the time, 'These young people cannot make their contribution without the long-term or "career" missionary being there. They need help in interpreting the new situation and in integrating into the foreign church fellowship . . . The short-term programme in no way supersedes the other, but is complementary to it and of growing usefulness in these days of cheaper world travel and fluid political scenes.'

BMMF's short-term projects developed through its 'Missionary Education Programme' (MEP), with an estimated forty per cent of short-termers going on to some form of longer-term work in cross-cultural mission. Some were school-leavers doing a 'year out' before going on to university ('SLOTers' – School Leavers Overseas Training); others were recently qualified as secretaries, nurses, occupational therapists and so on; others again were medical students. In 1984, for example, a young medical student from New Zealand called Paul arrived at Bombay to spend ten weeks doing his 'medical elective' at a small EHA mission hospital in rural India. Much of his time at first was spent observing, but gradually as he picked up some medical vocabulary in Hindi he was able to take case histories with the help of a nurse, to assist in the operating theatre and to share his faith with any who could speak English. He was one of about sixty-five people going to Asia each year from Britain, Ireland, Holland, USA, Canada, Australia and New Zealand with MEP.

Then in 1990 David Porter, at that time Interserve's Northern Ireland Director who had himself spent eleven months doing short-term work in Pakistan, was appointed

International Co-ordinator to the programme which became known as 'On Track'. Now participants come from around the world to serve in Interserve's various fields of work, going out on one of seven different Tracks which have been worked out to provide for those with varying skills, training and experience.

The seven tracks are these: the Youth Education Programme, for school-leavers; the Student Service Programme, for students during their long vacation; Student Electives – usually medical – for students who are required to do an elective year as part of their course of studies; the Graduate Training Programme, for graduates in the year following graduation; the Professional Service Programme, for skilled and professional people who have a specialised contribution to make; the Cross-Cultural Experience Programme, for any over eighteen who are not school-leavers, graduates or visiting professionals, and a Team Programme which covers all the above but for a team of people rather than in individual placements. Soon there were about one hundred participants in On Track each year, with about twenty-five people on location at any one time. Following the widening pattern of 'career' Partners, young people from Hong Kong, Malaysia, Singapore, Korea and India are now serving with On Track.

The opportunities are great, as are the benefits both to the participants and often to the churches and projects where short-term help is given. For the organisers, arranging the placements can be hard work. In Delhi, for example, I found Jeanette Short very apprehensive at the Interserve transit house as she awaited a new wave of seven On Trackers whom she was due to look after. She was supposed to be arranging a month's work for each of them, and it wasn't going to be easy. Sometimes people are so hard-pressed, that they can hardly find the time to show newcomers the ropes; sometimes there just isn't suitable work for them to do. However, the youngsters arrived; Jeanette welcomed them with open arms, and no doubt she found niches for them all. Erika Haug from Canada was one of them.

Philip Cansdale, from the UK, heard about the programme because his grandfather had known BMMF when he was an engineer in India. He had just had three very happy months at Gujranwala in Pakistan, teaching English. He told me, 'Before I came here I was not sure what I wanted to do in the future. Having seen people at work out here, I am beginning to think I would like to come back.' Nicola Brown and Lucy Guinness had already had some experience in Birmingham, helping Frances Iliff with MAB work. Attached to an Anglican church, they went round visiting families who had applied for their children to go to the church school. More recently, in Bombay, they had been working in creches helping to look after the children of slum families, seconded to Community Outreach Programme (CORP). Lucy stayed in the home of the teacher they were helping, and experienced first hand how other people live. Everyone slept in one room: grandfather, husband and brother-in-law on the floor, and the teacher, her six-year-old daughter and Lucy sharing the bed – an experience Lucy will not forget.

'On Trackers' are not exclusively young. Paul and Tineke Dodson from Australia, for example, whom I met at Butwal in Nepal, had been wondering how best to use his three months' 'long service leave' granted after ten years' work as an engineer back at home. They thought it would be good for their children to experience life in a developing country, and were eager to use their skills in helping needy people in the Third World. Through Interserve friends they were linked up with On Track, and after applying and being interviewed, they went to Butwal. Here Paul, a Department Manager with Shell Australia, was ideally suited to helping UMN in its strategic planning, as DCS (Development and Consulting Services) assesses the direction of future developments in appropriate technology.

Valuable though the short-term contributions are, Interserve has always been aware of their limitations. In 1983 Michael Roemmele wrote an article pointing out that it takes time to be effective in a new culture; that the pattern of the Incarnation is long term, and that the longer people stay, the more useful they can be. He urged young people to 'make it a career'. Nonetheless, the On Track programme makes its important contribution to the world-wide church, in helping to develop young Christians as followers of Jesus Christ with a big vision of God and his work in the world; in providing the first move into mission for the new generation, both from the West, and now from other parts of the world; in the contribution they make abroad at the time and in years to come, and in the enthusiasm and information which youngsters bring to their home churches on their return.

The energies of young people have been used in other ways – notably 'Christmas Cracker', a recent joint venture of *21CC* magazine and Oasis Trust with initial financial backing and publicity and other support from Interserve and TEAR Fund. Starting in 1989, the idea was to open 'Eat less pay more' restaurants in vacant high street shop sites for three weeks in December, and to mobilise Christian young people for mission, helping them to respond in a practical way to the problems of world poverty. One hundred restaurants were opened in the first year, and £400,000 was raised for indigenous Indian missions. Later, other countries benefited too, and in 1991 ninety 'Tune in pay out' Radio Cracker stations were launched, broadcasting throughout December all over the UK. For the young people it was valuable experience and good fun. Most importantly, they learned about world mission, became concerned about the needs and motivated to help. In all these ways Interserve has always been conscious both of the needs and of the potential of young people. And the whole Fellowship remains youthful in spirit, very much 'at the cutting edge', very much a mission on the move.

16

Where next?

In a series of four articles published in 1989 Michael Roemmele, then Executive Director, examined the directions in which it seemed to him that Interserve would be moving in the years ahead. He noted increased internationalism, as more and more countries recruited Partners; an increase in people in secular posts, and an increase in the numbers of 'midi-term' personnel – people serving perhaps ten to fifteen years. He foresaw, too, increased co-operation both with the churches and with other mission groups at home, and in co-operative ventures overseas. Increasing co-operation too with the Orthodox churches of the Middle East in Christian education and youth and relief work, as well as with the Protestant churches in Asia and the Middle East.

Interserve would be represented by smaller groups of personnel, with the structures within which they worked coming more and more under national (government or church) responsibility and control. Interserve's own role would become increasingly that of a catalyst – educational, advisory, providing tools for the job. Researching, for example, the most effective ways of reaching the major religious groups: ministry to Muslims and to Tibetan Buddhists; studying particular tribal groups with a view to advising on community development and evangelism. And as Partners going abroad into secular jobs seek to minister to work colleagues and neighbours, Interserve sees its main role in the production of literature, correspondence courses, cassettes and videos which they can use.

Another development within Interserve, already evident in what has been written, is an extension of 'the field' – the area within which work is done. When ZBMM began, as a mission running its own institutions, those very institutions defined the geographical limits of the work. Initially it was encapsulated in one country – India. As the institutions closed or were handed over, people were freed to meet the various needs which arose. BMMF moved from a position of running institutions to that of serving in them, a change eventually reflected in the change of name to International Service Fellowship – Interserve. Today Interserve is a fellowship of people working in partnership with others, some in groups seconded to governments (e.g. the UMN), and many as individuals either seconded to parachurch organisations and churches or with personal contracts in their professions. And as Partners, rather than working in a single institution all their lives, aim to work themselves out of a job or may have visas suddenly terminated, the very search for a new job in a given profession or linguistic region can lead Interserve into new countries. At the same time, some governments are increasingly unwilling to welcome large numbers of foreigners. This means that unless Interserve reduces its overall level of recruitment, as some missions have done, the trend towards lower numbers in any one country will inevitably widen the field of work, leading Interserve again into new fields, including that of the immigrant populations in the traditional 'sending' countries.

Another general trend in mission is the focus on religious and people-groups rather than on countries. Today mission strategists work in terms of reaching ethnic groups rather than specific countries. Experience gained in working with a particular religious group is applied elsewhere. Interserve, for example, has decided to try to reach Tibetan Buddhists across political boundaries following experience among them in Bhutan and elsewhere. Similarly as Partners are recruited from an increasing number of countries, their political, ethnic and linguistic links with other countries will contribute to determining where they should work. The Korean language, for example, belongs to the Urai-Altaic group, which is the same as Turkish. All these factors may well contribute to a widening of the geographic area where Interserve works.

As Interserve itself rarely places people in its own work, it is becoming steadily less of a controlling organisation and more of a support group. Support is provided in various ways: through local groups of Interserve Partners, like the one I visited in Delhi; through regular visits by representatives of Interserve and other groups, with co-operation among mission groups multiplying their usefulness (Denis Roche travelling round Pakistan as Medical Adviser was a good example of such visits); through seminars and conferences. These last have always been an important part of the life of Interserve. In sending countries there may be day conferences, weekend area conferences and national prayer conferences, at all of which information shared will fuel interest, support and prayer. And 'in the field', regional conferences are held which provide opportunity for communication and encouragement to Partners who may be quite isolated in their work.

Another very important source of support to Interserve Partners has been that of family and personal friends. Family has always been a strong strand in the life of the Fellowship, and there are families – some mentioned in this account – which have had links through several generations. At the UK Annual Prayer Conference at Swanwick, it was good to see grandparents, parents and children all together: parents and children possibly going to serve abroad for the first time, grandparents coming along to learn more about the fellowship their children were joining. Good friendships too often form between Christians working closely together, and these can be a tremendous help and support. A poignant example of this is Rosemary Taylor from New Zealand, ward sister at Thimphu Hospital,

Bhutan, who went through the traumatic experience of seeing her US friend and colleague slowly die of cancer. She went back to the States with her and nursed her there till she died – truly partnership and fellowship in action.

The other forms of support which Interserve provides are prayer and finance. Prayer support has always been crucial to the work of the Fellowship, and the prayer link among Partners themselves is a special feature of the Fellowship. This is fostered and maintained by the monthly prayer and praise notes which circulate within the world-wide Fellowship, and by regular meeting together for prayer in locations where this is possible. Many people who have never been abroad in the 'front line' have provided faithful prayer back-up, either on their own or in prayer groups, which has been absolutely vital over the years. As Michael Roemmele sees it, prayer support may become more specialised in the future. Already many people find it impossible to pray for all Interserve's involvements and personnel. Some pray just for those sent from their own country, or for those in a particular country or ministry. Some pray only for 'their' Partner, or for a few whose prayer letters they receive. Prayer more by 'focus groups' is already a trend, and Interserve may encourage and develop this.

Prayer support comes too from the Partners' home churches which have always been another vital source of strength, providing not only prayer but finance as well. Edwy Naismith, who has been the nerve-centre of BMMF/Interserve's International Finance for many years, throws light on the financial side of things for those supported by the Fellowship as follows. All Partners are given allowances on a 'needs' basis, which is dependent on the country in which they work. Those working in the Middle East, for example, need more than those in India. Allowances are not graded according to responsibility or experience, but a married Partner with a family will have an extra allowance for each member of his family. The allowances are adjusted to keep in line with inflation in that country.

Money given to Interserve is mainly of two kinds: *designated*, that given for the support of an individual Partner, and that given to General Funds as an undesignated donation. The support needed by a Partner may be a mix of these two. The larger part is usually designated, and some National Councils expect that it should all be so. This designated giving will either come from individuals, or from a church, or sometimes from a secular source such as government aid. All Partners have a team of people supporting them, by prayer and by financial support. These supporters are described in different terms in different countries: in the UK the term 'Team Support' is used, Partners needing to raise a specific number of 'Team Support Units' of financial backing; in the Netherlands support comes from the 'Home Committee' and so on. The responsibility for raising the necessary support is a shared one, the National Office and the Partner working together to raise the funds to enable Partners to do their work.

As more and more Partners are working as tentmakers and earning their livelihood from their secular employers, a new problem arises: accountability. What makes Partners, particularly those in secular jobs, accountable to Interserve if it is not paying them? Just what *is* Interserve, and what binds its Partners together? But first, the related topic of membership. Until the 1980s there were various categories of membership. There were contractual members – those who were employed and paid by BMMF – and there were 'Field Partners' – those employed by others. There were two sorts of contractual members: BMMF and ISA (International Service Associates), the latter working in a lay professional capacity rather than in full-time evangelism and church work, particularly in India, in HEED Bangladesh and in the Middle East. There were also different sorts of Field Partners, with different terms of employment depending on whether they were in secular employment or working in Christian institutions. It was all quite complicated, and to simplify the situation the International Council declared in 1987 that 'In the interest of unity and simplicity, it was resolved that there would be a single category of membership known as Partner, with different financial arrangements as appropriate.'

As fewer Partners have the accountability of being employed by Interserve, and as the diversity and distribution of people and areas of work increase, this brings us back to the question of what it is that defines Interserve's unity and commitment. What is it that holds the Partners together? The Fellowship has been likened to a religious order, the two vital things which bind its members together being individual commitment to Christ and corporate prayer. In 1989, with modifications in 1990 and 1992, a document called 'The Common Commitment of Interserve Partners' was adopted by the Fellowship. Its purpose was to define Interserve's unity and commitment amidst the increasing diversity of locations and financial arrangements within the Fellowship. It includes commitment to the aim of Interserve, which is to proclaim in word and deed that Jesus Christ is Lord and Saviour, and to its basis of faith. It includes commitment to support of Partners by prayer and fellowship; to an appropriate life-style which gives credibility to ministry; and to acceptance of different arrangements for financial support, with some Partners receiving full support through Interserve and some none. It includes commitment to involvement and participation in fellowship, and to the local church as a servant; also to the principle of servanthood in secondment, as there is no work in any field that has the label 'Interserve'. Finally, it includes acceptance of the spiritual authority and discipline of Interserve leadership and a commitment to the concept of long-term involvement, while recognising that this may include switching to different areas of work and from one means of financial support to another during a Partner's career.

The guidelines of this Common Commitment are general rather than detailed, reflecting perhaps a characteristic of Interserve mentioned by Brian Ringrose, Director of Interserve (Scotland): 'The scope for following personal guidance and showing initiative has always been great, and individualists and visionaries have found encouragement and support to a high degree. In a sentence, what appeals to me most about Interserve is the extent to which the Fellowship is cautious in directive, firm in support.'

So these are some directions in which Interserve is moving. Jesus likened his followers to the salt of the earth; here the salt is dissolving into smaller units spreading more and more widely – merging more and more, becoming less visible. To quote once more from Michael Roemmele:

> These new patterns of ministry may leave us feeling insecure. Will Interserve lose its identity as it further lowers its profile? I believe the paradox of the future will be that as Interserve's involvement in ministries grows further, Interserve itself will be less noticed. This should encourage, not alarm us. It is a biblical pattern as enunciated by John the Baptist when he pointed to Jesus and said: 'He must increase but I must decrease' (John 3:30).

As Interserve finds new ways and places to fulfil its aim of proclaiming in word and deed that Jesus Christ is Lord and Saviour, this is the pattern they determine to follow.

Select Bibliography

Anderson, Ken, *Himalayan Heartbeat*, Christian Blind Mission affiliated with Christoffel-Blindenmission, 1965.

Bell, Dick, *To the Source of the Yangtze*, Hodder and Stoughton, 1991.

Cleator, Margaret, *The God Who Answers by Fire*, Victory Press, 1966.

Cole, Michael, *Journey to the Fourth World*, Lion, 1981.

Cundy, Mary, *So Great a God*, BMMF International (UK), 1974.

Di Gangi, Mariano, *This is my Story*, Interserve, 1986.

Fleming, Guy, *There Shall be no End*, BMMF, 1977.

Fletcher, G.N., *The Fabulous Flemings of Kathmandu*, Dutton and Co., New York, 1964.

Foyle, Dr Marjory F., *Honourably Wounded, Stress Among Christian Workers*, Marc Europe, 1987.

Horner, Norman A., *A Guide to Christian Churches in the Middle East*, Mission Focus Publications, 1989.

Morris, James – *Heaven's Command*
  – *Pax Brittanica*
  – *Farewell the Trumpets*, Penguin Books, 1979.

Nicholls, Kathleen, *Asian Arts and Christian Hope*, Select Books, New Delhi, 1983.

Pollock, J.C., *Shadows Fall Apart, the Story of the Zenana Bible and Medical Mission*, Hodder and Stoughton, 1958.

Sikhar, *Braver Than the Gurkhas*, Word (UK) Ltd, 1990.

Sookhdeo, Patrick (ed.), *Sharing Good News*, Scripture Union, 1991.

Stacey, Vivienne, *Thomas Valpy French, First Bishop of Lahore*, The Christian Study Centre, 1982.

Stone, Anthony, *Hindu Astrology: Myths, Symbols and Realities*, Select Books, New Delhi, 1981.

United Mission to Nepal, *Nepal on the Potter's Wheel*, UMN, Kathmandu, 1970.

Index